TEACHER DEVELOPMENT SERIES
Series Editor: Andy Hargreaves

THE INDUCTION OF NEW TEACHERS

THE INDUCTION OF NEW TEACHERS
Reflective Professional Practice

Les Tickle

CASSELL

Cassell
Villiers House   387 Park Avenue South
41/47 Strand   New York
London WC2N 5JE   NY 10016-8810

First published 1994

British Library Cataloguing-in-Publication Data
A catalogue record for this book is available from the British Library.

Library of Congress Cataloging-in-Publication Data
Tickle, Les.
    The induction of new teachers : reflective professional practice / Les Tickle.
        p.   cm. – (Teacher development)
    Includes bibliographical references and index.
    ISBN 0–304–32746–8 : $70.00 (U.S.). – ISBN 0–304–32738–7 (pbk.) $26.00
(U.S.)
    1. First year teachers – Great Britain. 2. Teachers – In-service train-
ing – Great Britain. 3. Action research in education – Great
Britain. I. Title II. Series.
LB2844.1.N4T53   1994
371.1′46′0941 – dc20   93–43854
                                                            CIP

ISBN 0–304–32746–8 (hardback)
      0–304–32738–7 (paperback)

Typeset by Colset Pte Ltd, Singapore
Printed and bound in Great Britain by Redwood Books, Trowbridge, Wiltshire

Contents

Foreword

In Britain and Australia, they call it teaching. In the United States and Canada, they call it instruction. Whatever terms we use, we have come to realize in recent years that the teacher is the ultimate key to educational change and school improvement. The restructuring of schools, the composition of national and provincial curricula, the development of benchmark assessments – all these things are of little value if they do not take the teacher into account. Teachers don't merely deliver the curriculum. They develop it, define it and reinterpret it too. It is what teachers think, what teachers believe and what teachers do at the level of the classroom that ultimately shapes the kind of learning that young people get. Growing appreciation of this fact is placing working with teachers and understanding teaching at the top of our research and improvement agendas.

For some reformers, improving teaching is mainly a matter of developing better teaching methods, of improving instruction. Training teachers in new classroom management skills, in active learning, co-operative learning, one-to-one counselling and the like is the main priority. These things are important, but we are also increasingly coming to understand that developing teachers and improving their teaching involves more than giving them new tricks. We are beginning to recognize that, for teachers, what goes on inside the classroom is closely related to what goes on outside it. The quality, range and flexibility of teachers' classroom work are closely tied up with their professional growth – with the way that they develop as people and as professionals.

Teachers teach in the way they do not just because of the skills they have or have not learned. The ways they teach are also grounded in their backgrounds, their biographies, in the kinds of teachers they have become. Their careers – their hopes and dreams, their opportunities and aspirations, or the frustration of these things – are also important for teachers' commitment, enthusiasm and morale. So too are relationships with their colleagues – either as supportive communities who work together in pursuit of common goals and continuous improvement, or as individuals working in isolation, with the insecurities that sometimes brings.

As we are coming to understand these wider aspects of teaching and teacher development, we are also beginning to recognize that much more than pedagogy, instruction or teaching method is at stake. Teacher development, teachers' careers, teachers' relations with their colleagues, the conditions of status, reward and leadership under which they work — all these affect the quality of what they do in the classroom.

This international series, *Teacher Development*, brings together some of the very best current research and writing on these aspects of teachers' lives and work. The books in the series seek to understand the wider dimensions of teachers' work, the depth of teachers' knowledge and the resources of biography and experience on which it draws, the ways that teachers' work roles and responsibilities are changing as we restructure our schools, and so forth. In this sense, the books in the series are written for those who are involved in research on teaching, those who work in initial and in-service teacher education, those who lead and administer teachers, those who work with teachers and, not least, teachers themselves.

No period is more important for the development of teachers than the initial induction into the profession. For too long, and in sad contrast to most other professions, many new teachers have been left to struggle with the complex and challenging demands of their first job completely by themselves, in professional isolation. Soldiering on without assistance, often with classes and in rooms that other teachers do not want, they have had at best to overcome indifference or neglect from more senior colleagues. At worst they have had to prove their mettle as organizers and disciplinarians by overcoming the trials of fire that it is felt all new recruits should endure. In recent years, a number of educators have responded to this problem by creating structured systems of support for new teachers in the shape of programmes of induction. School districts might periodically bring new teachers together to share concerns and discuss ideas. Schools might assign mentors from among the staff to their new teachers to take charge of their welfare, keep track of their progress and provide assistance and ideas. There are books advocating such programmes, and books describing what they look like. But Les Tickle's book, *The Induction of New Teachers*, goes further than this.

As an experienced educator who has been a teacher, a school administrator, a teacher educator and an educational researcher, Tickle describes and reflects on processes of induction in vivid detail; not just processes of induction that he observes but ones that he also actively creates. Tickle is no fly-on-the-wall observer, no dispassionate inquirer into other people's problems. He is actively and passionately involved in induction himself, committed to the development and support of new teachers, while also reflecting with integrity on the success of his and others' efforts in this difficult task.

Tickle's book is a richly described process of action-research into the problems and possibilities of induction. It is a process conducted *with* new teachers, not *on* them. It models collaboration and reflection as well as investigating them, seeing reflection as a process of collective review and dialogue rather than private introspection, within a community of thoughtful professionals. But induction and the study and creation of it are not, for Tickle, simply matters of cognitive contemplation — they are also suffused with passion and emotion — hope, joy, anxiety, frustration, excitement and regret. This is what being a new teacher and working with new teachers is like, and Tickle brings what he calls the curriculum of the emotions to the very forefront of induction.

As you read this book, you will come to understand the process of induction through the lives of individual teachers undergoing it. With the author, you will experience the struggles of trying to make sense of this process and make it better. And you will be able to reflect on and have resources for improving your own practice, as you draw on his rich resource of recommendations. This book will take you beyond the advocacy and description of induction to understanding what it means to work with new teachers in productive, reflective, collegial ways that bring support to the newest members of our profession, and the benefits of further growth to those who work with them.

Andy Hargreaves,
Ontario Institute for Studies in Education, Toronto
August 1994

This book is dedicated to all those who participated in the induction projects on which it is based, and especially to the eleven teachers who feature individually in it. I have to acknowledge an enormous debt to them for their contribution to my understanding. Chris, my wife, and Anna, my daughter, have also played an immeasurable part in supporting my efforts. The rewards of any success will be shared with them in gratitude. My colleague John Elliott has been a true mentor throughout the work, both in person and through the extensive contributions which he has made to the literature on teacher education and action research.

Chapter 1

Teacher Induction and the Concept of Reflective Practice

A RESPONSE TO A PRACTICAL NEED

I was presented with the practical task of devising an induction curriculum for new entrants to teaching. The task was to be in two parts: an initial one-year project for 16 new teachers, with a view to extension, based on the initial experience, for 150 new entrants the following year and continuation each year thereafter. The project was intended to enhance support for new teachers in order to help them develop their teaching. I had a central part in its design and planning and was responsible for its implementation, co-ordination and monitoring. It had a single major aim: *to promote the development of classroom practice and the capacity for reflective thinking about that practice.*

The initiative to develop induction was taken in the broader social and educational context which had led to the professional expectations placed upon teachers, and upon those responsible for educating and employing them being changed dramatically. It had also become widely recognized that the professional development of teachers should be a continuous long-term process undertaken for and by all teachers (notwithstanding contradictory views from the New Right in Britain about teachers needing no training at all). There was a reiteration by Her Majesty's Inspectors of Schools (HMI), and by teacher educators, of the importance of a period of induction as a crucial phase of development which linked initial teacher education and inservice education for established teachers. Preparation for the development project included a judicious review of policy on teacher induction in order to establish whether there were existing frameworks within which to proceed. The review showed that provision was patchy across England and Wales, as well as within localities and even within schools, depending on the individual schools or departments in which teachers were employed. The same appeared to be true in other western nations. While I had supposed, I think reasonably, that the period immediately after recommendation for qualified teacher status is a crucial one in the educational development of teachers, the best that could be said of it appeared to me to be that it was worthy of detailed research as a basis for the development of provision. That view was confirmed by the research literature.

For example, Doyle (1985), Griffin (1985), and Hall (1982) each reviewed the lack of research on teacher induction, in particular on the question of what and how teachers learn from their classroom experience at this phase. Research which was available largely focused on the purported 'survival' needs of new teachers (Brown and Willems, undated); on improving the technical functions of instruction (Kerry, 1982; Smith, 1983); and on the kinds of formal programmes run by employers for their new teachers. Reports based on HMI surveys of a sample of new teachers in England and Wales indicated the deeply problematic administrative and managerial arrangements surrounding their employment and induction and widespread experience of a complex adjustment trauma among teachers as they embarked on their careers (DES, 1982a, 1988a). While some schemes for the induction of teachers had been established, there was little evidence about the nature of induction and the educational experiences which it offers (see Bolam, 1973; Bolam et al., 1975; DES, 1982a, 1988a). That is not to say that new teachers are not evident in the literature. In Britain the Department of Education and Science (DES), now the Department for Education (DFE) sponsored projects led by Bolam et al. and related studies (Davis, 1979; McCabe, 1978; Taylor and Dale, 1971, 1973), and reports of the Inner London Education Authority induction programme (ILEA, 1980, 1985) have been supplemented by other reports on teacher induction (Clark and Nisbett, 1963; Collins, 1969; Cornwell, 1965; Evans, 1978; Hannam et al., 1976; Hanson and Herrington, 1976; Kerry, 1982; Patrick et al., 1984). In the USA reports on induction schemes (Andrews, 1979; Berliner and Tickunoff, 1976; Hunt, 1968; Schwalenberg, 1965) were surveyed and summarized by Grant and Zeichner (1981), and more recently by Zimpher and Howey (1990), confirming the British studies' concerns with programmes of formal activities, informal support for new teachers, and the nature of their working circumstances. Tisher (1982) provided an international perspective on these kinds of provision.

The reports have implications for policy and provision of teaching and learning conditions which need to be taken very seriously, given that the experience of teaching and learning is constrained for all teachers by the material, social and ideological circumstances in which they work (Hargreaves, 1978; Pollard, 1985; Sharp and Green, 1975; Hammersley, 1977). It is within those conditions that teaching is learnt. However, while acknowledging the importance of these factors it seemed to me that in particular the place of individual action by new teachers, as agents of their own education, had been largely disregarded by researchers. Hannam et al. (1988), Beynon (1987) and Zeichner and Tabachnick (1985) each provided detailed case study accounts of individual new teachers as agents of their own work, who respond with different social strategies to their circumstances. Even here, however, there was little emphasis on new teachers as agents of their own education, or the development of the practical knowledge of teaching and means of improving it during this phase. Aspects of how the practical knowledge of teaching is acquired — subject matter, instructional strategies, knowledge of pupils, and curriculum development — have been studied amongst experienced teachers from a range of different perspectives (Elbaz, 1983; Clandinin, 1986; Calderhead, 1987; Elliot, 1980,

1989; Holly and McLoughlin, 1989; Lowyck and Clark, 1989; Winter, 1989; and others). Similar work has been conducted among student teachers (Berliner, 1987; Brown and McIntyre, 1986; Feiman-Nemser and Buchmann, 1985; Phillips, 1988; Russell, 1987a; Schrag, 1989; Shulman, 1986a, 1986b; Tabachnick and Zeichner, 1991b; and others). However, only recently and occasionally has such research begun with new teachers in the first year(s) of full-time work (Applegate, 1989; Russell, 1988; Clark and Yinger, 1987; and see Zimpher and Howey, 1990 for a review of research in the USA).

Furthermore, recent developments in schooling have raised new questions about the institutional experiences of new entrants. The institutional contexts in which they were employed have changed rapidly, with more complex professional demands being made of teachers, including self-appraisal, relationships with a wide community constituency, inter-staff relationships for curriculum leadership and change, changes in curriculum content, organization and processes of teaching, and assessment arrangements. It was in this broader context of instability and potential changes in professional orientation (with tensions between pressure for teachers to behave as compliant technicians, and demands for them to act as effective tacticians), yet with an insubstantial research base, that the practical task was undertaken. Given that practical task of devising an induction curriculum for teachers, and the limitations of research on what and how teachers learn from their classroom experience at that phase, my own assumptions (albeit qualified by uncertainty) about teachers as reflective agents of their own education, explicit in the aim of the project, became an important feature of what was done. Because of those assumptions it seemed both necessary and desirable in the design and implementation of the initial project to adopt an open but optimistic perspective of new teachers. At the same time, given the limited research, I decided that perspective and my own underlying assumptions, and the curriculum practice based on them, would need to be subject to scrutiny through research.

The question which arose from the task was: what should be done and how? Whatever the judgement made about practical action there was also a research and theoretical problem: to seek to answer why? Thus the task was to implement action as a research endeavour. Since the project was to be mounted without substantial foundation of understanding about the nature of induction and the educational experiences of new teachers, it seemed reasonable to suppose that my own research into the induction period would reveal important characteristics of teachers' educational experiences, highlighted by what is commonly seen as a period of frenetic activity and learning. The illumination of those characteristics, I presumed, was necessary for the development of the induction programme. In short, it required an action research perspective. At the same time, I took the view that there was a need for interpretive case study in association with the conduct of the practical task, and that both the action and interpretive case study research endeavours could be complemented by more detailed scrutiny of induction policy in England and Wales.

The aim of the practical task and the action research related to it was to enhance the quality of induction for the teachers involved, not least by developing my own understanding, values, intentions and actions in relation to that provision. The aims of the interpretive case study research and policy analysis were to contribute to that, and to knowledge of teacher education, by:

1. Elucidating the education of new entrants to teaching through the study of individual teachers' experience of their first year in the profession.

2. Describing the contexts of support for new teachers' professional development.

3. Understanding the ways of thinking about and learning teaching which were part of the individual experiences.

4. Analysing national policy and contemporary issues regarding modes of teacher induction.

As part of that research and development however, my own presuppositions about teachers as researchers were central to the endeavour. The view of new teachers which prevailed in planning the programmes was substantially influenced by assumptions of research-based teaching. My application of those ideas to work with undergraduate student teachers was already documented (Tickle, 1987a). The assumptions are intrinsically optimistic about the part which teachers play in initiating, sustaining and appreciating their own learning. They reveal something of my own view of educational process as enquiry, of knowledge as uncertain and provisional, and of teaching as inherently complex and unstable (Stenhouse, 1975, 1979). They imply a set of expectations (or desires) that, beyond the basic techniques of practice, teachers treat teaching as problematic; that, in the right circumstances as teachers, we will engage in enquiry about teaching; and that such enquiry is a necessary feature of a particular mode of the 'professionalization' of teachers. Within this is a particular conceptualization of the teacher as learner. It is partly a conception about what is, and partly of what ought to be. Correspondingly there is a perspective on the role of the teacher educator: to extend and encourage what is, and to develop what ought to be, among all teachers through the promotion of dispositions toward reflection and the systematic analysis of practice. These ideas were, and are, the basis of my commitments to research-based teacher education, within which the induction projects were devised.

However, as I will show, while the underlying ideas about the nature of teacher research and reflective practice seemed sufficiently clear, at the time, to form the basis of the central aim for the project, it is those ideas themselves which became increasingly problematic for me. I enjoyed a growing realization of the lack of conceptual clarity – on my own part – around research-based teaching, action research and reflective practice.

The problem arose in particular in the juxtaposition (and interchange in use) of the notions of 'reflection' (used as shorthand for 'thoughtful deliberation'), and 'systematic analysis of practice' (used as long hand for 'action research'). Through the work of the projects and the analysis of the data, numerous questions about this juxtaposition and interchange arose. Initially, however, my interest was one of the 'application' of the ideas, as I then held them, with new teachers, among whom, to my knowledge, such ideas had not been previously explored. Nationally and internationally, experience of such professionalization through teacher research had mostly been built on work with established teachers – often those in positions of responsibility in schools and/or those engaged in study for advanced qualifications. There was and is a growing interest in the application of principles of research-based teaching and its implications for student teachers in initial teacher education (Ashcroft and Griffiths, 1987; Pollard and Tann, 1987; Tabachnick and Zeichner, 1991b; Zimpher and Howey, 1987). The assumptions of the approach – that practical knowledge and action will be enhanced through classroom research – had not been examined at the crucial period between initial teacher education and INSET for experienced teachers. I saw this application as new ground to be explored within the field of teacher education.

ORIENTATION OF THE PRACTICAL RESPONSE

In taking the view that in my own case there was a need for action research, interpretive case study and policy analysis, I was cognizant of the claim that findings derived from empiric-analytical or positivist research, critical theory and interpretive research have had a limited effect on or application to teaching practice (McIntyre, 1980, 1988). Some researchers working in this variety of social science research traditions continue to argue that their work forms a basis for formulating practical hypotheses for professional practice and for discourse about teaching. This may be so in its own particular ways. However, the difficulty of the relationship between 'outsider' research and 'insider' practice had led in Britain to a particular drive toward resolving the problem through a reconceptualization of educational research. It was begun by Stenhouse at the Centre for Applied Research in Education in the early 1970s, and was developed by Elliott (and others) in a series of action research projects, the establishment of the Classroom Action Research Network, and continuing elaborations of research-based teaching. I was also cognizant of adaptations of these developments. For example, Bennett and Desforges (1984) summarized a range of strategies to devolve research activities to teachers in attempts to bridge the perceived theory–practice gap. These are said to include a 'harder try' to persuade teachers of the value of research; monitored workshops based on the transmission of classroom 'competence' outside classroom settings; and the involvement of teachers in research processes. However, in these approaches the researchers did not (and do not) engage in practical teaching;

nor do the practitioners engage fully in the research. In the case of the induction projects it was necessary to be both practitioner and researcher, and I regarded the pursuit of educational action research, interpretive case study and policy analysis as an appropriate orientation to the task. There was a background to that choice.

My own commitments to action research as a teacher were translated into advocacy of it when I became a teacher educator. Yet both as a teacher and teacher educator I was also persuaded of the value of other modes of research, especially qualitative case study from a symbolic interactionist perspective (Tickle, 1979, 1983, 1987a, 1987b). Faced with a substantial practical professional task I determined to use what I regarded as complementary approaches. The precedent for that had a good pedigree. The research model initially adopted by Stenhouse, involving teachers directly, aspired to incorporate elements of 'pure' empirical research conducted by professional researchers; the evaluation of programmes in which curriculum practice/development was critiqued by observers to inform project developers and teachers; and practice which was internally researched by those responsible for it, into 'a more scientific procedure which builds action and criticism into an integrated whole' (Stenhouse, 1975, p. 124). The development of interpretive modes of research in the social sciences appeared to offer more 'appropriate', but none the less problematic, means of studying educational contexts and practice (Stenhouse, 1975, p. 151). In some instances interpretive research had studied, and continues to study, teachers' perspectives and practices and their physical, social, political and economic contexts, in order to describe and explain teachers' work. Symbolic interactionism in particular has sought to describe and explain action from the position of whoever forms that action (Blumer, 1962, 1969). Its application to education grew through the use of case study in particular educational sites (Hargreaves, 1967; Lacey, 1970; Ball, 1981; and for a summary of these developments see Walker, 1985; Morton, 1988; Munro, 1989).

Stenhouse's approach, which included the transfer of external case study research into internally researched teaching, was one of a number of strategies which have a history dating at least from the third quarter of the nineteenth century for tackling the 'insider/outsider' problem in social practice and research. Proponents of action research claim as its distinctiveness a particular set of relationships between investigation and action, and have sought to exploit those relationships for the development of teaching. But there is not a coherent or consensual image of what those relationships are. McKernan has shown how variants of this approach had been developed, taking a number of twists and turns, among the Science in Education Movement, progressive educators (especially Dewey), the group-dynamics movement, post-war curriculum developers, and contemporary curriculum action researchers. He has classified three types of action research traditions: the early North American 'science in education' approach; the teacher-researcher view of Stenhouse; and that derived from critical theory (McKernan, 1988, 1991).

What they have in common is an orientation towards blending research with practical experience. This orientation is reflected in a belief that the professionalization of teachers will best be achieved through their adoption of a critical/revisionist or reflective/ revisionist approach to change in educational practice, charging practitioners to engage in the research of their own practices and the experiences of those with whom they work, as a basis for improvement. Since Stenhouse (1975), that belief has variously been championed in Britain by Carr and Kemmis (1986), Elliott (1991a), Hopkins (1985), Hustler *et al.* (1988), McNiff (1988), Nixon (1981), Walker (1985), Winter (1989) and others. It formed the basis for the aims of the induction project as well as my own orientation to my role within it. Prior to undertaking the research with new entrants to teaching, I had represented the image of action research as follows:

> Action research assumes that curriculum proposals are to be treated as provisional and worth testing. That concurs with the learning experience of practitioners, operating on a basis of practical knowledge and experience, constantly testing out ideas to be assimilated into a repertoire of practice, changed according to circumstance and rethinking based on further experience. The challenge of action research is to establish a commitment to systematic questioning of teaching and a concern to test theory in practice, with the development of skills to enable enquiry and the implementation of effective practices. The recognition of curriculum as problematic; disposition to seek understanding of events; mastery of investigative skills; and the capacity to effectively conduct practice on the basis of the knowledge gained, are the central elements of action research.

The development of interpretive case study research and of action research in Britain has been extensive in the past 30 years. There is also growing interest in the nature of reflective practice as research. The fuzziness which is created at the boundaries between these three, as well as sometimes within them, can be blinding (see Copeland *et al.*, 1991; Hayon, 1990; Zeichner and Tabachnick, 1991). What is clear through it is that the central recurrent issue is the relationship between insiders and outsiders (Elliott, 1991a), subjectivity and objectivity (Winter, 1989), existentialism and empiricism (Schon, 1971), and even 'I' and 'me' (Whitehead, 1989). This reflects widespread arguments within the social sciences and especially the positions adopted within phenomenology and hermeneutics (see, for example, Holub, 1991). They are important in terms of the nature of both the teachers' practices and my own in the induction projects.

The conceptual basis and the methodological implications of interpretive research and action research are similar in some respects and complementary. In relation to the development of professional practice in particular, observer research and teacher research are closely connected in purpose: to discover what is done — either in someone else's practice or one's own; to describe how it is done; and most crucially to understand why features of it are as they are. The extension into action research of features of symbolic interactionism, and case study research which attended to its methodological implications, provides the opportunity for the practitioner to explore his or her own actions: in Blumer's (1969) terms, to make explicit what is taken into account in determining action, and to describe and explicate action. The ethnographic approach of the outsider researcher is, however, a step away from teacher-initiated self-analysis of practice through reflection. The essential difference is that in seeking to explore one's own practice, the purpose of the action researcher is to reflect upon and enhance that practice. Understanding it may nevertheless be enhanced by taking an outsider research stance toward phenomena with which that practice is centrally concerned. As I have said, the application of that understanding — i.e. translating understanding gained from the interpretive research into action — is a problem which action research has tried to address. But taking a rigorous stance toward the practice itself places the purpose and value of the research primarily and intrinsically in the domain of the practitioner.

Symbolic interaction in particular had drawn from and blended structuralist and phenomenological perspectives, generating extensive debates about the relationship between individual biography and identity, social interactions, and social structures. From those debates I had derived a dialectical view of persons as wilful creative actors, with their own individuality and uniqueness but who nevertheless are situated within and take account of their situations in social structures, in a constant process of negotiation and the 'social construction of reality' (Berger and Luckmann, 1967). It was this theoretical basis which led some educational researchers, including me, in the direction of interpretive case study as a means of illuminating life in educational settings. The growth of this and related approaches to the study of education, drawing from social anthropology, social psychology, and sociology, has an extensive literature and numerous illustrative examples of such research stemming back at least to Willard Waller's *The Sociology of Teaching* (Waller 1932).

Although I had adopted this research approach as a teacher, I had applied it to the study of other teachers' work as a means of understanding and changing my own practices in art teaching (see Tickle, 1983). More recently as a teacher educator I had pursued a similar perspective in studying my own work with student teachers learning teaching (see Tickle, 1987a, 1987b). The perspective had influenced my views of research-based teaching, to the extent that I regarded action research as a devolution of research power to practitioners, and the interactionist perspective as one which could help them illuminate their worlds as I believed it had mine. The appeal of this 'illuminative' approach was greater than just its ability to describe the texture of reality in social life. It was in the ways in which that description might inform professional judgements. That was a view shared by Stenhouse, who saw value in reporting such research in order that teachers might judge it against their critical assessment of experience (and vice versa) (Rudduck and Hopkins, 1985, p. 40). He also saw it being undertaken by practitioners in direct relation to action, in order that it might develop perceptiveness and prudence: 'the ability to discern the most suitable, politic, or profitable course of action; practical wisdom, discretion' (Rudduck and Hopkins, 1985, p. 52).

It was in this vein that both the policy analysis and the ethnographic case study elements of the projects were undertaken. In order to examine broader aspects of the how? and why? of the new teachers' learning experiences than those which I was intentionally trying to foster, and to understand the contexts in which my work and theirs took place, I assumed an interpretative case study approach, presuming this to be necessary in order to describe and explain their worlds in ways which recognized them as persons constructing ideas and actions through interpretations of situations which confronted them (Blumer, 1962). Blumer (1969) argued that concern with the ways in which individuals construct action requires that researchers should see its construction from the position of whoever is forming it. The adoption of this tenet of symbolic interactionism meant gaining insight into what the teachers took into account, and seeking to follow their interpretations as they went about learning teaching.

I had promoted the devolution (Tickle, 1987a) of such research to teachers in the role of 'second order' action research facilitator, as well as undertaking some 'first order' action research on my own behalf (see Elliott, 1985, 1988). In retrospect, it was not clear how the study of phenomena or events outside of one's own practice illuminated or directly influenced that practice (as distinct from helping one's understanding). I came to see some teacher research projects as minor case studies which were not necessarily directly related to their own teaching, or if they were it was difficult to know how. In the new situation of the induction projects such interpretive, interactionist research seemed necessary in order to help me understand the worlds of the new teachers, but it did not seem sufficient or satisfactory in itself. My own decisions, judgements and actions were so central in implementing the projects in the early stages without that understanding available to me, that a 'first order' action research perspective seemed necessary as a means of monitoring my 'second order' role of promoting reflective practice, the central educational aim of the projects.

The development of a hermeneutic perspective provided complementation to the interactionist approach to the study of education, especially one that can incorporate the idea of teachers (or teacher educators) researching their own actions. At face value, the potential of hermeneutics in the social sciences did not seem to me greatly different from interactionism. It was represented by Wolff:

> Incorporating the advantages of both the structural approach
> and, particularly, the phenomenological perspective,

> hermeneutic sociology is in a position to comprehend the
> diversity of levels of analysis as well as the various, and often
> contradictory, aspects of knowledge, in a dialectical,
> sophisticated framework.
> (Wolff, 1975, p. 129)

The framework is certainly provided in part by phenomenology, which takes into account the consciousness of the individual, and provides for the analysis of the existential meanings held by individuals. A complementary part of the framework is provided by taking into account social-structural contexts within which individual biographies are located. And a further dimension takes into account the historical contexts which attach to both individuals and societies. In itself, that framework might be little more, or less, than that developed in some branches of anthropology and sociology, and applied in ethnographic research of educational sites as the basis for interpretive case study approaches. As I said, I judged that was not sufficient for the conception of these projects, in which my own work as teacher educator was to feature, not only as an object to be studied but also as a potential subject to be changed. The central problem which I faced concerned the relationship between the various elements of the projects: the conduct of actions aimed at bringing about change in the induction experiences of teachers; my attempts to monitor my own role as teacher educator, and in the event to surface and reconsider the nature of research-based teaching; the need to research the ideas and thinking of the teachers, and the ways in which they learned; my recognition that my work and theirs had its own interactional relationship, but that both occurred within a broader social-interaction context located in schools and in the culture of teaching and teacher education; and the fact that all the interactional experiences occurred within a historical context of teaching, teacher education and teacher induction.

Initially I held a view of this complexity rather intuitively, and perhaps naively, and came to explore it more fully through the conduct of the projects and associated research activities. At first I imagined that these two aspects – my teaching and research roles – constituted distinctive 'insider' and 'outsider' approaches. As the undertaking began, the relationship between insider and outsider viewpoints became more self-consciously puzzling. It would have been possible, and certainly less complex, to have pursued an 'outsider' inter-actionist perspective through case study research of one or other of the groups of teachers in order to understand their experiences. Even then a hermeneutic perspective both permits and demands that the 'outsider' scholar of social interaction should engage in self-reflection. This involves acknowledging that the scholar is a part of the interactions which he or she studies, and therefore needs to declare and take into account the perspectives or prejudices which are brought to the research. It is a view of human interaction and thought which I came to see as having a more comprehensive contribution to make to the research than my earlier adherence to symbolic interactionism and its methodological implications for case study. The critically different dimension in the hermeneutic view is that, in terms of both the philosophy and the methods adopted in research, the researcher is seen as being included among the subjects of the research:

> Hermeneutics consists in the end in the individual,
> socially-situated, sociologist or historian understanding the
> existential meanings, symbols, expressions and values of
> another culture and its inhabitants, and simultaneously aware
> of his own historical consciousness and its role in this process.
> (Wolff, 1975, p. 132)

This perspective appeared to provide a logical framework for those parts of the undertaking which I had embarked upon as researcher. Yet my work was a step more complicated than even that. Given my declared interests in research-based teaching, and the importance of my own actions in the projects, the prominence of the 'insider' viewpoint was more than that of the 'socially situated sociologist'. It was necessary not only to declare and examine my own consciousness and role as researcher. My aspirations as agent in attempting to change aspects of the situation were central to the projects. The theoretical perspective and methods adopted therefore also needed to accommodate the insider as agent in the social interactions, as well as being in active pursuit of greater personal and public understanding. That insider viewpoint was also influenced by the research reviews and reading of theoretical literature, the historical policy analysis and the case study research, which were undertaken with a greater sense of being an 'outsider'. They were conducted with an intention to change my understanding rather than to change others. Nevertheless, changes in my understanding affected the nature and direction of my attempts to change others.

As the work proceeded, that development included an elaboration of my own understanding of the hermeneutic perspective itself, especially through the idea of prejudice discussed by Gadamer (1975). Gadamer pursued the argument that the attempt to purge bias from enquiry was a misleading and impossible trail. He developed Heidegger's view that being necessarily involves presuppositions and prejudices which will be brought to situations as foresight or foreconceptions, and that it is these which make understanding possible. Rather than seeing investigators' prejudices as an intrusion to be prevented, Gadamer argued that as an unavoidable attribute of human existence, they might be seen as constituting a condition for understanding rather than a hindrance to it. That is only possible if we approach material (he held some concern for the interpretation of written texts and art objects especially) with an openness to alternative possibilities of interpretation and understanding than those which our preconceptions would allow if they were not controlled by the discipline of 'openness'. That openness means surfacing our preconceptions, making them available for criticism, discovering distorting perspectives, and engaging in revision. That revision may be enhanced and objectivity arrived at by making available the presuppositions, the objects of interpretation, and the interpretations. A circular, conversational process is invoked to ensure continual openness, enquiry and checking. It is by means of this process that understanding is also self-understanding, as interpretation and self-reflection combine.

AN AUTOBIOGRAPHICAL NARRATIVE ACCOUNT

In the study of induction policy, of new teachers' experiences and of the development projects, there was perpetual interaction between the different modes of research. The research was a response to the starting-point of the enquiry: the questions what should be done, how, and why? in relation to the practical task. This report of the research seeks to describe what was done, how and why, in the conduct of the induction projects, and in the research which informed their development. It also seeks to elaborate on the ensuing methodological and theoretical issues which I had to address in coming to terms with the nature of the practical response as a research endeavour.

The first year of the fieldwork was undertaken in three parts: an analysis of policy for teacher induction in England and Wales; action research of the initial project and my work with six teachers within it; and a case study of five other new teachers. The three approaches offered distinctive and complementary perspectives on the experiences of new teachers and provision for their education. By pursuing all three it seemed possible to become broadly informed about those experiences and their social context, in order to use that understanding in formation of teacher induction provision more widely. An inherent and explicit intention was that the first year should provide a basis for the follow-up project for 150 teachers. The methodological framework of the first year of the study was one which took account of the interaction between my action research, interpretive research, and policy analysis. Associated with these modes of research were a number of methodological judgements or 'choices the researcher must make before, on entry to, during and after the field' (Munro, 1989). These are outlined below.

The initial phase of the research focused well beyond the experiences of individual teachers and their schools, in an attempt to locate the pilot project within a national and international perspective on teacher induction. The literature search, which proved fruitful to the extent that it showed considerable gaps in knowledge about new teachers' learning, corresponded with initial considerations of policy, provision and principles relating to teacher induction in England and Wales. Coincidentally with that review the heat of debate about the nature of teacher education in Britain increased substantially, as the introduction of the Education Reform Act corresponded with a crisis in teacher supply in some secondary subjects and, in the primary phase, in some regions. That crisis led to changes in regulations for entry into teaching and calls for radical changes in the 'normal' route into the profession through initial training. What began as a review of policy for the practical purposes of the development project seemed worthy of a more prominent place in the research in view of the external contemporary debate, since the debate raised fundamental questions about initial teacher education and induction. These questions concerned the content of teacher education curricula; structure of training programmes; sites of training (institutes of higher education/schools); staffing (lecturers/practising teachers); funding (grants/bursaries/salaries as well as costs of training programmes); and control of selection and assessment for qualified teacher status. In consequence I subjected both former and present policy documents, and arguments presented in the debate, to some detailed analysis in pursuit of understanding the assumptions underpinning the notion of induction itself, or particular forms of it. That analysis was conducted in the light of my particular interests in and theories about research-based teaching. The policy analysis was based on primary documentary evidence and secondary historical accounts. Twentieth-century historical documents were scrutinized first-hand and recorded systematically, so that selectivity in the use of some of their parts could be checked against my interpretations and accounts of the documents. In the case of older sources firsthand scrutiny was not practicable, and I depended on the work of historians' analyses, in particular Dent (1977) and Rich (1933). The account of policy derived from this analysis is reported in Chapter 2.

The action research of the initial project began as documentary evidence from its planning and field notes made during implementation were filed, to be available and accessible for later reflection and analysis. These were working documents prepared by me, used variously with colleagues and the project teachers, which recorded the central intentions and activities of the project and noted my perceptions on its conduct. From these I hoped it would be evident how my own values and perspectives were intended to, and did, affect the practical task. Those values were made explicit as far as possible within the documents and my own notes. An outline of the project, based on those data, starts in Chapter 3 of the book, and explains further the intentions behind it, and the actions taken toward realizing the development of reflective practice with the group of teachers.

As that suggests, I had invoked my own presuppositions about and hopes of the possibility of teachers researching their own practice at this stage in their careers. The initial project involved attempting to realize those hopes, and maintaining a watchful eye on what I did, and on other phenomena which might affect the realization of the underlying values of teacher research. This was the origin of the educational enquiry – an attempt to understand the limits and possibilities of achieving research-based teaching during induction, initially with the group of 16 teachers of whom I worked closely with six:

Pauline, Mike, Lesley, Richard, Anna and Diane. That understanding, I hoped, would help me to perceive more acutely the possible answers to 'what should be done? how? and why?', with a view to the extension project. In this part of the research the methods I adopted, in addition to records of the planning proposals for the project and minutes of meetings with other personnel, included the use of diary accounts of visits to schools and interactions with the six teachers and their colleagues, field note records of conversations with the teachers, and interviews. The field note records of conversations, and the interviews, formed part of the interactions in practice as well as a mode of recording those interactions. Diary accounts were kept as a way of recording some events and my own reflections on them and on the progress of the project. By these means the data which were generated, and recorded immediately or soon after events, provided an opportunity to describe my own actions and to make explicit what was taken into account in determining them, or to monitor my response to the actions and/or other phenomena which affected them.

The other phenomena included, first and foremost in this phase of the research, the ways in which the teachers themselves undertook their teaching, if and how they reflected on it, and ways in which 'experience' and learning occurred. I worked with the teachers throughout the year. My aims for the project were made explicit in discussions with them, which included negotiating my support role. They also knew that I would research my role, their experiences and their teaching contexts, and that I was interested in their responses to the project's aims and conduct as well as in other aspects of their experience in schools. With these teachers the method adopted can best be described as observant-conversational and reflective-conversational. I observed the contexts in which they worked and their practice, and listened to and discussed with them their ideas about both. In turn they were observers as well as participants in the project, and conversed with me about its aims and my conduct in it. At the first meeting with the group, data collection was negotiated on the grounds that discussions would be 'open' unless confidentiality was explicitly sought. This was deemed important in view of the support role I undertook, and links with other colleagues, with whom individuals' learning might need to be discussed. The data were collected around the theme of the new teacher as reflective practitioner, and how the teachers learned (or did not). The exploration of that theme was approached open-endedly, so that data which challenged my presuppositions (my professional hopes, manifest in the project's aims) could be taken into account. In order to minimize biases and to achieve accurate accounts and interpretations of evidence the records were discussed with individual teachers. That was done partly in my role as support-tutor and partly as evaluator of the school experiences of the teachers. Anonymity was guaranteed to each teacher. External evaluation provided additional data on which I could reflect, particularly at the end of the school year.

The locations, circumstances and requirements of particular posts, and the dynamic of the teachers' responses to initial experiences of full-time teaching, were recorded for each of the six teachers. Chapter 3 continues with a portrait of Pauline, one of the teachers. The portrait of Pauline serves to illustrate the complexity of the work of the individual new teacher, the nature of her learning within the peculiar circumstances of one school, and my support-tutor role in relation to that learning, in some detail. Portraits of Mike, Lesley, Richard, Anna and Diane, set in their school contexts, and my work with them during the project, provide other accounts of the experiences of the individual teachers. These sections use a journalistic style for the portraiture of each teacher, and for the reports of tutor actions undertaken in the project. This journalistic style is mainly based on the observation records, field notes and diary accounts, with some interview data. The data were derived from the action research of my own support-tutor role, observation of and discussions with the teachers, and observation of the contexts in which they worked. The conception of new teachers as individuals, each very different in temperament, perspectives on schools and pupils, beliefs about teaching, background experience, subject expertise, educational interests, ethics and values, and all those other characteristics which make up the person as teacher, combined with the peculiarity of each of their circumstances, became an important influence on the way the project developed. The portraits convey my experience of working with these individual teachers in their respective circumstances.

From the interpretive case study I sought further data about the nature of teaching experience, the learning of practical teaching, and the nature of reflections on practice, by deepening the conversational method with a group of five other teachers who were not part of the induction project: Dave, Debbie, Kathy, Liz and Sue. This was conducted thoughout the same year as the initial project. We met as a research group throughout the academic year at two- or three-week intervals. Data were generated through discussion within the group, and the conversations were recorded on audio-tape. A procedure for the handling of data similar to that used with the six project teachers was adopted with the research group, to whom transcripts were returned at each next meeting or earlier. All the teachers built a file of data as a record of the discourse which could be, and was, referred to as the conversation progressed. Interim interpretations, especially through the selection of issues from the transcripts, were discussed with the group at intervals. That procedure served to extend the data on aspects of their thinking selected by myself. The teachers also selected from the data issues which they wanted to elaborate. Some of the ideas had not been especially prominent in consciousness in the initial discussions. Others were. But their experiences, thoughts and responses to both became more elaborate during the year. Confidentiality was respected within the group, but clearance of the data for use in reports was granted without reservation at the end of the year. Chapter 4 provides a brief background to the research project, and an analysis of data from those recorded conversations. The conversational nature of the discourse has been retained so that the teachers might be heard to speak for themselves.

The policy analysis, the action research of the initial project, and an interim analysis of the interpretive research, contributed to the design, implementation and practice of the wider induction project the following year. That involved 150 teachers and 90 teacher-tutors, directed by myself. The size and logistics of the extension project were very different from the initial one, and activating it occurred when the data from the first year was partially analysed. The same questions were invoked for this practical task as those asked for the initial project: what should I do, how, and why? They brought different responses. My perceptions of new teachers' learning and my experience of working with the six teachers affected the way in which the aims of the wider project were defined, and activities devised to achieve those aims. In particular I was concerned to develop the role of support-tutors in individual schools, rather than the external support-tutor role which I had undertaken, for reasons which will be discussed later, and which will become evident in the portraits of the teachers' experiences. Further, my own ideas about the role of new teachers were affected by concepts of 'competence' (explained by Zimpher and Howey, 1987), and 'social strategy' (Lacey, 1977; Zeichner and Tabachnick, 1985). (These concepts are described and discussed later.) The aims, then, were not only about developing reflective practice on the part of individual new teachers (as the aim of the initial project was conceived). They were also about developing different kinds of competence which might, as I saw it, contribute to the fulfilment of each teacher's potential in learning teaching, and in contributing to the schools talents which go well beyond basic technical teaching skills.

The second year of the fieldwork was done as an intrinsic part of the project's development, by adopting a collaborative mode of working with the teacher-tutors and new teachers. The 150 teachers met in five groups at different teachers' centres. Their teacher-tutors also met in five groups at the same centres, on different occasions. I sought to link action and research in the design of the project and the conduct of all the meetings by seeking and using within the groups information about the appointment and professional development of the teachers, and about the role of teacher-tutors. By inviting them to provide data, and then using collated and anonymized forms of the evidence in order to 'problematize' issues about appointment, development, and support of new entrants for further consideration among the groups, the method was intended to stimulate discussion within both constituencies as well as between them, and to stimulate individuals into conscious reflection. My actions in these respects included generating, recording, collating and re-presenting data as a means of bringing into consciousness, acknowledging, and seeking to enhance the conditions which might promote 'the self-development of competences' among the teachers, and the contributions which they made to their schools.

The project provided an opportunity to seek more extensive data on aspects of appointment arrangements, teaching contexts and support provision. I had identified the importance of these conditions for the conduct of

supported self-development during the previous year. The initial data demonstrated the need, in my view, to sensitize some teacher-tutors to new entrants'
circumstances, and the generation and use of the more extensive data was one
way to achieve that. Also, among the issues highlighted by the first year's
research the need for carefully stabilized approaches to the teachers' learning
through support dialogue, and developing the role of teacher-tutors in schools
to provide that support in each peculiar case, was seen as crucial. There was
neither the practical possibility nor the strategic desirability to continue my
role as support-tutor. It was deemed necessary to work through the agency of
teacher-tutors in such a way as to develop the quality and functions of that
agency. I judged from the experience of the initial project that it was necessary
to act in ways which might create different learning environments for the new
teachers, especially in so far as those environments were in the control of, or
affected by the actions of, teacher-tutors. The form which the collaborative project took towards that aim was to generate data from tutors and new teachers
about the qualities of the teacher-tutors' work, and the nature of tasks which
they undertook.

The instrumental purpose of the collaborative project was to enhance the
teacher-tutors' role, the opportunities for new entrants' learning, and the fulfilment of their potential in contributing to their schools, by:

1. Engaging teacher-tutors in the construction of policy and
   guidance for practice, through consideration of the conduct of
   their role.

2. Identifying areas of new teachers' knowledge which needed to
   be developed, and means of supporting their learning.

3. Identifying ways in which the full potential of new entrants
   could be fulfilled.

These methods and intentions related closely to other contingent aims for the
project, and reflected values which I hoped to realize during that year. The first
was that the project might become the property of the teachers and teacher-
tutors through information being shared among them, and tasks related to it
set in such a way that they constructed principles and guidelines for teacher-
tutor support practices. The second was that this project would provide a major
contribution to the formulation of policy by those who employ teachers and
those who provide for their continuing education. Chapter 5 is a report of that
year's work, the evidence which it generated, and the policy documents which
the teachers and I constructed.

The fieldwork and subsequent analysis of data began with the notion of
a set of case studies

> developed as a means to promote the basic phenomenological
> viewpoint that events are singular and unrepeatable but also
> that they contain sufficient within them that is exportable by

17

> other interested parties who will infer from that garnered
> experience and apply it to their own situations.
> (Sanger, 1986, p. 37)

This book takes account of the everyday world of teacher induction, including the 'mess' of those worlds, and screens in rather than screens out the variables (Sanger, 1986, p. 27) which play and interplay with new teachers' lives and experiences.

Such mess was not restricted to the worlds of the teachers. The variables which played and interplayed on my own work have already been indicated. The interweave of particular research literature and theoretical perspectives provided a range of concepts which played a part in my thinking and actions within the projects, and which also influenced my analysis and understanding of the data. In addition to literature on action research and research-based teaching, the ideas of Lortie (1975) had a general influence on my perceptions and insights about the nature of teacher induction and the experiences of the teachers. Lacey's (1977) study of teachers' social strategies, elaborated by Zeichner and Tabachnick (1985), played an important role in the way the projects were conceived and conducted, and subsequently in analysing the action research and observational data of the six initial project teachers. Zimpher and Howey's (1987) analysis of competences provided a vehicle for organizing my ideas about the development of teaching among the six, and among the research group of five. Most of all, with the latter the work of Schon (1971, 1983, 1987) provided an extension to my own initial thinking about the projects. These ideas were subsequently elaborated in the light of current debates among teacher-educators concerned with teacher research. What this interplay of ideas and actions displayed in particular was that in the projects I played several roles: teacher-educator; observer; and scholar of theoretical literature. The report of the work is therefore autobiographical, presented as a historical/ narrative account of the action enquiry incorporated into my work as agent, researcher and scholar. Compared with 'single orientation' research, the interaction of these roles presented a considerable challenge, not least in the construction of this book. Yet it was deemed essential to meet that challenge, rather than avoid it, in the interests of consistency and integrity of my own beliefs in research-based teaching.

The ideas of reflective practice which I held, and the concepts of competence and social strategy which I had borrowed from the literature, were ideas which were explored throughout the projects and after. The extent and intensity of the extension project meant that the earlier data were, in the event, more comprehensively analysed, and the conceptual ideas more fully considered, only after the extension project had been implemented. Chapter 6 provides a review of the directions these ideas took as the practice within the projects, the research data and the conceptual frameworks were brought together with more time for deliberation.

Chapter 2

Problems with Policy:
Teacher Induction in England and Wales

CONTEMPORARY ISSUES

After a century of compulsory public education in England and Wales, in which some millions of teachers have worked, during which state and local funding has been a massive investment, and toward which academics and public servants have contributed their individual and collective wisdom, there is little known about the educational experiences of new teachers or how best to provide for their effective education. In writing my book *Learning Teaching, Teaching Teaching* (Tickle, 1987a), I uncovered a dearth of understanding and lack of established principles upon which the initial education of teachers might be based. As my attention was drawn to post-initial teacher education experience, especially in the first year of teaching, the dearth of understanding seemed even more acute. Particularly surprising were claims, for example, that little is known about induction except that teachers find it difficult and memorable (Hall, 1982, p. 54); that numerous research questions needed to be asked (Griffin, 1985, p. 43); and that the study of how teachers learn to teach appeared to be emerging as a specialization in educational research (Doyle, 1985, p. 32).

During the period of the shift in my focus towards induction there also emerged widespread and growing dispute about what kinds of experiences are appropriate for new teachers. The debate intensified in a direction which made it increasingly difficult to distinguish between initial and post-initial experience in the arguments presented. The very need to provide initial teacher education was challenged, especially by the Hillgate Group and its 'New Right' associates, and defended, especially by teacher trainers, as national policy was made to allow direct entry into teaching with 'on the job' concurrent training (see, for example, Booth *et al.*, 1989; DES, 1988a, 1989a; Hargreaves, 1989; Hillgate Group, 1989; Newsam, 1989; *Guardian*, 1989a, b; *Independent*, 1989; *TES*, 1988; UCET, 1988). More recent proposals (Clark, 1992) to make initial training substantially more school-based intensified the dispute. These debates and events will be discussed more fully at the end of this chapter on page 40.

Even before this intensification of debate and events, and while the separation of phases seemed distinct in both policy and practice, I had begun a search for principles of teacher induction based on understanding of the learning of new teachers. This was done for the very practical purposes of directing the projects. Such principles and understanding seemed distinctly elusive however, and I wondered whether that elusiveness could be overcome by considering the issues as they appeared in former and current educational contexts – from evidence of policy and practice. Perhaps steps toward answers could be taken by examining recent and current developments in new teacher education policy itself, within the context of education policy more generally. Perhaps the problem could also be illuminated and my curiosity satisfied by examining policy and provision for new teachers of earlier times, both before and since state education was introduced in England and Wales. In doing both, it soon became clear that the separation of initial training and the early years of teaching is difficult in terms of how learning teaching is discussed. In the past, and in very recent policy, school-based induction has 'blended' the phases of initial training and induction. At other times policy has attempted to define phased but continuous induction, while provision has distinctly separated the two. And in relation to both policy and provision, it appeared that some major issues could only be addressed and understood across the phases – particularly the question of how teachers learn.

In 1985 the White Paper *Better Schools* (DES, 1985b) presented the economic imperative for improving standards in education through, among other things, improvements in the quality of teaching in state schools in England and Wales (DES, 1985b, para 9). It reiterated much of the content of an earlier White Paper, *Teaching Quality* (DES, 1983b), on initial teacher training's selection of students, structure of courses and curriculum content, and on inservice teacher education. In addition it summarized other areas of the education service which would be subject to centralized quality control and laid out the mechanisms for achieving that control, following numerous policy initiatives from the Department of Education and Science. The summary manifested a four-pronged approach to the achievement of changes in education provision. As well as teaching quality, selected contenders for reform were the content and processes in the school curriculum; the examination and assessment of pupils; and the government and administration of schools. Most were already subject to substantial overhaul, which has continued with increased vigour since, both before and after the pivotal point of the 1988 Education Reform Act.

The wider background, and some more recent foreground, to the White Paper *Better Schools* and its attendant reports, pamphlets, discussion papers, memoranda and command papers, has been the subject of previous analysis (see e.g. Hargreaves, 1988; Salter and Tapper, 1981; Tickle, 1987a) about ideological and bureaucratic responses which attached themselves to identified or expressed capitalist economic 'needs' during the 1970s. The subsequent passage of some of the White Paper's detail (and other policies) into legislation in the Education Act 1986 and the Education Reform Act 1988 has also been widely reported and debated, though analysis is only just emerging in coherent or comprehensive form (Flude and Hammer, 1990).

While change to each of education's constituent elements for reform, called 'linked initiatives' (DES, 1985b, para 302), has been in its own way contentious, curriculum, assessment and school management had entered the public domain of debate rather more fully than had teacher education and appraisal. Heated debate about teaching *quality* had been generated during the late 1970s, providing an instrument which helped to lay the foundations of the other reforms. It was, at that time, the issue of teaching quality which spawned the Black Papers on Education (Cox and Dyson, 1969); the press coverage of the William Tyndale School (Auld, 1979) and Bennett's *Teaching Styles and Pupil Progress* (Bennett, 1976); and the unprecedented prime ministerial intervention in education in 1976 (Callaghan, 1976). Subsequent DES and government interventions focused the public debate more notably around youth training. The structure for curriculum reform was initially put in place through 'consultation' within local education authorities and higher educational institutions, followed by wider political debate and legislation.

In the case of teacher education, however, changes had hardly been noticeable in subsequent legislation, because the legal and administrative structures which were needed for ministerial power to be directly exercised on teacher education were already mainly in place. Until the late 1980s teacher education seemed to be less contentious and therefore less in the public eye. Perhaps it was assumed by policy-makers that if the structures were set in place in those other aspects of the education service, then teachers may be simply trained to work the system, leaving them little space to challenge the supposed 'consensus' of educational values (Hillgate Group, 1989) asserted from the right wing of the political spectrum, and reflected in the other reforms. Until the 1980s within the educational community itself, and particularly from HMI and the DES, there had been little enough debate about the nature and quality of teacher education. The major feature of the previous two decades had been a focus on supply, as the demand for teachers leapt, and just as suddenly declined, in the early 1960s and late 1970s respectively. Those concerns, together with associated questions of salaries and conditions, remained a preoccupation into the 1980s. The opening section of the White Paper *Teaching Quality* (DES, 1983b) outlined demand, supply and salary 'prospects' up to 1991, and *Better Schools* (DES, 1985b) also addressed these issues. However, *Teaching Quality* invoked new debates about the initial training, appointment and subsequent career development of teachers. These were seen as of 'vital concern to the Government and to the nation'! (DES, 1983b, para 1).

In *Teaching Quality* the Secretaries of State (for Education and Science and for Wales) confirmed the Government's adoption (in the much earlier *Education: A Framework for Expansion* (DES, 1972) of a target of an all-graduate profession, and the need to ensure depth and rigour in initial training commensurate with graduate status (DES, 1983b, para 53). The Government had commissioned Her Majesty's Inspectors (HMI) and the Advisory Committee on the Supply and Education of Teachers (ACSET) to examine teacher education curricula. *Teaching in Schools: The Content of Initial Training* (DES, 1983c) had signalled a shift from concern with numbers towards commitment to quality by HMI. That shift was analysed by Taylor (1984) and summarized in Tickle (1987a).

The Secretaries of State also reiterated in both White Papers the Government's acceptance of the *Framework* paper's case for improved induction arrangements for newly trained teachers − particularly appropriate workloads, professional support, and further training:

> there is no major profession to which a new entrant, however thorough his [*sic*] initial training, can be expected immediately to make a full contribution. Teachers in their first teaching posts need, and should be released part-time to profit from, a systematic programme of professional initiation and guidance, and further study where necessary.
> (DES, 1983c, para 84)

Furthermore, the Government made it clear that induction should be seen as extending beyond the first year, which in itself should particularly include reduced teaching loads and professional support. The White Papers acknowledged that 'financial constraints have limited progress' (DES, 1983b, para 55) and reported that few schools had a systematic approach to the induction of new teachers and career development for staff (DES, 1985a, para 22). In consequence there was a reassertion of the challenge to employers to improve the quality of teaching practices by building on the period of initial teacher education. The clear commitment to inservice teacher education during the period of induction was expressed as the employers' responsibility to:

> support and encourage professional development at all stages of the individual teacher's career. A newly trained teacher needs structured support and guidance during probation and his early years in the profession.
> (DES, 1985a, para 178)

The establishment of a triad of criteria for selection and training − personal qualities, academic subject knowledge, and practical professional skills − was the major prop of the shift in concern from supply to quality in initial training. The establishment of the Council for the Accreditation of Teacher Education (CATE) and the issue of Circular 3/84 was later reported to have given 'practical expression to these requirements' for quality (DES, 1985a, para 141). The development imposed a bureaucratic layer of quality control through mechanisms for the approval of courses. The CATE, however, generated less debate than it did paperwork and consumption of resources. The discussions and exchanges within the teacher education community which followed the establishment of CATE in 1984 were relatively quiet. There was little outspoken fundamental disagreement about the content and structures of courses which CATE required. The longest and strongest debate concerned the subject qualification (appropriateness to the school curriculum) for entry into primary teacher training, and the length and specialization of subject studies in primary training courses. Both issues were overtaken by the implementation of the National Curriculum, which served to sustain the CATE requirements by its subject specification. Renewed CATE arrangements provided only minor modifications to the original demands (DES, 1989b). About the principles of participation in teacher education by practising teachers and by lecturers in schools, there seemed to be widespread acquiescence. Indeed there was nothing about CATE's scheme which had not been said better before (McNair, 1944; Plowden, 1967; James, 1972). My own published criticisms (Tickle, 1987a) were about the minimalist and inadequate proposals, and the failure of CATE to be radically revisionist in the education process for teachers. Amid that criticism, and the alternative proposals made for linking theory and practice in learning teaching, a major concern was with the assumptions about subject knowledge and associated pedagogy and the demise of the study of education, which had barely gained a toe-hold in teacher education curricula in Britain.

During 1988/89, however, England and Wales witnessed a sudden upsurge in debate and dispute about initial teacher training, sparked not by the issue of quality, but by a question of supply. While the Universities Council for the Education of Teachers (UCET) deliberated about their own constructive alternatives for improving quality through a two-year Post-Graduate Certificate in Education (PGCE), the economic, demographic and political contexts shifted at a pace which five years earlier had been foreseeable yet largely unforeseen. The debate was made more intense by the events which occurred in those contexts.

The return of a Conservative government in June 1987 carried a mandate to urgently introduce its Education Reform Bill. The Bill, and the Act which gained Royal Assent in July 1988, reflected all of the major reform elements presented in *Better Schools*. It went further, with provisions for schools to opt out of Local Education Authority (LEA) control and instead to be funded by direct government grant. Financial devolution to schools (now Local Management of Schools – LMS), the removal of LEA control over admissions of pupils and the establishment of city technology colleges (intended to be independently funded) reinforced notions of competition among and accountability of teachers and their managers. However, central to the Act was the plan for implementation of the National Curriculum, and national assessment and testing. As far as the Government sought or had control of the economy, and as far as they could show the link between schooling and economic prosperity, there seemed to be a battle for control of education among the bureaucrats as well as ministers. The Department of Education and Science appeared to be rapidly losing ground to the Department of Trade and Industry (DTI) whose Manpower Services Commission (MSC) had introduced industrial training programmes and entered the schools' curriculum through microtechnology provision and in particular the Technical and Vocational Education Initiative (TVEI). The Education Reform Act, which was firmly in the hands of the Education Minister, could redress the infringement only if the curriculum it imposed, and its other provisions, satisfied the economic and ideological imperatives of the Government and particularly the Treasury. The rapid implementation of the National Curriculum without major additional cost was essential in these political terms.

During the formulation and passage through Parliament of the Education Reform Bill, a select committee of the House of Commons was established to examine teacher supply. Whereas prior to 1985 there had been a general oversupply, there had continued to be shortages of teachers in subjects seen as central to economic prosperity: mathematics, the sciences, technology, business studies and foreign languages. At that time there was widespread dissatisfaction, dissent and disruption in schools as teachers' morale, pay and conditions and career mobility were each (relatively) reduced through cuts in public spending and stringent financial control of local authority employers by the Government. In 1987 the Secretary of State for Education and Science withdrew teachers' negotiating rights and imposed pay and conditions of service determined by himself, within Treasury limits. The school population which had been in steep decline levelled, and in primary school ages (and secondary ages in some places) began to rise. These multiple phenomena, planned, unplanned, or arising from tactical responses to events, meant that the Education Reform Act's implementation became the duty of the Secretaries of State, LEAs, governors and headteachers at a time when it was becoming increasingly obvious that sufficient teachers might not be available to do the work at the sharp end.

The outline time-scale for implementation of the National Curriculum was imposed by the DES during Autumn 1988. Religious education and collective worship began immediately in all schools (it had already been required by the 1944 Education Act). Mathematics, science and English began in Autumn 1989 for five-year-olds; mathematics and science only for eleven-year-olds. Technology would follow in September 1990 for the same age groups, when English was also added for eleven-year-olds. These core subjects plus technology were introduced to seven-year-olds in the same year. With geography and history in 1991 and art, PE and music a year later, plus a foreign language (in secondary schools only), the picture of the curriculum was drawn. As a result of ensuing events, numerous details have since been redrawn, though that is a story for curriculum historians to recount elsewhere. These changes did not take account, either, of continuing demands for teachers familiar with information technology, business studies and nursery education.

In March 1988, the Interim Advisory Committee on School Teachers' Pay and Conditions used the DES's own figures to demonstrate demographic trends in pupil populations, and equivalent projected demand for teachers. The DES estimated then that by 1989 10.4 per cent of all graduates from English and Welsh higher education institutions would need to enter teacher training courses if PGCE recruitment targets were to be achieved. Some 8.2 per cent of all those pupils in schools who achieved two or more A levels would need to enter Bachelor of Education (BEd) courses. In mathematics and computing, PGCE recruitment targets would require 18 per cent of all graduates; in French they would require 54 per cent (Chilver, 1988). However, the Committee discovered that there was no national assessment or published targets for overall teacher numbers. It recognized the urgent need for such assessments in light of the introduction of the National Curriculum. Teacher supply planning, it seems, had not improved on past experiences of fluctuating over supply and shortages. The demographic trends which the Committee presented corresponded to the time-scale, as it later transpired, for implementation of the National Curriculum. While the committee asserted that the teaching force was relatively stable with only a modest turnover, they could not predict the effects which the Act and other factors might have on its stability or specific needs. During 1989 some LEAs experienced substantial instability, associated with their inability to recruit sufficient teachers. Nationally, 27,000 new entrants per annum (into a total force of 404,000) were cancelled out by 27,000 departures from teaching.

It became clear in May 1988 that the DES was seriously concerned about not being able to recruit enough teachers. The consultation document *Qualified Teacher Status* (DES, 1988b) set out the Secretary of State's proposals for 'significant revisions' to the regulations for granting qualified teacher status, to produce 'a simpler, more effective system'. The system proposed was to remove the 'disincentive to recruitment' (to teaching) of a 'period of full time study' for mature or overseas personnel. Such entrants were seen as 'likely to become a more significant element within the teacher force in the 1990s as a rise in the school population coincides with a decline in the number of qualified 18–25-year-olds.' The status of licensed teacher was proposed, for direct entry into teaching. That was followed in Spring 1989 by the announcement of the articled teacher route into qualified teacher status, by way of which new graduates could undertake part-time initial training while working 80 per cent of each week in school under the supervision of a teacher-mentor (DES, 1989a). With these events teacher education policy-making returned, in part, from a brief period of discussion about quality, to its early dominant feature – supply planning.

The reaffirmation of CATE's role, coupled with HMI monitoring, and now in a proposed modified committee structure for policing quality in teacher education courses, provided the bureaucratic response to the question of quality (DES, 1989b). A statement of competences was proposed to ensure consistency in the criteria and the expected outcomes of full-time PGCE and BEd/BA courses and new routes of licensed and articled teacher training (DES,

1989b, para 4.2). It seemed to be assumed by the DES that debate about quality and the means of achieving it however it was defined, could simply be replaced by the imposition of competence criteria. For non-standard routes to qualified teacher status there was, in the event, only guidance to LEAs and governing bodies of schools on competence criteria, with little indication of how 'expected outcomes' or the means of achieving them might be effected. Paradoxically it was these proposals for non-standard teacher training which sparked heated debate within the educational community about quality and provision, to a degree which had not happened in response to the initiatives of the early 1980s which had intended to raise the debate (DES, 1983b, c). The debate was substantially fuelled during 1991, and ministerial action was taken on 4 January 1992 with an announcement at the North of England Education Conference. Changes in initial teacher training which would require 80 per cent of student time to be spent in selected schools formed a central prop of the proposed reforms. Modified soon afterwards to two-thirds of time in schools for secondary students, with longer deliberation about proposals for primary students, debate became subsidiary to local discussions about the mechanisms for implementing new course structures.

However, even within the policy initiatives on teacher education, the relatively acquiescent and calm debate of the early 1980s and more vibrant recent reactions to policy, the question of induction into teaching has been given scant mention, despite the policy statements about the need to improve it. Apart from a substantial HMI report on *The New Teacher In School* (DES, 1982a) and a follow-up survey reported six years later under the same title (DES, 1988a), little had been done. The probationary year in particular remained quite untrammelled and unreformed both in policy and practice (DES, 1990) until it was suddenly disposed of altogether (DES, 1991b), and teacher appraisal regulations were applied to new entrants where previously they had been exempted (DES, 1991a). Though it has been given a low profile up until now, teacher induction highlights some key issues about what is (or ought to be) happening in the education of teachers in the early part of their careers. The new routes to qualified teacher status and proposed changes in initial training raise those issues to a level of importance which is unprecedented in recent times.

THE CHEQUERED BACKGROUND OF TEACHER INDUCTION

The requirement for graduates to undertake initial training was introduced only in 1982 (DES, 1982b). Until then, policy-makers, employers and teachers assumed that academic knowledge of a subject was the only qualifying factor for teaching, or that in itself it also provided professional skills and personal qualities, at least for secondary school teaching competence. On the other hand, for primary school teaching the implementation of graduate status training was introduced only during the 1970s. Prior to that the focus of their curricula was substantially on classroom skills. Academic requirements for entry into teacher education were, until then, five subjects at GCE O level, with English being the only compulsory one. This perhaps reflected the Lancasterian and Bell models of teacher induction in the elementary monitorial schools of the early nineteenth century which assumed, at first, that academic qualities and qualifications, if needed at all, were secondary to knowing how to 'teach the system'. These assumptions, which have persisted in policy until recent times, and which emerged again in more recent disputes, shows signs of deep differences in teacher education ideology and perspectives. They have an extensive background.

The Society for Promoting Christian Knowledge (SPCK), an Anglican church body started in 1699 and which established charity schools for the Christian teaching of the poor, selected teachers on grounds of age (25+), sobriety, meekness and humility. It also sought natural aptitude for teaching, literacy and numeracy (in men, not women, who did not teach arithmetic. They, but not men, had to be proficient sewers and knitters). Here were the beginnings of the criteria-triad invoked by CATE: personal qualities, professional aptitude and academic subject expertise. The Society's aspiration for developing professional skills centred on plans to allow new recruits to observe and practise with experienced teachers, providing an apprenticeship approach to learning teaching in some schools as early as the beginning of the eighteenth century. It is interesting that these apprentice teachers would learn their professional skills from those who had had no training, and about whom it must have been assumed that they were naturally talented or had learned by experience. Some of those teachers became the first teacher trainers, moving into urban and rural areas to teach other teachers. But the upgrading of promising pupils within a school to teach under a master's guidance as apprentices was to be the start of later, more widespread teacher training systems. To methods training was sometimes added academic knowledge – of the Church Catechism and divinity (Dent, 1977). However, the systematic extension of popular elementary education, and concurrently the systematic training of teachers through apprenticeship as monitors, was another century coming. The Quakers' apprentice-teacher scheme, begun in the 1780s, was extended by Joseph Lancaster, while Andrew Bell introduced an equivalent system for the Anglicans. These were systems of teaching whereby each school was organized and administered, and a curriculum transmitted under rules rather like McDonald's hamburger franchise regulations – each part of the job had to be done according to the intricately planned system. At the service-counter equivalent – the desk – pupils were served by monitors, who were overseen by senior monitors, all working under the direction of a superintendent. The Quaker scheme monitors (who were young children aged 7–12) were trained by superintendents in both the content of lessons and teaching methods. Superintendents were trained in the system and how to work it at a centre overseen by Lancaster, who issued a teachers' certificate as credentials of training (Dent, 1977, p. 5), giving them the franchise to set up the system in schools around the country. While Lancaster included elements of personal education — 'lectures on the passions' — in his training of superintendents, Bell argued that it was only by taking an active part in teaching in school that teachers would learn (Rich, 1933). Different viewpoints about teacher education curricula during the first decade of the nineteenth century have clear reflections in arguments presented in 1989, as I will show later. Thus Bell established a training institution for superintendents in 1810, the start of central schools as model training places for the Church of England's national schools. Like the Quaker-founded British and Foreign Society, the Anglican National Society soon recognized the need to set selection criteria to ensure that entrants to teaching were literate and numerate, and to set examinations for certification after training. In 1813, The National Society also introduced an obligatory probationary period of practice before certification (Dent, 1977).

Training and probation lasted only one or two months. What or how the teachers learned from practice or from seniors in that time is unclear. Concern in the British and Foreign Society about lack of personal academic knowledge among recruits into teaching resulted in the addition of more of that element to the curriculum of Borough Road Training School — the first in Britain — and the later curricula of teachers' colleges elsewhere. However, the balance of time spent in those early model schools was tipped in favour of teaching in school, and apprenticeship. Apprenticeship was changed and more fully institutionalized in the mid-nineteenth century, following a pupil-teacher system known in Holland much earlier. Pupil-teachers were older than their monitor predecessors, and their personal education 'better'. They had correspondingly greater responsibilities, with a class of 40 pupils in a classroom, rather than ten in a schoolroom shared by many pupils and monitors. Apprenticeship was to a carefully selected headteacher for five years. Full-time teaching was accompanied by at least one-and-a-half hours' tutoring before or after school each day by the head, and annual examination by HMI. Apprentices were paid annuities, and heads were paid for tutoring, subject to HMI judgement of progress. Successful completion of apprenticeship led to opportunities to enter 'normal school' training and hence to gain certification for teaching, or to teach uncertificated in elementary schools. In the event, most did the latter so that apprenticeship to the headteacher constituted all their training (Dent, 1977).

The training system which developed alongside the pupil-teacher one, and which took most entrants from outside the pupil-teacher route, devised curricula which would be mainly familiar today, and these were formalized in the mid-1850s — subject knowledge relevant to school curricula; professional skills; and practical teaching. However, the combined routes into teaching showed another contemporary familiar element: issues of cost-effectiveness in the light of national economic restraint were raised. The 1862 Revised Code abolished grants for the employment of pupil-teachers and headteachers' tutoring of them. Apprenticeships were replaced by renewable half-year contracts, and scholarships for entry into training dropped. Training school funds were substantially reduced. Graded teachers' certificates, first awarded for length of training, were then awarded for length of teaching service, implying that quality of learning teaching and performance derived from experience – not necessarily automatically but, since there was no other way provided to improve professionally, this must have been the assumption.

The demise of the pupil-teacher route, as well as the direct training school route under economic restraint, was suddenly replaced by a demand for teachers to implement the 1870 Education Act, with its consequent doubling in school population in five years. Inducements to potential teachers were restored and improved; pass standards for certification lowered; and certification granted without examination to serving teachers on HMI recommendation. The apprenticeship of pupil-teachers, restored by financial inducements to schools and by 'many small School Boards and ... school managers ... shopping in the cheapest market' (Dent, 1977, p. 26) became commonplace again, along with the employment of uncertificated teachers. Raised age of entry (to 14 in 1878), the establishment of training centres and reduced teaching loads were invoked to improve the education and training of these teachers. Concern about quality continued into the twentieth century concurrently with apprenticeship, as the economics of teacher education and the school system in general sustained the cheap routes, and justified them on the rhetoric of the educational value of pupilage and apprenticeship. In contrast, by the late nineteenth century the training colleges ran examination-driven academic courses with curricula rather like secondary schools but with a modicum of teaching practice experience under controlled conditions in demonstration schools.

The bringing together, in the late nineteenth and twentieth centuries, of these different routes, experiences and syllabuses, through developments in central government policy, local education authorities, religious authorities and institutional practices, is a long and complex history, which has been recorded in part by Dent (1977), Rich (1933), Taylor (1969, 1978) and others. The point of reviewing its early stages, as reflected in these secondary sources, is to show

1. How contemporary developments in England and Wales are not entirely new.

2. How the debate about how best to train teachers has persisted, but not necessarily progressed.

3. That economic factors played a major part in shaping inexpensive teacher education for teachers in elementary schools for the poor.

4. The basic elements of teacher quality were set out long ago in terms of approved attitudes and personal qualities, aptitudes in

the classroom based on technical competence and limited academic knowledge to be transmitted to pupils.

5. There was no systematic evidence, and no attempt to gain any, of the educational experiences of teachers (or pupils). Policy was based on assertion, belief, and cost-efficiency.

6. Those beliefs and assertions eventually brought together but did not reconcile the practical apprenticeship and educational endeavours of student teachers.

7. The educational experiences of newly qualified teachers was largely ignored beyond certification.

   A major irony of the historical notions of teacher-apprenticeship in the twentieth century, and especially now, is that most teaching and learning teaching occurs in isolation from other teachers. I will show later that this is especially so at the stage immediately following initial training, where notions of tutored learning held over from the nineteenth century have persistently foundered on lack of funds in the twentieth century. In 1925 attempts to link initial training and the first year of teaching in a systematic, continuous training programme were discussed by the Government and aborted because of lack of funds (Evans, 1978). Revival of the issue in the McNair Report (McNair, 1944) made little impact on practice, though its recommendations have resonances heard again since 1989. For example, on the question of linking theory and practice, McNair proposed deeming some training schools as laboratories and scenes of field studies for student teachers to work in, with teachers to take on supervision and support of trainees in return for additional remuneration. It was argued that the combination of being a teacher yet also being a learner/student, with due recognition for the learner's needs, was the most productive curriculum combination (McNair, 1944, para 267). 'Outstanding practitioners' might be seconded for up to five years into colleges, thus guaranteeing that teacher trainers would have recent relevant experience of schoolteaching. Another consequence would be to provide a cadre of experienced teachers who also had experience of teacher education and who could thus better serve newly qualified teachers whom they would supervise (McNair, 1944, paras 271–279).

   For the probationary period (usually a year) McNair proposed the system of provisional recognition of qualified teacher status with the promise or expectation that 'they would make at least moderately good teachers' (McNair, 1944, para 278). Schools would be specifically staffed for receiving and supervising new teachers, in order to make the first year 'an effective part of training for all teachers, as a continuation of the full time training period' (McNair, 1944, para 280). However, McNair's recommendations are largely about 'catching them' – that is, about assessing and selecting candidates deemed unsuitable for teaching on grounds of lack of classroom competence. With regard to provision of support it attempted to establish, in principle, institutional structures based on perceived practice/theory gaps, and on the ability of outstanding practitioners to apprentice student and first year teachers successfully. There is no analysis of the assumptions about apprenticeship or of the nature of teachers' learning. Nor is there any analysis of training institutions' aims and methods. Discussion of teaching quality, of learning and of curriculum was displaced by proposals which reflect another recent feature of debate: the tension in teacher induction between mentoring and monitoring, advising and assessing, supporting and selecting (McNair, 1944, para 288).

Revival of the Board of Education's 1925 and McNair's proposals with regard to new entrants to teaching accompanied the lengthening of initial training and the expansion of numbers recruited to teaching in the 1960s (NUT, 1969, 1971; Plowden, 1967; Gittins, 1967). In tandem, DES memoranda to LEAs gave guidance on the assessment and support of new teachers. Administrative Memoranda 4/59 and 10/68 essentially reflected McNair. They saw the first year as an opportunity for tutoring and for testing, to provide learning, yet to secure selection procedures. Selection was framed in terms of assessing practical proficiency at minimal competency, after offering 'general help and guidance' within appropriate conditions of work. Responsibility for implementation lay with the LEA and schools (DES, 1968, p. 5). The evidence of new teachers' experiences at that time provides a stark contrast to policy aspirations, with support varying from area to area, and many teachers being abandoned to the isolation of the classroom (Collins, 1969). Teachers often did not have information about classes, syllabuses to be taught or support offered until close to the date when they began teaching, and more than a third did not meet an LEA adviser in their first year (Taylor and Dale, 1971). Confirming Collins (1969), Taylor and Dale reported that new teachers saw the year as a period of assessment rather than one of professional growth. This was hardly surprising, given that probation rather than induction had been the emphasis in practice with HMI responsible for approving successful completion and hence confirmation of qualified teacher status up to 1949, when the responsibility was passed on to employers (Collins, 1969). From then on, the LEA's formal responsibilities were to assess teaching, with HMI continuing to participate in cases which were not initially approved by the LEA.

Developments in the 1960s and early 1970s held some prospect of shifting the emphasis towards induction, in recognition of its potential for learning teaching, in ways which could subsume the formal requirements for the approval of teachers to work in schools. *Education: A Framework for Expansion* (DES, 1972) made very specific proposals for the support and induction of new teachers which looked like the pride of McNair with enhanced glow. New teachers were to receive help during their first year, with at least 20 per cent of their time devoted to inservice training. In addition they would be given a further 5 per cent of non-contact time and schools would be staffed to allow the three-quarters teaching load. Professional tutors would be designated and trained, and a network of professional centres would support induction arrangements. Assessment procedures remained unchanged, as did the formal responsibility of employers, but the emphasis on school-based learning, with structured provision to establish what were seen as necessary conditions for such learning, clearly shifted the emphasis from summative assessment of performance to formative appraisal for professional development. The shift was to be translated into practice through pilot schemes, with the aim of introducing a national scheme of induction for new teachers in the 1975/76 school year.

The pilot schemes, funded by the Department of Education and Science, were introduced in Liverpool and Northumberland (Bolam, 1973; Bolam *et al.*, 1975; Davis, 1979; McCabe, 1978). An emphasis on school-based support by experienced colleagues, together with out-of-school meetings of new teachers, were invoked as the main procedures for focusing on their individual needs. The reports of the pilot projects are important for several reasons. They

1. provide the first summaries of evidence relating to teacher induction in England and Wales;

2. reflect the views of numerous official reports, and report the effects of translating policy into practice;

3. show how the optimism of the time was short-lived, given more recent extensive evidence.

The summaries of evidence painted a picture of new teachers who began full-time teaching, with no systematic induction support, immediately after qualifying. A range of evidence and recommendations from other trial schemes (summarized in Bolam, 1973) and from a national survey (Taylor and Dale, 1971) suggested widespread dissatisfaction with that situation. The recommendations reflected the assumptions and aspirations of the various writers, teachers' associations, official committees and employers. The pattern of recommendations included appeals for:

- systematic co-ordination of administration of appointment and placement in schools;

- provision of information such as pupil lists, timetables, school handbooks, and induction procedures;

- early contact/orientation with the personnel and geography of the school and locality;

- pastoral support through meetings with peers, and guidance from colleagues;

- 'job-embedded' conditions, with reduced teaching loads, and release for orientation meetings, planning teaching, and observing colleagues;

- a structured programme of induction within the school, based on practical needs;

- a named teacher-tutor for the school-based support;
- a non-assessing mentor from outside the school.

Bolam presumed that, if such recommendations were met, the first year would not be characterized as a crisis situation (a common view represented in the literature which he reviewed). He also argued that the year was a period of missed opportunities which, if grasped, would enable initial, induction and inservice teacher education to be conceived as a continuum of professional learning for all teachers. That learning, it was asserted, would be most effective if based on practical classroom relevance and the individualized problems and opportunities of the teachers (Bolam, 1973). Of all the assumptions revealed, the Teacher Induction Pilot Scheme (TIPS) national evaluation report went somewhat further than this, setting out procedural arrangements (from appointment to end-of-year review) within the notion of context-based learning. Its stated aims of induction were primarily 'to provide the knowledge, advice and experience which will enable probationers to make their own independent professional judgements' (Bolam et al., 1975, pp. 12–13).

In one sense this was a curious aim. If teachers were (and are) characteristically isolated from colleagues and guided by intuition and whatever personal resources they have then it is inevitable that, in the nature of the job, they make their own independent judgements. Presumably, then, the knowledge, advice and experiences would provide for qualitatively better judgements. There is no evidence of how such educative processes would work, or their effectiveness. That they should be made to work, yet generally did not, was reflected in the second aim of the TIPS report: 'To promote professional growth and development, and not simply the acquisition of "survival" or "coping" strategies, for *all* probationers, including the able ones' (Bolam et al., 1975, pp. 12–13).

This alludes to a further characteristic of reports about the experiences of new entrants – that is, that teachers who 'cope' with the job do not receive support, and are left to their isolation. Yet there is also a view in the pilot project reports of such teachers being deficient – as if surviving and coping, presumably through effective use of independent professional judgements, was in some respect unsatisfactory and inadequate. In this, too, the report reflects certain typifications of teachers. It implies notions of restricted and extended professionals (Hoyle, 1969) without enquiring into the nature of or reasons for particular teacher strategies. Perhaps this was an artefact of a complex statement of aim, which might have rested at 'to promote professional growth and development' as the necessary supplement to making independent judgements. In short, the implied aim was *to promote professional growth and development in making independent judgements*. It was in that core and primary purpose that the TIPS project offered a radically different way of conceptualizing induction. Subsumed within the primary aims was the improvement of specific teaching techniques and classroom management competences.

It was presumably assumed, as Stenhouse (1975) argued, that that would stem from better professional judgements. The project also aimed to provide information and support which would enable judgements to be made in light of broader institutional contexts and 'wider professional issues'.

Again, while there were extensive and complex recommendations about organizational arrangements, programmes and personnel, there was no attempt to analyse processes by which professional judgement or other elements of teaching quality, or their development, occur. The 'components' of provision — LEA policy and programmes, schools' policy and programmes and tutors' roles — are essentially systems-building, to ensure that the minutiae needed for starting and sustaining a teaching job are catered for. Beyond that, the key assumptions about professional learning are that learning should be practice-based, individualized and continuous. The place of educational theory was that it would be 'applied' to practical problems and related 'to the experience of individual teachers over a sustained period of time' (Bolam, 1973, p. 180). Just how this might occur was not discussed.

The *Framework* paper and the pilot projects coincided with the publication of the James Report, *Teacher Education and Training* (James, 1972), which recommended many of the features of the White Paper and of the pilot projects. Its notion of a 'tricycle' of personal education, initial training and systematic induction, and longer-term inservice teacher education, formed the basis of all its proposals. The assumption was that initial training's purpose would be to equip a student 'to be as effective a teacher as possible in his first assignment' as a basis for further learning. This stage would concentrate on the 'functional' aspects of teaching, with 'conceptual frameworks', seen as contributory to effectiveness. The importance of theory was not challenged, but it was deemed to be more effective after some initial experience of teaching. Thus in the second year of the second cycle teachers would hold the status of licensed teacher, while undergoing training which was 'demonstrably very much more than merely an improved version of the probationary year' (James, 1972, para 3.21). The experiential/practical and the reflective/theoretical were again wedded in these proposals.

The 'ideal' provision and experience, juxtaposed to a typification of the 'reality' of new teachers' experience, was set out as if it were a campaign. The 'gross inadequacy' of practices for induction support was said to 'imply incompetence and irresponsibility' on the part of providers — LEAs and schools. The solution, it was argued, depended on changes in the structure of provision, and the establishment of principles. Among these the licensed teacher would have a special position, support of a teacher-tutor, and a curriculum of training in classroom practice and wider professional matters, both varied according to the context of the school but within 'universal principles'. In addition, new teachers would have 20 per cent of their time released for further training at a professional centre, with close liaison between the schools' professional tutors and professional centres, under scrutiny by regional teacher training organizations. The licensed teacher would thus have ' "a period of systematic induction, with proper supervision and support, and with time for reflection and study" to replace the "widely condemned" probationary year' (James, 1972, para 6.12).

James, the *Framework* and the TIPS project reflect each other very clearly. The perceived inadequacies of teacher induction were explicit; proposed new structures were presented; and a concern for the practice/theory relationship to be 'effective' was expressed. Notions of effectiveness in that sense, and the relationship of practical experience, study and reflection and professional competence and judgement, were based on an ideal view of teachers which corresponds clearly to more recent notions of the 'reflective practitioner'. However, provision was left with local education authorities. That would seem to have ensured a built-in failure mechanism for the establishment of 'universal principles', suggesting that James's new structures did not go far enough. Provision became, at best, patchy across the country and spasmodic within LEAs depending on the commitments of individual LEA personnel or teachers within particular schools. One perspective on the reasons for this consistent failure to provide adequately for the education of new teachers was summed up by Evans:

> So this fifty year story (since the 1925 proposals) ends with
> Government stating that induction during the first year of
> teaching is necessary, but there is very little money to support
> it. What induction will mean for new teachers is whatever can
> be devised within existing funds.
> (Evans, 1978, p. 15).

Certainly what were intended to be four pilot projects became two, due to economies in educational spending (Hanson and Herrington, 1976, p. 10) and the national scheme never happened at all. However, even if it had been implemented, another view would be that the expectations of Administration Memos 4/59 and 10/68 were quite inadequate to ensure extensive and effective commitments to teacher induction. They left the responsibilities of employers focused on the assessment of teaching rather than the issues of the quality of professional learning. The emergent principles based on ideals of reflection and study were not elaborated, and made little headway in the face of assessment based on performance skills. Even in James's ideal provision, 'the new entrant is seen as a passive receiver of geniality and advice from those whose perspectives are assumed to be fully professional' (Hanson and Herrington, 1976, p. 7).

This is reminiscent of the apprenticed pupil-teacher, learning a craft trade. It says little about making independent professional judgements or how such judgement-making can be developed. Running throughout these developments, then, but especially in the DES requirements, there was a condition of administrative and managerial prominence, without serious consideration of the nature of teaching as a problematic venture, or of learning teaching through reflection on practice. There was a bold faith, in the most constructive

35

proposals, that better professional judgements might ensue from problem-oriented reflection on practice, supported by teacher-tutoring. However, these stem from the aims of the national pilot projects and represent aspirations which never got beyond trialling. Indeed, Evans's 'fifty year story' continued, somewhat repetitively. The 1977 Green Paper *Education in Schools: A Consultative Document* (DES, 1977a), which heralded central government's interventions in the state education service in the name of improving standards and quality, said that the time was 'ripe to devise more comprehensive arrangements for supporting teachers in their initial period of service'. The statement continued with anticipation of a general spread of induction schemes throughout the country within the ensuing few years. Such schemes, for longer than just the first year of service, it was said, would enable higher standards of practical competence to be achieved (DES, 1977a, paras 6.19/20). It did not, however, say what kinds of competence or deliberate on what was meant by standards.

The provisions proposed clearly followed those of the 1972 White Paper — a notable irony that after five years the proposals for reduced workloads, professional tutors, interim teacher status and systematic support now appeared in a lower status policy document. However, the imperative for LEAs to act on support provision was upheld by the argument that a reduced rate of recruitment, consequent upon lower pupil populations, would mean less undue pressures on experienced teachers. It was also argued that this would allow the more rigorous application of requirements for passing probation 'than was feasible during the years of severe teacher shortage' (DES, 1977a, para 6.20). It is curious that while citing James, the pilot projects and the TIPS evaluation, the Green Paper saw no prospect of introducing changes immediately. While expecting a spread of LEA schemes, the only commitment from government was to 'consult the local authority and teachers' associations on the best way to embark on a *study* [my emphasis] of measures ... intended to improve the level of professional competence among teachers at the early stages of their career' (DES, 1977a, para 6.21).

Five years later the DES presented its own evidence that while individual headteachers and teachers in schools provided support for their new colleagues, less than half of secondary teachers and just under two-fifths of primary teachers received satisfactory LEA support. Even where support was said to be good, that was viewed largely in terms of reduced teaching loads, appropriate teaching timetables, and opportunities to meet support teachers and advisers. The survey said little about the quality of learning of new entrants or how to improve their level of professional competence. What is more, it was said that the number of LEAs providing support had 'tended to drop in the last year or so' (DES, 1982a, para 5.51). It is a matter of conjecture that this was inevitably linked to cuts in LEA budgets, and the growth in crisis management in local authorities. Ironically, given the Green Paper's hopes that fewer recruits might mean better provision, it is possible that the dramatic decline in numbers of new teachers being recruited also led to a decline in concern about their development. With small cohorts of new teachers scattered unevenly across the country, and with no clear pattern year by year, perhaps the problem of induction was assumed to have gone away. Whatever the causes, a consequence was that the experience of working with new teachers, and the development of induction processes, had receded rather than spread.

It seems that the rhetoric about needs was much the same as it was in 1925; by the mid-1980s provision by employers was poor and in national decline; and we still knew little about the learning experiences that new teachers have. Nor did we know how those experiences could be improved for the education of teachers. It seems that the view that the arrangements for entry into teaching are primitive compared to other professions and skilled trades (Lortie, 1975, p. 59) was quite accurate. Our understanding of what is needed to enhance the quality of those arrangements was certainly underdeveloped. A lack of central government lead, in terms of the philosophical and ideological directions for teacher induction, and lack of structures of provision with adequate resources, continued. New Education (Teachers) Regulations 1982 followed by Administrative Memorandum 1/83, *The Treatment and Assessment of Probationary Teachers*, set out to enable as far as possible a common minimum standard to be reached in the quality of teaching and of support provision (DES, 1983a). That minimum started by recognizing that while short-term temporary appointments for new teachers were to be avoided if possible, they certainly occur. The memorandum (in force until 1989) advised that the duties assigned to a new entrant, supervision, and conditions of work should be such as to facilitate a fair and reasonable assessment of conduct as a teacher (DES, 1983a, para 4.a). This of course could mean the teacher taking on the full workload rather than the 75 per cent timetable, supported by experienced colleagues. The fair test certainly included teaching classes of normal size, although it would not, if the memorandum was heeded, be conducted in especially difficult schools. Beyond that, support structures would follow the minimum basic information-needs approach – meeting staff, receiving a school handbook, timetables, syllabuses and schemes, information about equipment and resources, and about LEA support and supervision. Further support opportunities would be provided so far as practicable through an appointed teacher-tutor, observation of colleagues, visits to other schools and meetings with other new entrants.

The criteria for the assessment of teaching were also presented in Memorandum 1/83: class management; subject expertise; teaching skills; lesson planning; use of resources; understanding pupils' needs; and pupil and staff relationships. Assessment procedures, it advised, were to be communicated at all stages with the teachers themselves. This confirmation of a technical view of teaching and of LEA provision demonstrated, in my view, a lack of professional intellect and creative direction from the DES. The call for action does no credit to all the reports and policy statements which had emerged since 1944. Despite their shortcomings, those attempts to define policy stretched a long way ahead of implementation in practice, and of this memorandum. It is particularly paradoxical in one sense that the gap between policy and practice should be revealed, so starkly, concurrently with the publication of *Teaching Quality*, with its demands for part-time release for new teachers, professional initiation and guidance, and further study. On the other hand, the assumption of common minimum standards left responsibility firmly with the employers, who were also expected to finance provision of support structures. That let the Government neatly off the hook. Having said that what it required in fulfilling their duties was a minimum, low-cost endeavour, if LEAs chose to do more they would need to pay for it. At a time of severe financial stringency, and government-imposed cost limits on local authorities, it would be improbable that a high-cost endeavour would be advised by the DES itself, or pursued by LEAs. Not only the rhetoric, but also the reasons for it remaining just rhetoric, were exposed – and they were in part the same reasons cited for the failure of the 1925 Board of Education proposals to proceed to implementation, and for potential improvements being held back in the nineteenth century.

NEW DIRECTIONS?

Funding policy explains the failure to provide structures which might facilitate those basic conditions of work, support and preparation for the tasks of a new appointment which were described as essential prerequisites to successful induction by McNair, Plowden, James, and Bolam *et al.* Such provision seems eminently reasonable, given the acceptance of novice status and the normal (and arguably unsatisfactory) physical and material conditions in which teaching is conducted in state schools. However, financial factors alone do not explain why it is that these official proposals and associated policy statements since 1960 do not seriously address the educational status of new entrants and their learning. Nor do they explain entirely why explicit and articulated principles for the education of new entrants are so elusive to anyone, such as myself, interested in formulating curriculum for new teachers. But there are some important indicators from which we can infer reasons for these failures. Direct graduate entry (possible until 1982) and certificated teaching (prior to the all-graduate entry requirement of 1975) both carried implicit and explicit assumptions about learning the professional (i.e. practical) elements of teaching on the job either by 'experience' or by guidance from experienced teachers. The induction year had always been intended to rectify the inadequacies of these entry routes by providing additional learning through both experience and guidance; the probation requirement was deemed to ensure that such learning was tested and proven. The content of that learning continued to centre on the technical or craft skills of teaching, and its proficiency continued to be judged on specified, observable performance criteria. It is both this content and these means of acquisition which suggest that proposals for teacher induction, with the exception of Bolam's aims in the TIPs project, elements of the James Report, and some recent demands from HMI, have been based on a recurrent acceptance of the value of apprenticeship, without discussing that value or potential or consequences of apprenticeship.

Let me suspend for the moment the question of conditions and consider the value, potential or consequences of apprenticeship in its 'ideal state'. Apprenticeship, as Lortie (1975) points out, assumes a prolonged, rigorous and systematic induction, usually through a graduated process of being granted access to elements of a well-defined and established body of craft knowledge. In the guild system where it was the paramount form of training, and more recently in technical/industrial trades, the transmission of technical know-how by a master-practitioner, and the acquisition of know-how by the novice was the over-arching concern. Its principles constitute a process of initiation into the 'mysteries' of technical knowledge, and its practice carries with it systems of control to ensure procedural correctness in the utilization of that 'received' knowledge. The control systems are integrated into the system of instruction and/or assisted practice, and dominate its epistemology as a set of prescribed instructional objectives. The apprentice, monitorial and pupil-teacher approaches to training teachers discussed earlier were each in their turn based on assumptions that those teachers already in place, or those directors who established the schooling systems, were guardians of a proven body of transmissible knowledge, defined as performance objectives. The successors of those systems, the practicum elements, devices such as micro-teaching, 'performance-based' aspects of initial training, and the criteria prescribed by CATE, are based on the same assumptions as the earlier modes of apprenticeship.

It is not the idea of apprenticeship *per se* which presents a problem for me. The idea of prolonged, rigorous and systematic induction, with supported practice under guidance from a mentor, might provide a sound grounding in critical enquiry. That, I believe, would constitute something of high value, considerable potential and welcome consequences for those, like myself, who seek to develop a reflective/revisionist or critical/revisionist intellectual stance toward teaching and education. An apprenticeship into the rigours of the social disciplines and social enquiry was undoubtedly an aspiration of theory-based teacher education, and its successor modes of the curriculum reform and teacher-researcher movements. The views of teaching and teacher education represented by the New Right were being challenged within the nineteenth-century systems themselves, which led to the introduction of changes in initial teacher education, albeit gradually, during the first half of the twentieth century. (We should not forget however that entry to teaching in the state system without training remained possible until 1982.) They have since been further challenged, especially through the introduction since 1960 into teacher education curricula of the disciplines of psychology, sociology, philosophy and history of education. It is by way of derivatives of these disciplines that the farthest other side in the recent dispute can be located: the critical educationalist perspectives. In part, the development of these perspectives may be construed as an evolution from the disciplines-based (or theory-based) teacher education curriculum, which included new thinking as the curriculum reform movement (through curriculum studies) sought to develop inter-disciplinary practical enquiry in education, and especially among teachers themselves. It is those developments within which my own work, and the prejudices of the present account, reside, and which underly my concern about the uncritical acceptance of the value of apprenticeship and the continuation of conditions in which new teachers are expected to learn.

The problem, then, is *what* the apprenticeship is in, and how it is conducted – in other words, the underlying epistemology of particular kinds of apprenticeship. In the case of teacher education the kind of apprenticeship which has dominated policy and practice has, undoubtedly, been one limited to the pursuit of instruction in academic knowledge and technical classroom skills. It is that particular kind of apprenticeship and its consequences in a purportedly skilful but uncritical body of teachers which has been the target of action research and reflective practice reformists. In turn the reformists have been the subject of attack from the New Right as they have asserted a reinstatement of a particular, skills-based mode of apprenticeship which explicitly favours the socialization of new teachers into traditional modes of practice which are said to be proven in quality.

That side of the current dispute, represented by the Hillgate Group (1989), Lawlor (1990) and the New Right, challenged the need to have initial teacher training at all. They regard newly trained teachers from college-based courses as potential subversives of the established economic and social structures, and argued for the castration of critique and the reassertion of a 'new consensus'. In this view there are only two qualities necessary for effective teaching: the acquisition of knowledge, and the ability (and willingness) to put it across to others (Hillgate Group, 1989; O'Hear, 1988). The Hillgate Group condemns teacher training as intellectually inadequate, irrelevant, and biased (to the Left). In its place, it argues, should be direct entry into schools with the full training of new entrants carried out by teachers, bypassing LEAs and the DES, as well as academics in higher education. Quality control in their scheme would be overseen by HMI assessors in the mode of the nineteenth and early twentieth centuries. Thus the content of teacher training would be the skills required in the classroom, eliminating 'pretentious pseudo-subjects, uncomprehended smatterings, [and] shameless propaganda' (Hillgate Group, 1989). The Hillgate Group's uncompromising stance, attempting to use teacher shortage and licensed teacher proposals to assert its own political perspectives by removing what it regards as a route to critical education within higher education and schools, exposes an extreme opposition to any critical perspective. It also reveals, or at least highlights, the continuing power of the assumptions of any apprenticeship into purportedly established and proven practice. The triad of CATE criteria – personal qualities, professional skills, and academic subject expertise – is reduced to a minimum, and the notion that learning teaching is a continuous process is lost from sight. Perhaps this is a model derived from entry to teaching in the private sector, as much as it is based on notions of nineteenth-century monitorial and pupil-teacher apprenticeships. It is difficult to tell. Either way, what is explicit is the challenge to developments in teacher education which have been concerned to transform educational practice through research, and which stem from a different model of teaching (see Elliott, 1992a, 1992b).

What these differences demonstrate is that quite apart from the resource problems described earlier of putting in place an effective apprenticeship scheme for new teachers, teacher educators and teachers, as well as polemicists and politicians, have serious epistemological considerations to pursue. In relation to new entrants, for example, if unlimited funds became available there would still remain the question: how should they be spent? The prior question would be: what constitutes (or should constitute) appropriate teacher education during a phase of induction either before or after qualified teacher status recognizes formally that teachers are at least moderately good as judged, say, against CATE competences in the realms of subject knowledge and professional skills? (In Tickle, 1987a I asserted the need to ask such questions within initial teacher education, based on a further prior question: what kinds of teachers do we want? I still hold to that need and question the adequacy of CATE competences. See also Tickle, 1991 and 1992a, 1992b, 1992c.) It is these questions which, until Bolam *et al.*, seemed to be unasked in relation to induction. The lack of intellectual curiosity or failure to apply professional wisdom to such questions about teacher induction was, post-Bolam, apparently allowed to continue by demographic and political events. There were few, dispersed, new entrants for a decade or so. There were also other political and educational agendas in the limelight.

As I outlined in Chapter 1, the development of that professional curiosity took a particular direction in the action research movement. The ideas and their direction are complex, and based on a much older tradition of thought than their re-emergence in the past 30 years suggests. I will treat them in more detail as the book proceeds. For now put simply, the epistemological assumptions and pedagogical principles of these perspectives and those of critical educationalists share a common feature. Teachers (and student teachers) are viewed as active constructors of their own knowledge and understanding, and responsive participants in judging appropriate practical action which takes account of complex, often unpredictable variables. The elaboration of this epistemology and its implications for the continuous professional development of teachers has been conducted as a critique of a 'technical rationality' view of knowledge, which underpins both objectives-based curricula in teacher training, and technical skills-based apprenticeship to teaching. It is a view which takes account of the need for technical proficiency in practice, but insists upon a more comprehensive view of teaching and its development as an ethical social

41

practice. In particular it calls for the explication, examination and public discourse about the values which underly and drive practice on the part of individual teachers and the professional community at large (Carr and Kemmis, 1986; Elliott, 1980, 1988, 1989; Schon, 1983; Sockett, 1986, 1987; Stenhouse, 1975; Tickle, 1987a). As I suggested elsewhere (Tickle, 1992b), one professional slogan in teacher education which (inadequately) represents this epistemology, and which implicitly challenges notions of apprenticeship based on the transmission/acquisition of technical skills alone, is reflective practice. It was, I have to say, with that slogan in mind, used interchangeably with action research and research-based teaching, that the policy analysis itself was initially conducted. I set out in search of evidence of those views of professional development in the policy documents and historical accounts which I reviewed. As I showed earlier, these views were represented in the aims of the TIPS project in relation to new entrants to teaching. There was no evidence that they were pursued when the trials finished.

THE PUZZLE OF POLICY

Thus I believe I uncovered several parts of a complex puzzle. First, there were historically grounded widespread views of the learner teacher as an apprentice to a master practitioner in a particular kind of craft knowledge. These views carry their own perspective on the nature of teaching as a craft, the skills of which, it may be presumed, will best be learned on the job but through gentling in with a guiding hand. Both the craft and the component skills are presumed to be relatively stable and unproblematic, such that induction means initiation and socialization into pre-existing forms of knowledge. New teachers are seen as undergoing adaptation to fit the forms, learning in a relatively passive, certainly compliant mode to become technically proficient. Hence proficiency, competency, efficiency, effectiveness and quality are gained and assessed in practical experience, while knowledge is treated within one particular epistemological mode as easily measurable in the performance of observable technical skills.

Secondly, even if these were reasonable premises, there was, and is, no national apprenticeship scheme beyond initial training, and no funding committed to implementing one. There was a large chance element for each teacher which determined whether they got apprenticed to learn or were required to perform as full-blooded craftspersons. In both cases, and like any apprenticeship, there was, and is, tension between learning and performing. The criteria for assessment and approval as a qualified practitioner were set out in task terms, not in measures of learning. The first year was represented as a test of competence, not as a period of development, and the kinds of competences to be assessed were exactly those which were and are used in initial teacher training practices: the minimum technical skills of moderately good teachers (McNair, 1944, para 278).

Thirdly, this demonstrated that in policy statements there was no view presented of what progress, or improvement, means in learning teaching. Indeed there was an implicit contradiction between becoming proficient and continuing to develop which was not discussed in these documents. In the apprenticeship view which was invoked, mainly implicitly through reliance on conceptions of teaching as a set of performance skills, the aim is to become masterly in the constituent skills. Once achieved, continued skill performance would be all that was required. In that view the outstanding student or new teacher might learn very quickly and soon acquire a range of competences. However, most of the proposals and discussions imply different assumptions – about longer-term inservice education (ILEA, 1984, para 4.3.3) – not only in the case of changing circumstances but also assuming individual, professional growth. There was, up to the late 1980s, no notion about what educational experiences for new teachers might look like, or how they could accommodate the extended professional view (Hoyle, 1969). Even when it did emerge, the official view was more rhetoric than principled debate or explicit curriculum proposals:

> The notion of 'extended professionalism' is not a new one, but it is one that has not been fully and universally recognised. The expectation [for continued INSET] should be laid down during initial training, and the process should begin with induction.
> (DES, 1987, p. 30)

Extended professionals, in this view, were seen by Hoyle as those who maintain a learning stance in their teaching throughout a career. He distinguished such teachers from restricted professionals who did not seek to develop their practice and their understanding beyond the point of qualified teacher status. In this report however, HMI did assert that continuous commitment of individual teachers and groups to career-long professional growth and development should be based on initial training experiences of questioning, debating, analysing and arguing from evidence. In a typically Stenhousian statement they argued that new teachers should become accustomed to examining 'their own habitual assumptions'. Subsumed within that general notion of teacher enquiry and research, a range of teaching phenomena were identified by HMI to which such enquiry would be directed: planning, content, teaching strategies, relationships, pacing, imaginativeness of lessons, management of pupils and events, their own perceptiveness of situations, assessment of pupil learning, and so on. Here, we read of the process of learning which is different from the skills-based apprenticeship and a latter-day successor to the aims of the TIPS project: 'the ability to undertake self-evaluation successfully is essential if the students are to continue to develop their professional skills during their teaching careers' (DES, 1987, p. 129).

That view had been represented deep in the CATE criteria of Circular 3/84, which said that courses of initial training should provide opportunities for students to reflect on and learn from their own classroom experience, as well as to understand their role in a social context (DES, 1984, Annex, para 12). However, it was hardly noticed and was certainly not part of the application of the CATE criteria which followed. It seems as though the concerns which emerged in *Quality in Schools: The Initial Training of Teachers* (DES, 1987) were a timely reflection of *Quality in Schools: Evaluation and Appraisal* (DES, 1985a). Yet the principles of self-appraisal, let alone critical enquiry, were either not passed, or did not survive the passage from HMI to CATE. In the renewed criteria (DES, 1989b) reflective thinking was not mentioned.

Fourthly, the understanding about learning teaching which had been gained through research was splintered and dissipated. It was also subject to interpretation and application with underlying and sometimes conflicting values, or else ignored in attempts to ensure quality control in teaching. The latter was reflected by Chilver's view of what needs to be done to ensure that teachers will be 'of the required quality':

> greater attention must be paid in future to ensuring that
> teacher quality is monitored and maintained at all stages.
> High standards and strict quality control are needed both for
> admission to and graduation from teacher training courses;
> thereafter, that same regard for teaching quality must govern
> each subsequent step of the teacher's career.
> (Chilver, 1988, para 3.8.2)

The dominant concern for measuring output performance had not led to sustained and systematic research into how to improve that performance, or to ensure that it may be continually improved. It also deflected seriously any concern about the learning experience of new teachers, and the development of alternative conceptions of competence or associated curriculum paradigms.

This combination of the historical traditions and assumptions, the economic and financial limitations, the political and ideological assertions, and the lack of intellectual and scholarly influence, seems to form the conundrum which made agreed principles for teacher induction an elusive phenomenon. The elusiveness of principles and substantial gap in knowledge about the experiences of new teachers had sustained the rhetoric of induction, while other political and educational agendas appeared to allow lethargy and incompetence to flourish in actual provision and practice, and to leave the experiences of induction to chance. The Education Reform Act 1988 made no requirement or provision for the induction of new teachers. The major gap in the Act left the conundrum to flounder on, leaving new entrants to the experience of idiosyncrasy, dependent largely on their own intellect, as they tried to make sense of their world.

As that world continued to be reshaped into the 1990s, policy on induction experienced yet another nudge from the DES. In July 1991 proposals to remove the requirement for employers to assess the first year as a probationary period were attached to the identification of induction as a specific grant within the Grants for Education Support and Training (GEST) funding for inservice teacher education. Yet, as if to reinforce a sense of shifting sands of policy, these proposals were made concurrently with those for teacher appraisal which maintained the category of probationary teacher, and exempted that category from the appraisal process (DES, 1991a). Within six months (January 1992) the intention to locate the initial training of secondary teachers mostly in schools, conducted mostly by teachers, was announced. Decisions about primary teachers' training were to follow. The distinctions between initial training and induction were again blurred, and the conundrum potentially extended.

Chapter 3

Testing Reflective Professional Practice:
Pauline, Mike, Lesley, Richard, Anna and Diane

Within the unclear and incoherent world of teacher induction the practical problem had to be addressed: how to devise and direct the initial project for the education of 16 new teachers for one year, with a view to introducing enhanced provision the following year (and thereafter) for 150 new teachers across all age phases and subject specialisms. The initial project and the worlds of the new teachers who participated in it needed to be the subject of enquiry for several reasons: to record and evaluate the project; to provide evidence of the teachers' experiences, and understanding of their needs; and to redress the dearth of empirical research on the education of new teachers. As I concluded in the previous chapter, the wider educational world which the teachers entered when they joined the profession was (and is) scattered with widespread and growing differences of view and even dispute about what kinds of experiences it is appropriate to try to provide for them. The diversity of views is governed by historical tradition, assumptions about how teachers learn, political and ideological assertions about the purpose and conduct of schools and teachers, economic policy and financial controls, demographic instability in student and teacher populations, and political and administrative decisions within schools about the deployment of new teachers and provision for their professional support. Given these various influences on provision of learning opportunities for new teachers, it was important to ask: what was the nature of their immediate habitations, and what was their sense of them? The aim of this chapter is to report aspects of the initial project and the teachers' circumstances in schools.

As director of a project which sought to enhance their professional development during the year, I was a part of their worlds. Their educational experiences were intended to be changed to some extent by the decisions and actions which I took. Those decisions and actions were based on aspirations which I hold for the professional self-development of teachers – on a set of values and beliefs which I began to make explicit in Chapter 1. In *Learning Teaching, Teaching Teaching* (Tickle, 1987a) I adopted an optimistic view of the educational development of undergraduate student teachers and their supervising teachers and tutors as partners in learning. That approach was based on the assumption that classroom technique as a predominant feature of teacher training is a limited and limiting conception of competence in teacher education. (The construct of competence in teaching will be discussed later in this chapter on page 53.) Through case studies of individual students within an undergraduate programme I explored how much of a shift could occur beyond what Stenhouse (1975) called mere competence, in a way which could actually enhance classroom technique but which could also develop the capacity to engage in reflection and research. I sought to show how Stenhouse's notion of subsuming the technical competence of classroom teaching within teacher research could be achieved even in the early experiences of student teachers. In part, that incorporated the development of problem-solving, for instance in planning for classroom teaching, anticipating situations, orchestrating the many variables of classroom life, and reflecting on events to improve judgements. I also argued that the development of judgement through reflective practice linked closely with growth in confidence, identification as a teacher, and the ability to relate classroom experience and theory. Together, these characteristics of growth in some students' professional knowledge, I claimed, offered their emancipation (and that of teachers and tutors) in the educative sense. As they became more aware of their own actions, more skilled in the use of evidence, and more knowledgeable both in teaching and about teaching, they seemed able to identify and analyse the consequences of their actions. I also argued that that kind of professional development had the potential to raise awareness of the effects of institutional characteristics, the conditions of schooling, and of social phenomena reflected in classrooms. The assumptions of the programme on which that research focused reflected those of action research and critical enquiry: that such awareness would enable students to respond to situations by seeking evidence, and to develop understanding which could improve not only their own teaching and their pupils' learning, but potentially also the social circumstances in which teaching and learning occur. Such an educative approach to teaching, I asserted, would constantly enhance teachers' knowledge – of subject matter, of self as a teacher, of pupils, of instructional strategies and learning processes, of schools as institutions, and of their community contexts (Tickle, 1987a). Furthermore, I argued, it was an appropriate way to establish dispositions towards continuous and sustained professional self-development.

The work undertaken in the project reported here was founded on the belief that the approaches adopted in the undergraduate programme could be extended to, and could facilitate the learning of, new teachers. The development of an educative approach to teacher induction which could enhance a teacher's knowledge and improve (or sustain) dispositions toward teaching as a problematic venture became a central purpose in working with new entrants. My initial ideas were a set of beliefs, reflecting my own central values in teacher education curriculum. There was no experience or evidence to substantiate or sustain the beliefs in relation to new teachers. I did not know if research-based teaching could work for them. Initially therefore, I wanted to explore the possibility of new teachers adopting research-based teaching approaches to learning. Whereas action research had been developed extensively and internationally among experienced teachers there was no evidence of whether or how it might work in the professional development of beginners. Yet it seemed from the evidence of initial teacher education that there was a need to address the problem of how new teachers learn, or might learn most effectively. In particular there seemed to be a need to discover how the initial teacher education of individuals could be advanced immediately and continuously after entry into teaching.

But action research is only one mode of learning available to students and teachers at whatever stage. So as well as wanting to explore its possibilities with new entrants as a way of confirming or denying my own faith in research-based teaching, it was also necessary to research the learning experiences of new teachers more widely, and to examine the worlds in which they work. In doing so I hoped that it would be possible to set the evidence of the project in its broader context: the educational and school worlds of new teachers.

The initial project was designed to encourage teachers in the development of reflective practice. That was intended to extend my work with student teachers and my aspirations for developing enquiring dispositions described on page 47. I saw this as a means of recognizing the baseline of recommendation for qualified teacher status as an acknowledgement of proficient classroom technique, and seeking induction provision which could extend and improve on that. The reason for adopting a view of *the possible* was to break out of a minimum requirement perspective on classroom skills development during the first year, to challenge the survival orientation of reports on teacher induction, and explicitly to test out at this early stage of teaching whether the assumptions of teacher research were or could be adopted by new teachers. My participation in the project was as a non-assessing support tutor, external to schools and employer and therefore neutral in the formal assessment of the teachers. In the professional development of the teachers I was not neutral. The design of the project and my part within it centred on the following aims and principles:

1. To promote the development of classroom skills and the capacity for reflective thinking about teaching.

2. Tutors will negotiate with the teachers the best means to support that development, outside of the formal assessment of teachers.

3. Opportunities for discussion about the development of their teaching will be sought among the project teachers and, where appropriate, with their colleagues in school.

These principles were discussed with teacher-tutors from each of the schools, as well as with the teachers during an induction day two weeks after term began. However, the project boundaries, my role and the principles were tightly defined within wider provision and experiences of the teachers. Those boundaries were defined at the planning stage with representatives of the teachers' employers:

1. It was taken as understood that all matters concerning the appointment and employment of the teachers, including formal assessment, would be conducted by the employing body.

2. Early contact/orientation with schools and information provided by the employing body and by schools would continue as before. No attempt would be made to modify that provision, or to advise schools how to help new teachers to adjust to their new posts.

3. The shared responsibilities of subject advisers and officers for the oversight and assessment of new teachers was recognized. Generally, subject advisers dealt with secondary teachers, while officers dealt with primary teachers.

4. There was a need to distinguish between statutory oversight and assessment, and induction for developing teaching. While advisers and officers might engage in both, their status and lack of opportunity for regular and extensive contact with the teachers provided little hope of systematically developing teaching quality. The role of the 'neutral' tutor was to concentrate on the development of teaching.

5. Co-ordination of the various support provisions was impossible, even if it were desirable, because of the diverse involvement of administration personnel, advisers, headteachers, teacher-tutors, heads of department and 'neutral' support tutors.

6. Teacher release for inservice was presenting difficulties in schools because of cost, and supply teachers not being readily available. The structured programme would concentrate on school-based induction as far as possible to overcome that problem.

7. Further, it was felt that the development of teaching within the teacher's own classroom context would be most valuable. The programme would thus be largely individualized and seek to operate within schools. Contact with other teachers and schools however was regarded as desirable.

8. New teachers often did not have vehicles; distances to teachers' centres can be considerable, and public transport is often unavailable. This provided another reason for the programme being school-based.

In summary, it was agreed that a structured programme of induction would include a 'neutral' tutor. The intention was to supplement the work of teacher-tutors and existing provision within schools. The programme was largely school-based, individualized, and concerned with promoting the development of classroom practice. Resourcing meant an allocation of neutral tutor time equivalent to one day per teacher per term, to be used flexibly in negotiation with the teachers. Telephone contact and/or evening meetings were not limited.

Fourteen teachers attended the induction day. Two others were appointed a week later. I became tutor to eight and a colleague to the other six (and two more who joined later). During the induction day the support role intentions were explained and contact arrangements negotiated. Invitations were received from all the teachers to make initial visits to schools during teaching time, to observe teaching and discuss it with them. Specific visits were later arranged by telephone. I also extended an invitation to telephone me at work or at home. This was taken up by three teachers who telephoned regularly to discuss issues about their teaching. Telephone conversations were also held with the others when appointments were being made. In agreement with the teachers I adopted the practice of making diary records of observations and conversations, giving or sending copies immediately to individual teachers. Those notes formed the basis of the next visit, and often focused on aspects of teaching which the teacher might develop, and how that might be done. In the spring term I arranged to meet each teacher when they were not teaching, seeking to extend discussion rather than observation. Discussions were sometimes tape-recorded, or summarized in follow-up notes, with transcripts sent to the teachers as a record and for comment.

Striving to achieve the aims of the project provided a focus for my own action research, for which the diary records, field notes and transcripts provided data. An evaluator was appointed specifically to research the support tutor role. He attended the induction day, interviewed me during the project, and surveyed the teachers by questionnaire towards the end of their year. Data and the report from that evaluation were available to me.

As well as being support tutor to the teachers I had contracted with the employers to research the schools' provision for them, and their experiences of induction within schools. That was done by questionnaire, observation, discussion and interview. Together, the range of data provided a picture of the worlds and experiences of this small cohort of new teachers. The 16 teachers worked in varied circumstances, and experienced different initial school support arrangements for induction.

The details of the contexts and the formal arrangements of induction indicated some of the major differences, and some similarities, between the teachers' circumstances. The type and size of schools and number of teacher colleagues varied, unsurprisingly, between the primary and secondary teachers. A difference in non-teaching time between these two groups was also obvious, with potential implications for opportunities to develop teaching in ways which involved gathering, recording and analysing evidence. The majority worked in one, two or three rooms, providing relatively stable bases in which equipment, resources and ways of handling pupils' work, for example, could be developed. One teacher worked in seven rooms within a three-day week contract. It might be anticipated that this offered little chance or incentive to develop such aspects of teaching except in nomadic form. All had an appointed teacher-tutor, usually a senior teacher or head, and all but one had been provided in advance with a school information handbook of some sort, enabling the basic routines of the institution and the job to be learned quickly, with a named support teacher to turn to. Three had no curriculum guidelines to work from, and the majority had very limited contact with the school prior to starting. Two had none at all, so that the initial tasks of planning and preparing for teaching would have been difficult. Nine of the teachers were on temporary contracts for either one, two or three terms, with implications for the ways in which they might view their own development and that of their teaching. These circumstantial similarities and variations were pertinent to the establishment of the project. They provided some indication of how well prepared the schools were to help the teachers get established, by providing the opportunities, information, and conditions which might be deemed to be prerequisite to beginning teaching (James, 1972; DES, 1983a, 1988a). But they also indicated the diversity of teaching arrangements, some of the detailed implications of which are illuminated in the qualitative data of individual cases which follow. The quantitative data provided the basis of more extensive surveys, with other groups, which are reported and analysed in Chapter 5. But to these circumstantial indications can be added the human factors, the actions of the teachers and those with whom they worked, including myself. It is within those activities of beginning teaching as part of the initial project that the texture of experience developed.

Breaking into the possibilities of constructively working with the teachers for the development of their classroom practice provided the major challenge of the project. At the first meeting there was a general question about the extent to which this might be possible, given: i) their (presumed) limited experience of reflective practice; ii) limits on the amount of contact time available between tutor and teacher; and iii) their concerns about the assessment of basic classroom skills. There was also an immediate recognition of the diversity of school situations, individual responses to the tasks of teaching, and specific practical needs of the teachers.

The biographies of these teachers, and especially their most recent experiences, demonstrated a complex range of persons, circumstances, and responses to the requirements of teaching, as well as to the aspirations of the project. The individuality and idiosyncrasy of the teachers' lives and their present circumstances emerged during that induction day. I highlighted three aspects of the fieldnotes which were written impressionistically and spontaneously immediately after the day. The first was the tapestry of emotional responses, and the sense of self, which were evident in the interchanges. These aspects of teaching, and of professional development, also emerged as important considerations from data provided later by the research group of five teachers. The second was the concern among the teachers with the formal assessment of their classroom performance. That assessment was based largely on technical skills, deemed to be a requirement of all teachers in all circumstances. It contrasted somewhat with ideas of individual personalities with idiosyncratic emotional conditions governed by unique events which emerged as a picture of the group. The juxtaposition of those characteristics provided a certain puzzlement for me, which was to emerge more fully only later. It grew, in part, in relation to my reflections on the third aspect of the field notes, namely my assertions to Pauline and the group about reflective practice, and in particular my implied rejection of conventional models of action research in favour of thoughtful trial and error practice which I actually deemed unsophisticated. What this description displays in effect are my own assumptions at that time about reflective practice and action research, and their place in the daily and busy lives of teachers. It was these three issues – personal emotional experiences; notions of competence; and the nature and place of reflective practice – represented in emergent form in these early notes, which became central to the development of my ideas and which were gradually elaborated as I proceeded towards this book.

The encounters with individuals became more complex as they came to include contacts both in classrooms and outside schools. Visits to schools, classroom observation, and further discussion allowed me to develop conversations with individual teachers around some of the issues which were of concern to them. The range of these, and their complexity, demonstrated the need for supportive, reflective conversation which could help the individual teachers to explore and (hopefully) resolve some of their concerns. These included such matters as:

- the work rates of pupils, and how best to improve them where it was needed;
- how to motivate fifth year low achievers in maths in order to improve their mathematical capability;
- how to adjust/vary expectations in mixed ability classes, yet maintain high standards of work;
- how to achieve sufficient 'coverage' in GCSE economics in a one-year sixth form course;
- whether satisfactory work was being set for infants across the whole curriculum;
- to adapt classrooms in order to conduct the kind of curriculum activities regarded as desirable, in order to achieve satisfactory standards of learning;
- how to introduce computer-assisted learning;

- how to provide for children with special educational needs in a primary classroom;
- what extent of theory to include in design and technology;

and so on. There was a clear pattern to these concerns. All were about achieving the highest possible quality of learning for the pupils through the most effective teaching which could be offered. What characterized the conversations most notably was the goal of achieving effective learning for every pupil. The teachers were involved from the start in redefining their own practices to suit specific situations. Some were concerned with changing the situation in order to make that performance more effective, or in order to suit their own preferred practices.

It was at this point, in trying to make more sense of the teachers' reflective practice and my own role within the project, that I read the work of Zimpher and Howey (1987): *Adapting Supervisory Practices to Different Orientations in Teaching Competence*. In their analysis of forms of teaching practice supervision, and their place in different 'orientations' (or what may be regarded as different ideologies) in teacher education, they drew distinctions between four kinds of teaching competence which, they argued, can be detected in the central aims of the different orientations and supervisory practices. The competences, set out briefly, were as follows: *Technical Competence* refers to the effective use of day-to-day teaching skills employed in classroom instruction and the employment of craft knowledge in teaching strategies; *Clinical Competence* includes the ability to make judgements about problematic situations, and to solve problems, through reflective action and inquiry; *Personal Competence* is the achievement of 'self-actualization' especially in terms of a willingness and capacity to develop values through 'self-confrontation' as well as through dialogue with others; *Critical Competence* is the capacity to engage in the critique of social institutions, social structures, and the norms and values, or ideologies, which operate within them.

Although Zimpher and Howey argue that these are not hierarchical, and that each might have within it different possible levels of development, my interest in the classification was partly because it allowed for both a hierarchical and developmental view of professional learning. My disposition toward such a view was undoubtedly affected by a particular notion of professionalism and by the assumptions of action research. Stenhouse, for example, referred to technical skills in classroom practice as *mere* technique. I had developed a view (in Tickle, 1987a) of classroom technique as a prerequisite to professional credibility, but as insufficient in itself for professional 'growth'. Hoyle had implanted a hierarchy of restricted and extended professionals. MacDonald *et al.* (1986) and Sockett (1986) had argued the case for professionalism to be based on the making of situated judgements rather than just the acquisition of practical technique. HMI were now seeking not just skilful but thoughtful and self-critical teachers. The extensive and growing interest in a continuum from initial training, through induction, into inservice professional development, assumed a mantle of hierarchical and not just cumulative and lateral professional growth. In addition, my own disposition towards particular notions of apprenticeship, based on the acquisition and application of prescribed and proven, and therefore unproblematic, skills was a negative one as I have already recorded. My interest in Zimpher and Howey's classification, therefore, was that on the one hand it helped me to locate my aims for the teachers in the project within a broader view of assumptions and values in teacher education and teaching generally, provided by their review and analysis of orientations to teacher education. On the other hand it also helped me to read the data from the work with the project teachers in terms of these different kinds of competence, as they were manifest in my view of their practice and my interpretations of our discussions. As I proceeded I adopted these constructs while recognizing that the relationships between technical, clinical, personal and critical realms of competence, and indeed their internal characteristics, needed to be tested against the data from the teachers.

What this meant in particular was that, since my aims for the project had been substantially derived from my attachment to the ideas of Schon (1983) and Stenhouse (1975), I found myself exploring my role with the teachers and my impressions of their work and working contexts around the relationship between the technical and clinical areas of competence. I sought confirmation of the demonstration of technical competence, since it had been agreed in devising the project that we should assume this came with recommendation for qualified teacher status. I was more interested however in the use and development of clinical competence, taken as meaning the capacity to effectively undertake certain chosen courses of action. In short, I recognized that I was seeking to engage the teachers in deliberation by way of which they might develop their capacity to make judgements and solve problems. It was less clear to me to what extent I was concerned with encouraging them to question their own values, and to engage in processes of change in their schools. These distinctions were not well articulated within the aims and work of the project, which were loosely framed under the notion of developing teaching and the capacity for reflective practice. It seems now that that notion needed a good deal of clarification, which has only since emerged through the study of the teachers' data and my further consideration of the construct of competence.

Certainly I used reflective practice interchangeably with research-based teaching, and with action research. In my use of them they took on a mantle of homogeneous concept. Yet I had previously articulated and still had in mind certain distinctions between, for example, the development of classroom technique subsumed within action research; enquiry into practical judgements made in teaching; systematic research of phenomena and events in the educational domain; self-questioning of assumptions and values underlying one's own teaching; and social critique of the values, aims, practices and consequences of institutions and social structures. These dimensions of reflective practice or action research were conveniently articulated by Zimpher and Howey's constructs of competence. They provided a model for making sense of the data, and a catalyst for re-examining the notions of reflective practice and action research which I had assumed.

In still seeking the answers to the practical task's problem of how to best proceed in the development project, I also attached myself to concepts of social strategy presented by Lacey (1977) and elaborated by Zeichner and Tabachnick (1985) which seemed to be linked to the notion of reflective practice. Zeichner and Tabachnick (1985) considered, through a detailed case study, the degree to which new teachers adopted the cultures and traditions of the schools where they worked; the extent to which they maintained the perspectives brought to their first jobs; and whether they could be viewed as 'making substantial contributions to the quality or strength of their own induction into teaching (Zeichner and Tabachnick 1985, p. 4). They used a model of social strategy developed by Lacey (1977) which recognized that socialization into teaching is a process of negotiation in which individuals can influence situations as well as adjust to them. Three varieties of social strategy are defined by Lacey. Strategic compliance would, in my present application of the concept, be when a new teacher complies with requirements which do not fit his or her own values and beliefs. Internalized adjustment would occur when individuals are in accord with the expectations and values of others in a school. Strategic redefinition would occur when institutional change is brought about by the activities of the new teacher, whether or not that teacher has the formal power to bring about change.

Zeichner and Tabachnick were conscious of the complexity of notions of culture and traditions of occupations such as teaching and institutions such as schools, recognizing in particular that the ethos and belief systems in particular schools may be dominant and relatively cohesive, or disparate and splintered. (There is an extensive literature on occupational and institutional cultures in teaching, and the socialization of teachers, among which the work of Waller, 1932; Lortie, 1975; Munro, 1989; and Hargreaves, 1986 provide valuable insights.) From the point of view of working with the project teachers it was interesting that Zeichner and Tabachnick demonstrated how teachers reacted uniquely to school situations. With four who were tracked through their first year of teaching they showed how two demonstrated internalized adjustment, finding themselves in congruence with the school situation. Two showed a dominance of strategic redefinition in the social strategies adopted, one of them successfully, the other not so. However, the authors asserted that 'all the teachers engaged in some form of strategic redefinition and introduced at least some new and creative elements into their schools' (Zeichner and Tabachnick, 1985, p. 12). They argued that new teachers can have a creative impact, but define clearly the lack of success in making creative contributions where an opposing dominant ethos is encountered (see Beynon, 1987; DES, 1988a).

Specific aspects of culture and tradition within teaching which concerned me in the project included the characteristic of privatism, dependence on 'survival' strategies, and what are deemed to be difficulties of articulating professional knowledge. These are said to stem from beyond particular institutions (Lortie, 1975) and to be part of teaching's occupational culture, but it is within individual schools that they will be encountered by new teachers. I believed that in such circumstances where these characteristics of teaching predominate, induction may be to sink or swim in private, to survive or not, without expectation that issues or problems should be articulated. I also thought that reflective, self-critical teaching may even pose a threat to some colleagues of new teachers, in which case the likelihood of reflective dispositions being developed in supportive situations would seem slim. On the other hand, if a teacher started a career in a school with an ethos of collegiality, supportive criticism and systematic reflection on practice, it might be assumed that similar dispositions would be encouraged. Part of my rationale for the orientation of the project and my work within it was a belief that the way out of privatism, 'survival' and inarticulateness for individual teachers, institutions and the profession as a whole could be through a corresponding development of classroom practice and associated enquiry skills, and a concern to generate and explore questions about teaching in public. Such a widespread action research approach would assume individual and collective intent toward strategic redefinition for the improvement of teaching. That aspiration reveals my own position *vis-à-vis* the orientations of teaching and teacher education described by Zimpher and Howey. In that respect I saw a potential link between their construct of competences, the construct of social strategy, and that of reflective practice. The nature and location of that potential link became of increasing concern as I pursued my role and juxtaposed these ideas as the project got under way.

Implicit in Zeichner and Tabachnick's study is a view of new entrants to teaching who have brought preformed perspectives to their school situations. An educational view of teacher development, I thought, would not assume that perspectives are wholly preformed and stable. New teachers (and old ones!) would be prepared to modify their beliefs, attitudes, values and purposes in the light of new experiences and understanding. That understanding might be gained among professional colleagues committed to the development of teaching. I regarded the interplay of individual intent and institutional constraint as a crucial feature of the educational experiences of new teachers. I argued within my own deliberations that the concept of strategic redefinition should be extended to include introspective activity in individual teachers' perspectives and practices. These linked constructs, to include the redefinition of individuals' professional practice, would have to be cognizant of the need to develop 'a sensitive and self-critical subjective perspective [through which] illusion, assumption and habit must be continually tested' (Stenhouse, 1975, p. 157). It would not of course necessarily constitute a social strategy if it remained an introspective activity. However, the point about redefining one's own practice is vital to the question of whether new teachers could be seen as making substantial contributions to the quality or strength of their own induction into teaching. A priority in the education of new entrants would therefore seem to be to harness any disposition towards self-development, to make it public, and to sustain it against the tendency towards privatism and 'survival'. Then the skill and culture of teaching could be seen in a framework of construction and reconstruction through individual and collective action research. But what were the chances of such an approach to induction succeeding?

The aim of the rest of this chapter is to consider these matters, based on data from the six teachers and the contexts in which they worked. These teachers represent other meeting points between the aspirations I held for research-based teaching and other aspects of those contexts. Each case is unique. They represent in brief and selected pictures of the teachers and their worlds the complexity of situations faced by new teachers, and the ways in which individuals respond to some of the variables in their circumstances.

PAULINE

The classroom where Pauline spent all her teaching time was a characteristically (secondary school) sparse, upper-floor square box of a room, with windows all along two sides, a blackboard on the wall in which the entrance door is set, and a minimum of display space on the opposite wall. Conventional box desks were set in rows facing the blackboard. A door at the back of the room led to a computer room which Pauline said was unused most of the time. Next to the blackboard were maps of France and of Europe, semi-permanent fixtures covered with a sheet of clear acrylic. A French lesson began soon after I arrived, and I made notes:

> Nineteen year three lower set pupils are in the lesson. Pauline takes charge with authority over the social behaviour as the pupils come in. Business is brisk and the work of the lesson begins immediately, with Pauline handing out Scrabble sheets, to be worked on in pairs co-operating to provide French vocabulary. The rules of Scrabble are briefly recounted by Pauline, and not fully, resulting in some misunderstandings as the work proceeds. But generally the pupils know how to play, and from the start word BONJOUR immediately find a vertical addition to get the game going. They talk excitedly. One boy exclaims loudly 'This is brilliant Miss.' The enthusiasm is widespread − so are the frustrations as they find difficulties of fitting words within the rules. They search for appropriate words in their books, from the few pieces of pupil work on the

wall, from each other's memory bank. The scoring is kept by
the players themselves. Pauline moves around the room, as I
do, joining in answering questions about the rules, checking
that the rules have not been transgressed – and finding that
they have been in numerous cases. After 20 minutes the game
is drawn to a close by Pauline, the scores are totted up, and
the winning claimant's score checked. Throughout, the children
have been excited, lively, interacting with Pauline and each
other. A change of activity to Blockbusters continues the
enthusiasm. The blackboard is rolled round to reveal the ready
prepared chart – not the visually impressive multi-coloured
television version or even a facsimile of it; rather two chalk line
drawings, one for the heats and one for the gold stage. That
doesn't deter the keenness. The class is split into two teams.
The questions are presented in French; the first hand raised
gets the chance to answer; incorrect answers provide a chance
for the other side. No thinking time is allowed after the hand is
raised. For difficult clues the pupils confer within their team.
At the end of the heats, two pupils go for gold, encouraged by
their respective teams.
(*Notes*, 9 October)

The participation of the pupils, their continued concentration on a task and
their enthusiastic responses, were notable features of classroom management.
As we discussed afterwards, the tension between maintaining that enthusiasm
and participation, and ensuring that command is maintained over proceedings,
was noticeable. I suggested that with the nature of the subject and the need
to teach it in such circumstances that tension may be inevitable.

The formal and sparse setting seemed to make a difference to the lesson,
particularly in the Scrabble game. I discussed with Pauline the possibility of
using visual resources from which the pupils could work for information, ideas,
vocabulary. I also wondered if the environment could be made less formal,
more amenable to a range of learning activities and modes of organizing classes.
It was used as a form room – what problems/constraints did that impose? We
talked about using techniques of presentation other than the blackboard –
work needed to be prepared in advance for the children, Pauline said, so that
she could devote the whole time to activity and control (rather than wasting
their time while she drew/wrote on the blackboard). How could that be overcome? There was a shortage of materials. She was already concerned about the
amount she had used in preparing activities like Scrabble. Where would large
sheets of paper come from? How could self-produced resources be developed
so that they were more attractive, and kept for future use? Clearly the limitations which the space and furniture placed on teaching were acute. Even with
different tables I suspected that the possibilities for more flexible teaching and

learning situations would be limited. However it was worth pursuing. (From *Notes*, 9 October.)

From the beginning, discussions with the head, the teacher-tutor and Pauline confirmed my impressions of enthusiastic and outstanding teaching performance, which was backed by clear and firmly held theories of language teaching in particular and education in general. Classroom practice was further characterized by charisma which brought subject matter, pupils and situations together in an atmosphere of sheer excitement, respect and commitment to clear intentions to bring success in learning language to every pupil. All of these views were judgemental. There remained the question of how the world looked to Pauline, and how her own reflection on practice could be supported.

Classroom conditions were not ideal for this teacher's aspirations for active learning. We were able to consider other ways in which they might be improved and the opportunities for doing so – developing the notion of 'stations', and the use of labelling, say, the floor area to provide route signs or other activities. Such opportunities were available because Pauline was the only teacher using the room; she did all her teaching there; and it was available in her non-contact time. I had the sense that over time such changes would be an inevitable consequence of the kind of teaching which she intended to pursue.

My role was non-assessing with regard to the formal requirements of the first year. Classroom observations, however, involved making and sharing (with the teachers) judgements about the quality of teaching observed. As far as possible these judgements were made as neutral observer or as professional colleague. But it was difficult initially to shake off the mantle of the teaching practice supervisor. The conduct of the observations and discussions required different approaches which were tested out at different times. In particular, I felt a sense of responsibility to praise Pauline (and the other teachers) for the quality of work and ideas. Not to have done so would have left her (and them) wondering what I was thinking. Suspended judgement could have led to wrong, negative impressions. In some cases where there were negative criticisms of teaching quality, a different tension occurred: in a supportive role, how far did my jurisdiction extend for imposing judgements? Where openness in conversations about teaching occurred between teacher, teacher-tutor and myself it was possible to solve that problem by balancing judgements and sharing ideas in a constructive atmosphere. That kind of experience was enjoyed from the start in Pauline's case. Communication was achieved through the medium of notes and conversations with Pauline and the teacher-tutor, sometimes together. But was it necessary to stimulate discussion in this way?

An important characteristic of the conversation with Pauline was the extent to which she sought out a sense of success or failure. That happened with regard to a very wide range of teaching events, towards which there was constant evaluation. Evaluations were both on-the-spot and longer term. The ways in which success or failure were identified was intuitive, the criteria unspecific, and the reasons unclear. In some cases there was a sense of puzzlement. The reference point was sometimes teaching practice experiences, but with clear recognition that this situation was different, as a conversation half-way through the year revealed:

> I was never worried about shouting at anybody or anything on teaching practice. I think, for some reason when I started this year, in the back of my mind, I was thinking if this doesn't work what is the effect going to be next year, and the year after that and year after that. It wasn't in terms of 'are they going to like me or not?' because I came with the attitude where I was thinking I don't mind if they don't like me to start with as long as they know what my rules are. So, it wasn't that but I think it was the fear 'if I get it wrong now, am I going to be able to pick up the pieces later' and looking back now after seven months or whatever it is, I can say, 'yes, I did make mistakes, but I have managed to pick up the pieces and things are now working in my favour.'
> (Discussion, 17 March)

There was an indication of the importance given to discipline, though not just for its own sake. In the lessons there was no difficulty with discipline as such. The problem was much more complex:

> Well, the big one is still, I think, going to be discipline and relations, rapport with the class, that, I think, is a great concern of mine, in particular in relation to the language situation. This idea of letting the kids know where to draw the line, but not inhibiting them speaking, because that is exactly what we want them to do, we need them to talk, there's been a geography or a maths class, when they've been round the school and they've stamped down, they come into a classroom like this where you are trying to set up some sort of an atmosphere, and I think it's difficult because if you do stamp them down, I as a pupil would automatically assume, 'Oh, well, this is the normal run-of-the-mill school discipline situation', which I don't want to create; but if you don't stamp them down they go haywire.
>
> Having said that it troubled me quite a lot to start with because it didn't seem that anything I was doing was getting anywhere at all, it seemed that every time there was a break at half-term or something, we went back to square one, but I sat and I thought about this last night, things have changed quite dramatically, I can say one word now, and even the worst of my class has stopped and listened. And I think the challenge at the moment is to try and work out why that's the case. The

answer I came up with last night was consistency, the fact
that I kept the same thing right the way through, and sooner
or later it dawned that they were going to be treated in that
way, that I would allow them a certain amount of freedom, but
that they mustn't take me for granted, I wasn't here to be
walked over. Now taking that in terms of what do I do next
year, or actually what have I done and how do I do it, and
how do I improve on that, I think that's going to take a bit
longer. I am more conscious of what I'm doing and why.
(Discussion, 17 March)

While it was important for Pauline to judge successes from the beginning
of the year, and in particular to correct any failings which may have been detectable, actually doing so was exceptionally difficult. Half-way through the
year the evidence for success and the criteria against which to measure it were
still hazy, intuitively held and in a realm of 'general and overall' judgements.
Some very specific successes were much clearer – the improved motivation of
the 'worst pupil'; the implementation of less formal arrangements; noticeable
improvements in vocabulary use within teaching groups new to the subject
were described. The basic competences of teaching seemed to be taken for
granted in our discussions, although they were dealt with overtly by the
teacher-tutor in assessment observations under headings such as preparation;
classroom performance; control; voice; questioning; pupil performance; contact
with children; monitoring; blackboard. From the start, impressions of success
in most of these competency areas had been established. It was the less tangible
aspects where relationships, content, teaching methods and pupil assessment/
performance 'met' in a web of 30 or so individual pupils in each of several
classes, at different stages of progress, that the information for judging success
was difficult to disentangle. This raised important questions about how Pauline
would be supported yet challenged by aspects of teaching which could still be
developed, but which she seemed only able to consider intuitively and unclearly
from within a realm of tacit knowledge.

Some of the competences discussed formally with Pauline by the teacher-
tutor have already been mentioned. Arrangements for assessment of teaching in this case were clearly set out so that they were understood by the teacher.
Observation sessions were agreed and impressions discussed, with a written
account agreed and signed by both teacher and teacher-tutor. The formality
was said to provide 'professionalism' in a difficult activity by making assessment explicit and recorded. It was complemented by being set within regular,
frequent meetings which provided collegial supportive tutoring, through informal discussions and advice. In Pauline's case that was considered successful
(by both) because mutual respect and 'openness' and willingness to share feelings, ideas, views and observations were quickly established. It was less clear
that this was as successful with the head of department, but a colleague new

to the school also provided an important source of support, as did the general staffroom atmosphere:

> In this particular school I wouldn't say that I felt the need for a support group because I have had marvellous support here, and especially from Valerie, the German teacher, who started the same day that I did, and fortunately we got on from the word go. It's great, I mean, I can go into the staffroom, I can say anything I like and, you know, I can vent my feelings, I do get a lot of support and it's a very nice free easy staffroom.
> (Discussion, 17 March)

It is worth noting comments by the teacher-tutor that previous experiences in these circumstances did not have the same success. The contribution of the individual teacher to successful support was in this case also paramount.

It was a central assumption on my part, influenced by the work of Schon (1983), that reflection-on-practice and in practice is an intrinsic part of the nature of teaching. The extent to which different teachers showed that to be the case varied. The ways in which reflection occurred also varied, in relation to different events, and as time went by into the year. Further, it was not always easy in the time available to uncover the thoughts of the teachers in conversation – either for them or for me. Pauline was interested in hearing/reading my observations of lessons as a stimulus for reflection and development after the events. She held a strong belief in the value of collegial openness, raising questions about how that could best be used for developing teaching. In discussing my role, the only previous experience Pauline drew on was the supervising tutor in teaching practice, which was an imposed and assessing role. She talked of her responses to supervisors' comments as listening, accommodating to or rejecting the views of the supervisor. Devising one's own reflective scheme was a new venture, and it was unclear how that would work (from Notes, 9 October). The attempt to make it work was undertaken in this case co-operatively and through conversation based on Pauline sharing classroom events. Her willingness to engage in conversation about her teaching was very refreshing for me. It seemed from my discussion with the teacher-tutor that that aspect of her teaching characterized it throughout, enabling them to develop a close professional relationship. But it was also necessary to make more explicit my own beliefs about the project, and about the value of its underlying principle assumptions. That process – making explicit the ideas about reflective practice – had started at the induction day and had been challenged by Pauline. I found myself reiterating my ideas in my notes to her. Conversation, I argued, would be best if it was based on the sharing of classroom observations – not least because two pairs of eyes can be better than one, different perceptions can be compared, and the meanings in the discussion can be based on practical knowledge of the situation. However, for most of the time that was not possible, and reflective 'conversation' with oneself, I noted, was undoubtedly occurring in her case. The prospects which that offered for advanced professional development seemed considerable, though even then I asserted it would be good in the future if Pauline could use some of those reflections to lead some part of our conversation along her own agenda (from Notes, 19 November). It did not prove easy for Pauline to take a lead in that way, at least within our conversation. It was difficult for her to initiate the ideas and issues even though there were very real concerns of which she was aware in her work. The difficulty seemed to be in making a judgement about what to discuss out of the many considerations which occurred day to day. That in part was a question of what others might think it worthwhile to discuss:

> As I said right at the beginning, if I can think of something to talk about this will be great. When I'm actually put into a situation, if you had come in and not said I was looking at those notes, what's happened about such and such, I think I'd have spent the first couple of seconds, even if I'd thought 'oh yes, I'll talk to him about so and so', I'd have still spent the first couple of seconds thinking – 'What do I want to talk about that for?' 'What is going to leap into my mind as something worth talking about?' and I think that's probably a fault of my student years, in that instead of just taking something that comes into your head as being important otherwise it wouldn't be there, I'm always thinking 'Yes, but is there a great educational significance or is that totally irrelevant, is that worth talking about' – value judgements that aren't necessarily right. I think more often than not the things that come into your head are the things that are important to me at the particular minute, be they of great philosophical value or not.
> (Discussion, 17 March)

The question I asked at the time was: how can we promote reflection on teaching so that the questions and issues are shared and regarded as worthy of consideration? That was a key question for Pauline and for myself. My support as a rather distant, irregular visitor proved particularly problematic. Getting to know the teachers and their situations sufficiently to develop a detailed and prolonged conversation about their teaching was not possible. Even less possible was the intention to work alongside teacher-tutor colleagues towards that aim. The time was not available. Contacts often bypassed teacher-tutors, perhaps because they were teaching. Even in Pauline's case, with good links with the teacher-tutor, there was little opportunity to discuss ideas. It was also difficult to determine my status in relation to teachers as employees. As 'guest' worker, and guest in each school and classroom, sensitivities were required which would ensure that I was regarded as a partner in seeking effectiveness in developing teaching. This aspect of the project proved to be crucial, and led to my seeking ways of achieving what I came to call *intervention without imposition*, through the conduct of conversation with teachers. In some situations it was relatively easy to act as 'adviser' with supplies of information. For example, a specific area which Pauline was interested in developing was the use of computers, particularly with the 'lower achievers' in French. The availability and proximity of the computer room made that feasible; Pauline believed the pupils would have skills in using micros; but that she had not. Nor did she know about the availability of software. I suggested she might take advantage of the university resources to gain basic competence and knowledge of materials. Later I checked out further on that, and informed Pauline about the Centre for Information on Language Teaching and Research, invited her into the Resources Centre at the School of Education, and put her in touch with someone who could help her learn how to load software and work the machines. I also informed her about *Granville*, a computer program produced by Homerton College, Cambridge and published by Cambridge University Press for the BBC, and suggested she contacted Sue Hewer at the IT and Languages Unit, St Georges School, Sleaford (Notes, 9 October).

Such situations and conduct on my part did not fulfil the principles of the project. Yes, they were instrumental in the development of practice, potentially, and an important part of it. There were other recognizable ways in which support from outside was seen as valuable, or potentially so. Pauline identified the tensions in the role of outside support, as well as possible advantages:

> What I tend to think about your coming, I agree totally that coming in in lesson time wasn't necessarily a brilliant idea, but at the start I was one of the people who said 'come in make notes on what I'm doing and help in that respect' – looking back I'd say, 'well, yes, but all that that meant really was you were a sort of supervisor, our education colleague, you know, so that wasn't perhaps a good thing when you've got so many other people doing that particular role. But what I think now, this sort of situation could be is more in the sense of if you could really build it up so that both student and person – what do we call you – (laughs) that it isn't a supervisory role, it's more in the sense of a counselling role, then we, I, the other people can use that, a) as a springboard to say 'look this is what I'm thinking, am I thinking in the right way?' and so on. And on the other hand perhaps vent our feelings about things that have been happening, you know.
> (Discussion, 17 March)

The sense of being able to contribute to the quality of work in the school was important to the teachers, and played an important part in Pauline's year. In the early stages that came from doing a thorough and successful job of teaching. Time was spent doing the 'essentials' of the job – preparation, marking, finding resources, display, orientating herself to the school, discussion with colleagues, and effecting her aims in the classroom. In the instance of the latter, for Pauline that meant effecting physical changes to the classroom environment. On a later visit, such changes had been made to the arrangement of desks and we discussed those changes:

> Oh I spent hours in here. I just got fed up with it. I didn't like
> the formal rows anyway, so in that sense I feel more relaxed,
> more informal, which I think is better for language teaching
> anyway. And in terms of role-play, which is of course the great
> thing we use in languages now, with my café up that corner
> and my supermarket over there, my tourist office every time I
> put a load of leaflets and things on that one, I can actually do
> situations now. I can see so many more possibilities in this
> room, really since I've moved the desks, than ever before. It's
> taking on a different character, I enjoy it now.
> (Discussion, 17 March)

Through this kind of concern for the quality of work there were sometimes unintended contributions to the school. Pauline's teacher-tutor talked of the quality of teaching which she had brought, being such that the teacher-tutor had already 'borrowed' a number of lessons as excellent examples of how to work with lower-ability foreign language pupils. In Pauline's case, the quality of teaching and the determination to develop it was a platform for other contributions to the school.

> They've now got a language master, French master actually on
> the computer program, but this is vocab based really – give
> yourself ... seconds to spell this – but we've just, on Friday,
> sent off an order for a lot of new tapes – asked to see
> inspection copies, try them out and then, hopefully, it will be
> through that door and increasing the area of my classroom.

Pauline had also been co-opted into the Staff Development Committee, a steering group which determined policy for school-based and other INSET activities, encouraged by the teacher-tutor to join the group. The teacher-tutor saw Pauline as having a valuable contribution to make. Pauline viewed the opportunity positively:

> I'm quite happy to be on that group, I think it could be very
> good. But I'm that sort of person I like any opportunity to get
> to know more about what's going on anyway, and well, just to
> be able to do something ... I think probably I'd see my role
> more in terms of listening, not being a mole, but listening to
> things that are going on, being able to report in a general

fashion back, being a voice for the staff, if you like, as other
staff on that group will be. And at the same time having the
opportunity of having got what's going in middle management
eyes, to come back and say, 'yes, but actually there is a
possibility of this happening' to be able to give that sort of
counselling role, guidance role, I suppose, it's fairly big-headed
of me as the youngest member of staff to go in and say, 'look,
I'll give you all the advice' (laughs).
(Discussion, 17 March)

In another important respect, Pauline had by now been able to make a
substantial contribution to the department. In September she had felt reluctant to offer the expertise she had, for fear of offending senior colleagues by
making them look less expert in a specific area than she was. Increased confidence and growing relationships added to her willingness to put her own ideas
forward among colleagues:

I mean, to a certain extent the particular degree of expertise
we were talking about then was the fact that having done a
year and a half study of GCSE in its conception, I had a
greater knowledge than somebody who had done two or three
INSET days on it. I've already been able to put that into
practice and was sent on the GCSE conference for languages
and so on, as someone who didn't know the other system too
well to go in, pick up the points that they were saying and
bring it back; and on our INSET day I had my spiel, I do feel
quite chuffed being asked on the committee to be able to say,
'ok, you are the youngest member of staff, but you have got a
role anyway, and do voice your feelings'.
(Discussion, 17 March)

Pauline represented a view of teachers entering teaching feeling, and being,
competent in different ways in different aspects of the job. She was able to
identify specific areas — the use of Information Technology (IT), for example —
where she was incompetent in her own terms, and to act on them. The
knowledge required included that of sources and support expertise, resources,
personal skills in using equipment, matching these with curriculum intentions,
and classroom techniques for demonstrating and guiding pupils in the use of
IT. This signalled a rather obvious problem with the assumption made about
the prior acquisition of technical skills being represented in the recommendation for qualified teacher status. It also signalled the difficulty with the construct of competences as being hierarchical, which was how I chose to regard
them. The need for these kinds of knowledge and skills might best be regarded
as different from reflective judgement-making. They seemed also to be com-
pementary to, but not the same as, other conceptions of teacher knowledge,

especially subject knowledge and pedagogical strategies around which teacher education policy revolved. But with regard to pedagogical knowledge the introduction of IT did include certain capabilities used in judging which materials were suited to individual pupils; judging pupils' responses to this mode of learning, and managing its introduction and use with groups of pupils while maintaining success in other, tried methods of teaching. The innovations once trialled might lead to greater understanding of these new forms of practice to match other areas already well developed.

Underlying the approach to new, as well as developed, knowledge was a disposition to improve teaching. That disposition was based in part on a set of ideals to be achieved, or at least worked for. The ideals were centred on concern for the quality of language learning of every pupil, and thus concern for the quality of teaching. Hence the big question for Pauline was the maintenance of good rapport, with effective language teaching within classroom discipline: uninhibited oral work under good management! But the challenge was to establish the evidence for why techniques and judgements had apparently succeeded. She recognized that gaining the evidence about 'what have I done and how do I do it?' as well as working out 'how do I improve on that?' would take time. But being 'conscious of what I'm doing and why' held out the prospect of moving beyond tacit knowledge. The tacit know-how of teaching might sustain what she was already doing, but it could not answer this challenge. That required the shift into reflective, evidence-based testing of theory against classroom experience or development of theory from it. The willingness to do that seemed to be related to the existence of confidence in other aspects of teaching, even though these might in themselves be tacitly held areas. Identification as a teacher (rather than student) and recognition by colleagues as an equal seemed to be important factors in that confidence. This use of, or rather aspiration towards reflective, evidence-based learning appeared a crucial step for Pauline in the development of professional competence – linking practice and theory leading to initiatives, and the adoption of strategies for changing her own teaching (if change was judged to be appropriate) or changing the circumstances in which it occurred.

In my own role these distinctions in the type of knowledge and of competence were important. From the outset I sought to define the conduct of that role, through discussion and negotiation with the teachers but within the parameters of the aims of the project. The provision of information (such as the locations of resources) helped to increase a particular kind of 'know-what' as well as the potential to develop 'know-how'. Had I offered advice on teaching strategies as a 'sort of supervisor', I might have enhanced that increase in practical knowledge (if Pauline had judged my views sufficiently worthy to take them into account) as one of the 'many other people doing that particular role' – head of department, teacher-tutor, headteacher, and adviser. What Pauline (and I) realized (as I sought the strategy of intervening in the teachers' thinking without imposing ideas, and Pauline sought to work out 'what do we call you?') was the value of having 'a springboard to say, "look this is what I'm thinking, am I thinking in the right way?"' Success in that role depended on whether 'you could really build it up'. It seems now, on reflection, that building it up would mean finding ways in which the ideas underlying her teaching could be considered, discussed, assured and/or improved – recognizing and being seen to value the work and ideas of the teacher as an equal, yet agreeing a dialogue which allowed those ideas to be drawn from the realm of the tacit, or raised to a level of being worthy of discussion. In many respects the conventional supervisory role had an inherent potential to undermine that possibility, because of its assumed status, knowledge and power relationship to the new teacher. The apprenticeship view of learning assumed in conventional supervision and assessment of teaching, i.e. in giving information or offering imposed advice, would not, in my view, enable such dialogue to develop. As Pauline made clear, her response to such support was to judge the value and relevance of advice in her terms, and to accept, act upon, store or reject it in her terms, and according to her perception of the problem, situation and potential of someone else's knowledge. Such offerings are in any case isolated in time and space. They were a minor part of the many considerations which Pauline made and which other new teachers make; they are few and far between, are rarely followed up by the supervisor, and are made by numbers of different personnel, sometimes with conflicting viewpoints. What was crucial in Pauline's case was that her values, theories and practices were based on such strong conviction and will to realize her aims for all pupils to learn a foreign language. What mattered most was to be able to meet the challenge of gaining a more lucid view of those theories and practices by way of evidence, to examine what she had done and how, and to judge how to improve it.

MIKE

Mike was teaching in a secondary comprehensive school. In the first meeting he sought reassurance that the neutral tutor role offered him a phone number, Samaritan-like, as a point of contact in his isolation and uncertainty. He never used the number. My first visit to his school in early October was one of familiarization in which we had agreed I would join a class while Mike was teaching. We had also agreed that we would discuss which aspects of teaching Mike was concerned to develop. The visit first revealed something of the working context. The school was a former girls' high school, remembered as such by the senior teacher who was also teacher-tutor to Mike. The building façade was the grandiose red brick, partly ivy-covered, double-storey architecture of between the wars grammar schools. Inside the entrance the impression was of a mock-gothic attempt to emulate the public schools, with wide corridors, high ceilings, portraits and roll-calls and trophies. That impression disappeared quickly at the back of the school, with extensions, temporary classrooms and a brand new sports hall fitting uncomfortably together, a kind of mini-urban sprawl. Mike was teaching in the workshops in the midst of this sprawl. The teacher-tutor was quick to discuss Mike's progress in terms of 'he's doing alright. There are no problems'. He seemed to think that was what I was there to find out. The idea of developing teaching in a systematic way whatever the judgement about classroom performance seemed to have been missed (that had been the main message of a teacher-tutors' meeting five days earlier). Now he talked of Mike as an asset to the school; senior staff were 'very happy with him'. We went to meet Mike's head of department, who spoke in glowing terms of Mike: 'the best new teacher I've ever had'. Mike arrived and the others left; classes were due to start.

Mike's fifth formers were doing a project in plastics, within the design and realization mode of Craft, Design, Technology (CDT) in the GCSE course (though only a few of them would take the exam, he said). There were 11 boys and three girls. He had said in advance that he was concerned that they were not working fast enough, not producing enough, they seemed lazy. In this session they were at the stage of making a working drawing to full scale to apply to the backing paper on a sheet of acrylic, so that Mike could cut the sheet up to working-size pieces for the production of a notepad holder. The design brief was to produce a container for paper to be used as a telephone notepad, so that when holding the telephone in one hand the paper would stay in place for writing with the other hand. The 'design line' model was written up on the blackboard. There was an illustration next to it of how to produce a working drawing. Mike introduced the lesson with instruction based on that illustration. All the pupils had their own sketches and finished isometric drawings. They were now ready to carry out the next stage described on the blackboard. The result would be to produce a pattern around which to draw on to the acrylic.

The pupils set to work. There was a sense of calm, quietness, getting on with the job. Mike circulated, checking, asking questions. About ten minutes into the lesson he detected some problems in understanding what was required and called the group round a bench to reiterate the working drawing instructions. The pupils went back to their own benches and continued. I noticed most of them drawing margins around their paper – using the conventions of design drawing – and was surprised, given that they would cut out the working drawing from the sheet and discard the edges. Quite some time was spent on margins. When one boy cut his, I asked why he had drawn the margin. He did not realize that the intention was to make a pattern. He thought the drawing would go in his folder, along with all the other working drawings. The folder was to emerge as a central piece in the story; it was where all 'theory' was stored, where homework was done, and where the record of the process was catalogued. The misunderstanding and the importance of the folder illustrated the range of graphic work involved – ideas, roughs, working drawings, finished drawings, prototypes in paper/card – all these were in evidence. By the end of the session three pupils had transferred their pattern onto the acrylic. I asked what experience they previously had in working with plastics. Some had done a keyfob two years previously. Mike had demonstrated basic shaping techniques this term.

In discussion with Mike after the lesson he said the pupils had clearly been affected by my presence: they all seemed ill at ease and not as interactive as usual. That had made him a little uneasy. We discussed the following:

1. Ways in which he might ask questions of pupils during instructional sessions so as to establish if they understood, or as a way of reiterating without himself repeating, thus using 'contributory' methods.

2. Making and using exemplars to illustrate stages, rather than depending on blackboard/verbal instruction, and possibly asking pupils to demonstrate techniques.

3. The advance on previous experience which this piece of work represented for pupils in some respects.

4. Ways in which work rates and levels of expectation could be determined, both in terms of products and in terms of the extent of pupils' learning.

5. Ways of linking the theory with workshop practice – the concern here was to ensure maximum use of workshop time, and to get the pupils to a stage of seeing results in production as a means of ensuring continued motivation.

Mike also commented on how different full-time teaching seemed compared with teaching practice, even though he had not yet been as long in the job as he had spent in one practice. It felt totally different. There was excellent support from staff. Familiarization with the school building was not complete; even within the department there was a need to do things which were not familiar. For example, ordering materials was a particular problem, as was devising a store-room system to suit himself (all workshop tools were neatly racked and displayed). In particular there was a concern to introduce multi-media activities, though the workshops were not set up for that.

At this early stage it was clear that Mike had established his presence in terms of required performance of teaching. That view was held by his head of department, teacher-tutor and assessor. Although my own role was supportive and non-assessing I felt impelled, in early December, to compliment Mike on the quality of work being done by pupils, and to thank him for the pleasure of being a guest in his classroom. My written notes to him on that occasion also said:

> I hope my presence has not been too disruptive, and that
> we can now jointly consider what developments might be

undertaken in your teaching, and how best to proceed with them. In the brief conversation it is not really possible to begin a proper and useful dialogue, and I think that in the future we might consider meeting for discussion rather than me observing teaching. We can then work out the best ways to help/support the development of teaching. I am especially keen that the ideas/issues should be your own, and that I should not impose. (Notes, December)

The issues which (re)emerged included the problem of introducing multi-media activities, questions about discipline procedures, and Mike's own style, which he saw as too laid-back and undemanding of pupils' work. These continued to be among themes of development. In a February meeting we extended discussion on the topics. They emerged as concerns with teaching technique, organizational skills, judgement about pupils' work rates, and confidence in and possibilities (or lack of these) for bringing about changes in the department's organization of resources and approach to teaching technology. Using questioning as an instructional technique had been the first point of discussion earlier. Mike had tried to develop that:

> I've certainly made efforts towards that end. Sometimes I sort
> of catch myself and I think that I haven't asked them anything
> for a bit, I'd better – because if you've prepared your spiel,
> what you are going to be teaching, then there seems, with me
> anyway, there seems to be a danger if I don't constantly keep
> thinking to myself exactly what I'm doing then I will just keep
> telling them what to do now, this and that, but I do now ask
> them questions at the end on what I've been talking about to
> see how much they have understood.

This was not merely a question of technique, or of memory, but of also establishing a climate of trust in which pupils would initiate questions. That in turn required 'appropriate' personal relations. However, these were tempered by considering other techniques – of discipline – and the different relations they required:

> I've always said that I'll be pleased if they do [ask questions]
> rather than anything else because it will tell me where I'm
> going wrong, where I have to emphasize things more. I try to
> make myself as approachable as possible. But then there is a
> very fine line between that and becoming, if you like,
> over-familiar, because of the discipline side of things.

The link between technique and judgement was seen by Mike as an 'overlap, a sort of grey area'. These grey areas presented the greatest cause for reflection as solutions to perceived problems were sought. The work rates of fifth year pupils were too low for Mike. His timetable was predominantly with fifth years, many entering for GCSE. They knew the programme, with interim targets for coursework, and had been provided with extensive resources:

> I've helped them as much as I possibly can help them without
> doing it for them because, as it is, an examination is 30 per
> cent of the [total mark], I can't do too much of their project for
> them, but I've tried every angle that I can think of so there is
> not a great deal more, short of me sitting down and doing it
> for them, which is probably what they'd like me to do [laughs].

Short of doing the work for them, Mike had tried a range of techniques: producing visual aids, visits, photographing the students' work, providing information about the exam, photocopying notes, presenting a stage-by-stage time-scale on requirements and so on. 'But it [was] still a question of motivating them.' Other year-groups were well-motivated with high work-rates, and offered a measure against which fifth formers were judged. It was with fifth years where Mike's confidence was challenged, where technique was insufficient, where explanation was sought, in reflection, about dimensions of pupils' experience beyond his control, such as their previous experience of the subject. Work-rates and lack of motivation were linked to the problem of discipline which Mike also reflected on regularly and tried (unsuccessfully in his terms with a few pupils) to resolve. Here too he had tried to balance judgements, tolerating some behaviours to avoid confrontations and to maintain good relations (approachability) with other pupils, which was seen as a key to maintaining and improving motivation. In these judgements Mike saw himself as unsupported, not by colleagues but by lack of a structure or framework within which to act:

> I find it difficult without, I don't feel that there is any
> structure or framework for me to know where to draw the
> lines, really ... that I can go by. It seems to be very much left
> up to me, to make my own decisions, I'm sure it is the same
> for every teacher, but when you come new into the profession, I
> think possibly it might be helpful to have some sort of guidelines.

The 'red area' for behaviour was defined by workshop safety, and protection of equipment and pupils' work. Minor offences – such as 'little niggly things' like flicking paper – left Mike unsure about what action was available to him to take. That, he determined, was because he had no real powers. But the situation arose in the first place, he knew, because he was seen by the fifth years as 'the new boy'. He had not had an opportunity to establish authority with them. Even then, however, Mike was well aware of the structural limitations affecting disciplinary measures. His view of these (as well as other matters such as a dislike of mixed ability grouping) had been confirmed by colleagues. 'Virtually every teacher in the school' who he had talked to said:

it's all very well taking away various sorts of punishment,
various sorts of power, but they haven't replaced it with
anything, and that they are almost teaching without power,
and they are teaching on bluff ... you can't pinch the
misbehaviour, if you like, in the bud when it first starts,
because there's no real power there to do so, at least I can't see
where it is.

Constraint, lack of determination over one's own decisions and actions,
were in that case related to European Community regulations regarding corporal punishment. Other constraints were located closer to the classroom, such
as the department's approach and organization for technology. An important
intention for Mike was to introduce multi-media activities for pupils, using
combined wood, plastics, and metals (as well as card, paper and other
associated design materials) in problem-solving. Mike was trained to teach such
'true CDT' but could not do so effectively because the school facilities reflected
the separate woodwork/metalwork approaches of other teachers. Changes in
policy were necessary, in his view, at department, school and local authority
levels:

There should be a county policy, if you like, to get those
workshops changed because you can't teach CDT as such, as it
stands today. CDT has been going now for a few years, and it's
just difficult to put into practice what I've been taught at
college. I'm having to compromise and adapt everything that
I've been taught here, and I don't particularly like doing it, I
like to let the kids if they want to do something, some sort of
project that involves three materials, I like to say, great.

Such changes were outside Mike's power, except to the extent of letting his
head of department and adviser know his wishes. There was the possibility that
the aspirations would be lost, and that without policy changes Mike might 'sort
of just trot along and start doing rather what I consider boring projects and
just become rather staid and just go with the flow, if you like, but I hope that
doesn't happen'.

However, minor actions towards achieving his ideas were taken. A disc
sander had been brought into the workshop. Woodwork benches were being
negotiated with the woodwork teacher. A bandsaw and set of woodwork tools
were being sought, and storeroom conversion considered. However, far from
the aspirations of the project for developing teaching, Mike's teaching was
clearly in danger of regressing in terms of the use of expertise gained in training. Implementation of that training required resources, a challenge to other
teachers' perspectives and practices, changes in department policy, and
changes in the timetable/organization of the whole school. Mike was very well
able to articulate the problem he faced. His difficulty was solving it: 'I can't

really start saying that I want this and I want that — it's difficult, I can express my views, but ...'.

A degree of reticence, in recognition of his own status and newness, meant that Mike did not 'push it'. He had made judgements about how far he might act in each respect — money, colleagues, policy and timetable: 'I don't really want to be too pushy, I don't feel confident enough to be too pushy, to be quite honest.'

In the longer term strategies would be determined, either to instigate changes or to move to another school. In the meantime, concern to develop technical teaching skills and judgements to reconcile discipline, good rapport and motivation and increased work-rates within the limitations of the department's approach was undaunted. Beyond the dialogue established in the project Mike saw that development as a matter of gaining experience in identifying and solving the problems of teaching:

> they will develop with time, that's all, I mean, I can't say
> specifically what will happen, but I'm sure that all experienced
> teachers, it just naturally comes about — I'm not totally sure, I
> mean, I can make some decisions myself, if I can recognize a
> problem, I can make certain decisions as to how I can try to
> rectify, but I think the solution, the correct solution to that
> problem will only come about in time, possibly I'm wrong, but
> that's how I see it.

However, he could clearly see that the range of teaching problems which he would meet were governed partly by the constrained context in which he worked. The opportunities and experiences of the pupils were determined by taking that context into account, and limitations placed on what they were allowed to do. So long as Mike acquiesced, then even what he learned by experience would be in the realm of context-bound problems. Such compliance would not mend the dislocation between his own values and practice. Unable to pursue his desired teaching (based on desirable learning for his pupils), he was also unable to meet the kinds of problems which that desired teaching might present, and unable to gain the experience which he himself saw as the key to his professional growth. On the other hand, he was perhaps learning political strategies for implementing change which he would not learn if he had entered his ideal-state department. In the meantime the pupils' experience was curtailed:

> I try and structure them so that they are very pointedly
> directed towards metal. Well, I have to make their
> problem-solving much more limited than it would be because I
> am having to structure it so much, and to tell them almost.
> [LT: The solutions are fairly well-defined?]
>   Yes, they have to be otherwise they'd start doing things

that I have said no to – it's a bit negative for me as well as for them having to say no all the time.

Mike's capacity for identifying problems and issues in his teaching, and his willingness to reflect at length and in depth about them, and about possible solutions, was evident. Some were matters of instructional strategy, such as using questions so that pupils contributed actively to instruction sessions, or asking pupils to demonstrate craft techniques as exemplars to others. More searching reflection was apparent in the attempts to judge effective action to enhance both classroom interactions with pupils and pupils' work-rates. There was a lack of evidence especially about why fifth year pupils seemed to have low work-rates, and whether these were consequent upon his own 'laid-back approach'. The evidence of practice depended upon changes to teaching which might stimulate higher work-rates. Yet some changes – to multi-media teaching – represented critical but unavailable shifts toward meeting his own desired approaches. Some actions, which could lead to evidence of different pupil response, could not be taken. Mike needed to take careful, detailed and serial political action to change his situation before he could conduct his preferred teaching, which he believed would improve the motivation of fifth formers. However, such action (or lack of it) seemed to depend on his own lack of confidence and sense of low status. In terms of social strategies he was, predominantly, biding his time while making minor changes where he could. This is different from compliance. There was not necessarily a loss of intent, but rather a judgement about whether the context could be changed, or whether transfer to a school more in accord with his own values would be necessary. However, while Mike displayed this kind of critique of his context he did not seem to engage in self-critical enquiry about his own aims and values. He had come from college 'equipped' with a 'true CDT' approach which could not be tested in these circumstances. Even if that had been possible, his view of his own learning was to allow 'experience' to accumulate 'naturally'. He declared that he was uncertain just how that would happen. In our conversations it seemed that Mike could certainly identify problems both in classroom processes and interactions, and in his teaching context. He was certainly thoughtful in puzzling out strategies to solve these problems. Yet his thoughts were confined to the realms of instructional techniques and clinical judgements about rapport with students, and how to establish conditions to effect such technical knowledge. Questioning of his underlying values was less evident. That was exemplified by his regret at the loss of corporal punishment and imposition of mixed ability grouping, as well as attachment to 'true CDT'.

LESLEY

Lesley returned from taking a class swimming. A child had lost a silver ring and they had been delayed until it was found. One of the work experience helpers had failed to turn up – he had reportedly joined the Marines. She had been left with two groups to supervise, one at each end of the pool. That had proved traumatic. The class of 9–10-year-olds in this junior school were based in their own classroom alongside the school hall. This was part of an extension/annexe to the older building, and was some distance from it. There was another classroom next door, the deputy head's. The room was well organized, with materials and equipment trays labelled clearly. There was a computer, video and audio-stereo in the room. Lesley explained that she had responsibility for recording programmes for other staff, hence the equipment. The computer was shared, one day per week to a class. Displays on the wall were colourful, headed with interesting, large and bright titles in self-produced lettering. The work was mounted in interesting ways; for example, a holiday jigsaw with pictures and writing by pupils. The environment was resourced and resourceful, books displayed, objects available. The tables were grouped and pupils arranged in sixes where they could converse across the tables. In the corner on the display board there was an impressive display of Chinese dragons produced out of cardboard boxes, tubes and other materials for the heads, and fabrics, which had previously been curtains, I guessed, for the covers of the dragons' bodies. The whole atmosphere of the classroom was one of visual variety.

Lesley took over from the deputy head, who had substituted for her own class while she was taking swimming. Quickly and efficiently she introduced the groups to their topic work activity. TIME was the continuing theme; each group had different activities, based on worksheets which were written out by hand and photocopied. Listing timing devices, drawing some of them, fitting in key words to sentences, etc. began with enthusiasm. Lesley asked the groups to discuss their ideas – a request which raised some issues later as some refused to discuss and even engaged in building barriers between the sexes. An interchange of activities took place as each task was completed, so that all pupils would deal with the range of tasks eventually. The computer was in use throughout, as groups of three interchanged for their turn, using the same programme. The minimal amount of class instruction was administrative and organizational. Other interactions by Lesley were with groups or individuals as she moved around the room, answering questions, checking progress, etc. There was an atmosphere of productive activity.

In later discussion Lesley talked of the experiences of preparing lessons and keeping up with the work. She worked until 9 p.m. every night and by self-discipline stopped then to take a break. She was away from home; her fiancé in London; and had no life outside of school in the new setting so the workload did not concern her in the way of interfering with other priorities. She was lodging with a teacher from the high school – aged 31 and 'of another generation!' Lesley could tell that from the way she talked about life at university in 'her time'. Being with another teacher helped, because she understood the pressures and workload and was sympathetic to the conversations which resulted. In school she felt a little isolated: the newness, as a stranger; being based in the annexe – 'they put all newcomers out here, it seems'; and being aware of the micro-politics amongst the staff and cautious not to ally with or alienate any faction. She said the head arrived late and left early, so she didn't have a chance to talk with him – a contrasting picture from the one he presented to me earlier. Her main interest was in developing teaching materials and visual aids for classroom use and she felt regret that time didn't allow her to follow that interest. She was not clear about what other aspects of teaching might be developed. At that stage she was just feeling that she had caught up with herself in the preparation and marking of work and was looking forward to half-term to plan in advance the next half-term's work. That would provide a different perspective on the relationship with the job and the demands it makes.

Our discussions later raised two related and major long-term issues for professional development. The first was about matching tasks to pupils, a complex area on which very little work had been done, but Lesley knew it was crucial to begin to understand it if effective teaching in mixed ability classes was to be achieved. That issue related to the question of what it means to talk of getting to know the children. Of course establishing personal relationships and getting to know how individuals respond to particular approaches, what their attitudes are, how they relate to each other, and the million other variables of classroom interaction, were an essential part of the practical knowledge being built up. Getting to know appropriate curriculum levels needed to play a central part, and a systematic approach needed to be developed over a longer time-scale. Somewhere between the two was another major issue – how to develop in the children attitudes to learning which would ensure that they would spend time on tasks, within demanding expectations about the disciplines of learning. How to develop self-directed, self-disciplined approaches to learning within a carefully structured curriculum was the challenge. There were at least two aspects to that. Those who did everything they were told when they were told and didn't think for themselves, made no decisions, took no initiatives, etc. provided one kind of problem. Those who quickly lost attentiveness, were distracted, or found amusements which disrupted the flow of learning or the flow of teaching, provided a different problem. There were others in between.

The search for a systematic approach to these problems contrasted with other early learning experiences in the job. We talked about the first technology lesson that Lesley had taken. She had mentioned this lesson on the telephone when I rang to make the appointment. She said technology had not been mentioned at college during her course and she had done none before, and she certainly had done none at school, where such subjects as technology, or even art, were frowned upon. The staff in the school had some contact with the technology teacher adviser, who had begun to get work going in the local schools. The deputy head, who taught in the classroom next to Lesley's, had started producing boats with her class and his; he took both for technology.

In turn, Lesley took both classes for art, which was her specialism. They had agreed this between them, since Lesley said she knew nothing about technology and he was happy to do it. It was a new introduction in the school as a whole. When the deputy head had been off sick the previous week, a supply teacher had come in. The supply teacher had asked 'What's technology?', at which Lesley laughed. It had thus come about that the supply teacher had taken the art classes and Lesley the technology, since she said that she was willing to have a go. She had seen that the children were shaping and cutting boats, so she knew that she could cope with the work. In fact, her response was that it had been interesting, but that there was a lot more to it than just woodwork; it included measuring, forward planning, testing things out, and she had seen the possibilities for links with science and particularly with topic work.

By February Lesley talked about the rest of the work with her class in a way which was very different from my earlier impressions of the previous term. She seemed like a different person, more confident, more aware of all that was going on, and full of ideas and thoughts and activities, which she began to describe. The words flowed out. First, she talked about how much better it was, knowing the capability of the children. The process of learning how to match work to pupils continued to be learned, and used in predictions and planning. She had planned the whole term's work in outline and knew what she would be doing in each area of the curriculum for the whole term, and then set to plan the half-term in detail. She would plan the next half-term in detail during the half-term holiday. In particular, she said she found it possible to produce plans for varying the activities for different capabilities amongst the children. She referred to individual children to exemplify how she did that and she referred particularly to the way in which she had achieved such matching during the work for measuring the school in order to produce the scale plan of the buildings. Furthermore, she described how she was able to adjust the activities when she realized that the children were either under or overstretched so that her planning in detail was also adjusted on the basis of judgements made in action. This was dependent upon the responses that she noticed amongst the children. For example, she had tested out with the 'brighter group' the use of six figure location points on the map so that they might be able to use these in drawing the plan and in extracting information from it. She had found that they were quite capable of that work, and had thus proceeded with it. She had expected them to be capable of it, but needed to check it out just the same. Others in the group seemed unable even to measure from a particular point in the classroom to, say, the school wall, and she thus had to give considerable support, or to change the activities for those pupils. She gave other examples.

There did not seem to be any concern about the techniques of classroom instruction. Lesley appeared to take such activities as the use and distribution of resources, organization of pupils, questioning and instructing, display, marking, hosting discussion, and the rest of the skills deemed to be the qualifications for successful classroom teaching, into her stride. What was much more evident in our discussions was the constant search for information from which to analyse the effects of teaching, on which to base judgements, and make predictions. This formed a key part of the development of experience with the pupils. The knowledge needed for technology was different. Neither subject knowledge, instructional strategies, nor even her knowledge of her 'self' in relation to them (Elbaz, 1983) had been developed in training. Only a broader sense of personal confidence allowed for that to begin – a willingness to have a go, alertness to what the children had been doing with another teacher, and theories about children learning through testing things out, applied to new activities. Other kinds of new learning were also sought through other means. We talked about inservice study. First, she had made an arrangement to visit a colleague's class, with supply cover provided from a county INSET budget. She had also made arrangements to visit the infant school to see how Beginning Reading starts, in order to see better how to help the poor readers in her class. On the latter, she said that she had done the theory at college but really needed to see the work in action with Beginning Reading so that she would have a better idea of how to implement work which was suitable for those particular children for whom she had responsibility.

In visiting the colleague's class Lesley had been commissioned by him to observe his poetry teaching. He was very keen on poetry, but was not satisfied with the way in which the work was going. He wanted her to come in and observe, to see where he was going wrong, or what in particular he was doing which might in some way stunt effective teaching, especially with the 'remedial' pupils who were grouped round a 'remedial table'. That in itself, she said, would be a different experience for her because it seemed from what he said that his grouping at tables was arranged according to particular abilities. In her own class this was not the case; instead the children were grouped according to friendships; she allowed choice and seated them in such a way that their friendships could flourish, but also so that they could work effectively. There was therefore no arbitrary teacher choice about the grouping in her own class, so that she was interested in seeing the differences in her colleague's grouping arrangements. On this occasion, when she was to visit his class, she had deliberately taken on a tight brief, i.e. not to go in with just an open agenda but to have a specific purpose to observe the teaching in the classroom. He, in turn, would visit her classroom, and would observe a new grouping arrangement which she was going to introduce. This had been an idea picked up on an inservice course, and was described as jigsaw networking. The idea was that the groups of pupils would be given a range of tasks, and one person from each group would carry the responsibility for a specific topic within the broader project. For instance, if they were working on local studies, one pupil might have sole responsibility for discovering information about transport. Each person with that responsibility from each of the groups would go to the tables and collect the resources available on that particular topic. They would thus have to gather as much information as possible and become the expert of the group.

Each person in the group would therefore become an expert in a specific aspect of the project. They would report back to the group and would contribute to the production of either a book or a newspaper, or a report of some kind.

The intention behind this exercise was to motivate all pupils and to provide them with responsibilities within active learning, so that there was not a tendency amongst the lesser motivated pupils to sit back and allow others to do the work for them. The plan had been carefully thought out and the recognition that a wide range of resources would be needed was also discussed by Lesley. She talked of going to a film archive to look for information about the town, to the library and to other sources. More generally she talked about the extent to which inservice activities appeared to go on in the locality. She was surprised, she said, that such a range of activities existed in a rural area. Her college time had been spent in London, where she expected that there would be far more in the way of inservice activities for teachers. However, she had not been aware that the teachers in the schools where she spent her teaching practice undertook anything like the amount of inservice activity which she had encountered amongst the teachers locally. She herself spent two evenings a week on inservice activities, and such activities were always being advertised which she felt she would be interested in undertaking. This appeared to be the case for many of the teachers in the region. It had allowed her contact with teachers from other schools with ideas and had also allowed her to begin to feel very much a part of the established teaching group in the area.

We also talked about how she had begun to feel in terms of being on the staff. She said she now felt able to contribute and to be part of what was happening generally in the school. She shared ideas and discussed things with the rest of the staff as though she was one of them, although, she said, she still retained a certain distance from the micro-politics amongst the staff, recognizing that she did not want to ally herself with one group or another. In talking about classroom practice it was very clear to me that Lesley had developed a sense of awareness of all that goes on. She talked about how it was unnecessary to have someone else observe her classroom and to make comments upon it. She said, in particular, that where things went well she knew they had gone well, and usually why they had gone well. Equally when things did not go so well, she could usually tell why and knew what to do about them. It was often explicable in terms of when she had had a very busy time, she was overworked or she had a cold or was not feeling well. She knew that the pupils' responses indicated when things were going badly or well, so she would make adjustments accordingly if things were not going so well. She thus felt the need for a teacher-tutor, or any outsider, to observe her classroom to be rather an imposition. She herself felt competent and capable in evaluating her own teaching. I asked if there was a possibility that she might be missing things, and referred, for example, to the arrangement she had made with her colleague for mutual observation. Yes, she agreed, that was possible, but in general terms it was reasonable for her to make those judgements about her own classroom. That was what she normally did anyway. She commented that she had not had written reports from her formal assessor who had visited her and observed her teaching several times. He had simply commented that he had had no criticisms, and she had thus assumed that things were all right in terms of the assessment of her teaching. She had then received a report from the deputy head, with whom the assessor had discussed her work during the head's absence.

The teacher-tutor, who was also the head, became increasingly irrelevant to Lesley. She had virtually no contact with him as head and none at all as teacher-tutor. When he left to take up another post she was indifferent to the idea of a replacement teacher-tutor. The close location of the deputy head's classroom and some exchange teaching seemed to offer no further learning opportunities since the technology experience. The deputy head's replacement by a supply teacher, as he became acting head, might offer more:

> So I shall have a supply teacher next door, which could be a
> good thing, especially if it's the one that we normally have,
> who comes to the school once a week anyway, that could be a
> good thing because it could mean I actually get a chance to
> work with another member of staff, I mean, I don't work with
> the deputy head we just agree to differ, I mean, I don't know
> what he's doing, I never know what he does, so, um, that could
> be quite useful.

Lesley sought the chance to learn from other teachers, though the opportunities were limited as she had no non-teaching time. The chance was seen as one which could confirm or deny one's isolated classroom experiences:

> I'm always fascinated, not only to see other schools, but I'd
> like to see what goes on in other classes simply because when
> you're in your classroom sometimes you think to yourself,
> 'Well, am I doing this right?' even if it's going well, if it's going
> right, well, you know it's going right but some days you think,
> well, is this how everybody does it, obviously people are
> different but you do wonder, do other people have these
> problems. I mean, you know that they probably do, but you
> never actually see it particularly.

The idea of being observed teaching in the supervisor sense, as a means of identifying problems, was not seen by Lesley as a productive way of learning. Problems in that sense meant failings, rather than issues to be resolved. The instinct which Lesley felt for knowing when classroom events were succeeding or failing was sufficient for her. In particular she felt able to diagnose her own failings in planning, preparation and classroom management, and to rectify them by her own actions. The active interest in learning teaching included the pursuit of improved technique by these means, but self-evaluation could achieve that. However, learning through self-evaluation went much deeper. It was about testing out theories: 'I mean, I've done the theory of it at college, but I've never actually been with children who are going through those stages.'

Those theories came also from the advisory teachers, from other colleagues, from INSET courses, from reflection about the needs of pupils, and by testing one's own ideas in new experiences of practice. The active search for new ideas, tested against experience and compared with colleagues' experiences, proceeded alongside a sense of confident expertise in classroom practice. Lesley also held formal responsibility for the use of audio-visual aids by the entire staff. Within that responsibility she was required to act as technician, recording programmes and overseeing equipment. She also needed to use her knowledge of audio-visual and computer software, checking these out against their classroom value for children's motivation and learning, and sharing that knowledge with colleagues. Through this work she also actively sought to increase her knowledge of herself, and how confidently she worked in a staff-relationships/leadership context. That in itself demanded knowledge of the material resources; of instructional strategies (gained through whatever means she perceived to be at her disposal: discussion; trying out software; leading staff training; observing pupils' use of resources; reading instruction manuals; and attending courses). In this work at this stage Lesley operated at the level of gaining technical expertise, which needed to be applied to provide experience on which further judgements could be made. These kinds of expertise – i.e. in the realm of technical and clinical competences – may well be the precondition of confidence and the ability to theorize about practice, not only of teaching pupils, but also of teaching colleagues.

This sketch of Lesley's approaches to developing her teaching shows her moving actively among sources and resources for information and ideas which might be applied and tested in practice, as well as testing out, against experience, what she had learned in theory at college. This was a largely private quest, rejecting the role of any external evaluation, yet potentially shared through mutual evaluation with a colleague. The air of self-assurance about knowing when, and why, classroom events had worked well or otherwise made it difficult to even discuss matters of teaching techniques and classroom strategies. That made it difficult to know how Lesley thought about those aspects of her work. She was, simply, alone with those thoughts, and this was normal. Yet she was willing, even eager, to work with other teachers and to explore some of the complexities of the classroom and her own ideas and values: matching tasks to children's abilities; engaging all children in activities with equal motivation; and generating a sense of independence in active learning approaches, were themes in her teaching which seemed to be constantly under review. Even in these, however, it was difficult to know how Lesley went about those reviews, and impossible for me to play any serious part in them.

RICHARD

Richard was teaching in a modern, single-storey, purpose-built middle school on a suburban housing estate. He was appointed after term began, a temporary one year, part-time (70 per cent) 'floating' teacher, peripatetic to other staff and all pupils. His post and appointment fulfilled an organizational need: to release other teachers for non-teaching periods. He had no classroom base of his own, and he met no group of children for more than a short session at a time. Duties began the morning after being appointed (which was in itself in the late afternoon), under the guidance of a teacher-tutor who was also new to the school and who had been allocated that role on Richard's appointment. The teacher-tutor had no experience in the role, and felt very unsure of her ability to support a new teacher. She taught a full timetable, with no non-contact time, and had responsibility for developing special needs provision throughout the whole school.

Richard moved from class to class teaching each class *in situ* in their own classrooms, dealing with the full range of subjects and classroom activities according to different teachers' requirements. The range of subjects, at different age levels and for different pupils within each age group, had to be taught within the organizational arrangements, resourcing, and management regimes determined by the different teachers. Richard had to adjust to these as he moved, learning what he could of each aspect of each classroom as best he could to enable him to teach at all. He also had to know the children in each class. The demands made on his learning by this context were considerable; not least they highlighted aspects of Richard's self as he tested out his stamina, temperament and orientation to teaching:

> Particularly at Christmas I had a real sort of crisis over the feeling that you had to go in that class, not yourself but as somebody else, I just found that the most difficult thing, as a part-timer not having your own class, and seeing somebody has one hour a week, or perhaps half an hour a day or ... knowing that you really have to follow on from somebody else and not really being comfortable in there. I found that difficult. Or having children who just didn't respond to your way, could only seemingly respond in one way, and not in different ways. They couldn't suddenly see 'ah different teaching methods, I can cope with this' — I found that very difficult — at Christmas time.

Richard felt ill-equipped for the broad spread of subjects he had to handle in terms of subject knowledge. That feeling was compounded by insecurity in instructional strategies for different subject content and for different ages and abilities of pupils. He also felt ill-equipped in classroom management expertise. Although acutely aware of the need to establish technical competence there was no opportunity for sustained experience, reflection, and adjustment in any location or subject, or with any group of pupils. Identifying problems was not difficult; they were myriad. One difficulty was not having time to get to know individual pupils, to confirm diagnoses of their learning needs and to check these against further experience. But the major problem was that even if that was possible Richard could not plan for teaching or take action on his own account. He was constantly subject to the controls of other teachers and established classroom expectations, rules, and resources. He could not orchestrate all the variables, nor implement decisions based on his own judgements, nor try out his own preferred theories of teaching. We discussed at length a range of classroom teaching skills which Richard wanted to improve, but he was constantly frustrated by circumstances. When the question of developing teaching arose, the lack of opportunity to implement and evaluate his own preferred modes of teaching was a recurrent theme. Making the adjustments which the context required seemed like constant crisis management of the array of information needed for coping with each lesson. However, as the year progressed, coping with the application of technique and subject knowledge began to develop into reflective and predictive adjustments to planning and teaching:

> I feel that as the year's gone on I've accumulated more ideas
> for myself, so that I know that sort of thinking with
> September in view, I have a much better overview of how a
> course should be set out really – the various work programmes,
> the outlines of work, and I think I've got a much better idea of
> how it would go ... because I have different age groups as
> well. Yes, and again that's been good experience to know – up
> to fourth years – how different things work. I think I've got a
> much better idea of the ethos of the school as well now than at
> the beginning ... I think I've learnt a lot about what activities
> work with certain classes, and what doesn't, even though
> theoretically I feel other approaches would be better for them,
> I feel that would be a better strategy of teaching, it hasn't
> necessarily worked in the class, and they are not used to it.

Richard adjusted to the demands and expectations of other teachers by ditching his 'ideal' perspectives for teaching and learning, and even ditching what he knew would be pragmatic responses to 'what worked' in his own classroom. He was advised by colleagues to adopt more 'formal' approaches, giving children 'controlled things' which were 'teacher-centred'. This went against his own wishes, for he believed it would lead to disruption in the classroom as pupils became bored. Active group work, with variations in activity and organization were preferred, but were unworkable in the circumstances. Adjustments were made also with regard to expectations for standards of work. These were partly based on 'experience', but mostly on reference to work seen in other classrooms and other schools:

I think I've got a greater awareness now of what I should expect – as opposed to at the beginning I didn't [have] ... it might be one week somebody's creative writing work is so much better than it was two weeks ago, and then obviously I can look back and see two weeks ago that child, either the ideas inspired them, or I should have expected something much higher, really ... looking at the work and comparing and also looking outside at other classes. Our modes of working, as well, I think that's one of the things that has worried me most, or been uppermost in my mind – do I expect them to work, for example, in total silence if they are doing something, or, when don't I, and perhaps I haven't really cleared that up in my own mind, and I've had to follow somebody else, and not be very comfortable.

Adapting to expectations, to conventions of practice, to the ethos of the school, had created a number of dilemmas for Richard. He was committed to ideals developed at college, but had become unsure about them in light of experience in these new circumstances. He sought the opportunity to deal with the tension between 'what I personally want and also what is just best for ... them [pupils]'. That was linked with a desire to discuss philosophy as well as the practical, to talk about his views with colleagues rather than feel an anomaly. That would also allow for the development of his own underlying ideas, which he accepted were subject to change, but he also had to accept that he was denied the opportunity to test them. Even discussion consistently eluded Richard:

Yes I sort of came to the point where I thought well, irrespective of whether I like it or not, I've got to do this, for the sake of them [pupils], otherwise it wouldn't work. Sometimes it leaves you feeling frustrated because you think well, that's not how I want an English lesson to be. I think at the beginning I just thought 'oh, I feel frustrated', I thought I want to teach better, you know, I want to be a better teacher basically, and I don't feel – I feel things frustrating me, and then you question whether it's your ability or whatever, you have to have faith in yourself to be able to deal with that ... I mean, as I said, partly you think well does the fact that a middle school and a more structured timetable, is that automatically going to change, obviously will change styles, as opposed to a primary situation where you've got the whole class all day, it's not structured, go outside when you want, obviously ... just like the style of a building is going to change the style of teaching and different things, they are all contributory factors, aren't they, so, I think the fact that in a

> middle school, I'd quite like to know more about middle as
> opposed to primary as well, I think I'd find that quite
> interesting. An interesting thing, really, to know more about
> what middle schools in general, their approach as opposed to
> primary and which tends to work better – does one work? I
> think that's another thing – trying to judge which works better
> for different reasons – you know, styles of teaching again, or ...

Frustration at not being able to examine these ideas either in practice or in discourse with colleagues continued, but were overtaken by events which caused greater concern – even anxiety – during the summer term. The teacher-tutor was absent from school for medical reasons; and Richard was deemed by the head to be insufficiently successful in his teaching. It was unclear if there would be a post for him at the school the following September. He telephoned me to ask for advice. My diary shows the following record:

> It was difficult to interpret what [the headteacher] meant. I
> asked if Richard was getting into a state about the matter, and
> he said he was, he would like to talk with someone outside of
> school as a matter of urgency. I agreed to meet him during the
> week-end. Richard met me, with his wife. They are expecting a
> baby in September, and his wife finishes work in July. Richard
> is confused – thinks he is not free to apply for jobs for
> September even if offered no contract at his present school.
> Unsure if he will be offered a contract – has to apply with
> anyone else for a vacancy. The head has advised that he
> intends to deem Richard as 'unsatisfactory' – and that staying
> there is tightly tied to that assessment. I suggest he talk with
> the formal assessor to clarify the assessment situation, and
> with the head to clarify the applications situation and
> possibility of Sept. contract. It is late in the year. Richard
> fears he may be unemployed in September and is obviously
> worried. I agreed to see him in school later in the term.
> (Notes, 10 June)

Two weeks later (23 June) Richard heard that he was to stay at the school, teaching a class of first years. He was working on plans for that already. At the final contact in the academic year we discussed the situation and I recorded the discussion in my diary:

> We talked about the developments within school, and the news
> that he will be employed there, and teaching first years. He
> explained that the head had made clear to him that he only
> offered the job to Richard for two terms temporary, under
> pressure from the LEA officer. Two permanent full time jobs
> had arisen, and new teachers had been appointed to them.

Richard had been told that should he apply for one he would
not get it. A well respected teacher on the staff, who had
taught in the school for two years on temporary contract had
also been refused a permanent post, causing considerable
resentment amongst the rest of the staff as well as herself. The
atmosphere was very sour in school with acute antagonism
towards the head.

Richard was careful about how he related this information, but it was clear that
there was a serious breakdown in relationships with the head. I was also told
later that a serious breakdown had occurred between Richard and the teacher-
tutor. Richard had indicated a problem when I met him, saying that the tutor
would not have fought for him to have a class of his own if she had realized
that it would be her class. He had been given her class for the summer term
while she was on maternity leave. A new teacher-tutor would need to be agreed.

The circumstances in which Richard had been appointed, the conditions
under which he worked, the acknowledged (by the head and teacher-tutor) lack
of support or even opportunitites for discussion, and his personal financial
circumstances, conspired, in my view and that of his formal assessor, against
the effective development of Richard's teaching. The assessor acknowledged to
me several times that Richard was struggling against high odds created by the
headteacher, who was eventually persuaded to at least allocate a class to
Richard. Even then, with the absence of a teacher-tutor and difficulties in staff
relations throughout the school, Richard was isolated. Further, whatever he
learned from experience did not readily have relevance in the application of his
own teaching theories. Although he believed that there was value in experiencing teaching all-year groups he could not 'use' the experience, which had
perpetually frustrated his own aims, predictively in anticipation of future
teaching. He did not know in which school or age group, if any, he might be
teaching.

In this case the aims and principles of the project were thwarted; the promotion of classroom skills and the capacity for reflective thinking about
teaching seemed like a high ideal for someone who had no classroom, nor even
any personal space, to work from. There was no chance for Richard to exercise
his own values, or to test those values against experience. The application of
second-hand advice was commonplace as a coping strategy. And the best means
to support Richard's development became the use of counselling in support of
whatever self-confidence he could retain. At the end of the year, 'having faith
in yourself' seemed to be put to even greater test, and it was difficult for
Richard himself to know how far those ideas which he believed would make him
'a better teacher' had been compromised by institutional norms and the lack
of opportunity to put his aims into practice.

ANNA

Anna entered teaching after having a family. She already held a doctorate in mathematics, and trained in a secondary PGCE course. Because of family commitments she had negotiated a 60 per cent contract. The timetable was arranged to allow her two complete days off. Within the 60 per cent contract she also had an allocation of non-contact time. The 900-pupil, 11–18, secondary comprehensive school was in a small country town. It drew pupils both from the town and an extensive rural catchment area to modern, rather sprawling buildings typical of recent educational architecture – large, glass-fronted entrance hall flanked by administration suite, dining facilities, assembly hall and staffroom front the long dark corridors to conventional teaching rooms. Beyond these are outer doors to 'mobile' classrooms, sports hall, and practical subjects facilities, as well as playing fields. The corridors and outdoor paths are packed with students outside of lesson time and during changeover.

Anna was on duty. When I arrived at lunch time she was due to go outside to supervise pupils between the finish of lunch and entry to school for the afternoon. At the end of the afternoon, she had the task of supervision from bell to clearance of the outside areas as buses departed with the last pupils. These were additional to the other concerns of teaching maths in a comprehensive school. The timetable involved teaching a full range of groups in five different rooms, only one of which was a maths base. The latter was used for 'lower attainers' because it contained practical equipment which, it was said, they needed while the others presumably did not. Moving constantly from room to room while carrying books and basic equipment had presented its problems. Arriving to find no chalk, no drawing instruments for blackboard use, etc. and thus having to send for things to colleagues had been mastered. But it still appeared to be a problem as she finished duty and hurriedly gathered together the basic needs for the next lesson. The explanation was that there were only three maths rooms, and seven classes were taught maths at the same time. Over half of the pupils thus experienced maths in non-maths environments.

The first lesson I observed took place in a geography room with displayed posters on cocoa cultivation, mountain-building, the face of the earth, and world maps. There was no sense of a mathematical environment. It was a fourth year second set, 29 pupils (two absentees), algebra for a double period. Initially, Anna handed back books to the pupils as they sat down and went over the homework which she had recently marked. She had selected some common problems which she identified during marking. I was interested in the way she asked some questions; for instance, 'what is D?' where I might have asked 'how do you calculate D?' Where she was asking for direct answers, I thought it might be appropriate to ask pupils to demonstrate the process in order to detect where problems lay, or to demonstrate methods used. Instructions and explanations were given by Anna, rather than inviting them from the class, which I thought might be more effective for motivation, checking understanding, reducing passivity, etc. I was interested in this classroom technique and how it might relate (or not) to the circumstance in which homework was actually done, presumably by and large in isolation, where the calculations have to be sole attempts and where problems encountered cannot be discussed. Is there a way of translating the solitary homeworker into the class of passive receivers of instruction? Or is there a way of accommodating to the problems encountered by individuals during homework, and exploring them in the classroom? These were my own puzzles which I might get a chance to discuss with Anna.

The quality of the blackboard surface was poor. Given the dependence of this lesson upon it, that was a pity I thought. Anna addressed the class frequently as 'fourth years'. I wondered if they felt a sense of depersonalization from that, or whether there might be an alternative way of addressing them as a group while maintaining a sense of addressing each individual. Pupils worked in their books on reducing and expanding simple equations. Concepts such as factor were reiterated, and the processes were returned to in demonstration at frequent intervals. The giving of instructions and explanations again interested me. Some pupils clearly did not understand what was required. There was a failure of communication. They were puzzled but did not say so. It took time before that problem was resolved. Consideration of this aspect of practice would be worthwhile, I later suggested. The pupils worked diligently and responded well to the lesson. I got the impression that the work was stretching their capabilities.

After break the lower achievers fifth-year group of 18 pupils provided a contrast. Social-behaviourally, there were some who obviously provided a challenge to the authority of the teacher. Anna was very conscious of this – we had talked about it previously. The majority were presented with a numeracy test which they worked through in isolation. Two others were given a different worksheet because they were regarded as 'more able'. I joined them. They skated through the sheet with ease, completing it in a few minutes. I talked about it at length with them and how they regarded the worksheet. It was 'kids' stuff' – the calculation of simple measurements as percentages of a metre or multiples of metres. They even corrected a mistake in one of the questions! I asked Anna if there was other work for them, and she provided books with graphs involving calculations of distance on a bus journey. The boys had no problems explaining to me how to do these exercises, and provided the answers orally. They said they would enjoy maths which was intellectually challenging, implying that they usually found the challenges through messing about. On the other hand, one boy doing the test was clearly in deep trouble with his calculations; conversation revealed that he seemed to have no concept of the basic units of measurements or how to apply or calculate them. What's more, he claimed that he never had cause to use measurement in his home situation. The teaching problem in this circumstance was acute. Here were questions of how to make the Cockcroft Report work in practice for this range of pupils.

In discussion with Anna later, she revealed the sorts of difficulties which she was encountering and the feelings she had toward teaching the lower achievers. We agreed that the development of appropriate strategies for teaching maths to the range of individuals in this group was a worthwhile focus of attention; seeking examples of good practice with lower achieving fifth formers was one way to be explored. Other ways might come from discussing the issues involved with the pupils themselves, working out negotiated activities which were meaningful and individualized. It was recognized that, at this stage, social behaviour was potentially such that practical activities out-doors would lead to loss of control rather than to enhanced mathematical learning! Resolving that dilemma provided substance for the development of teaching in Anna's case.

At a very early stage there was consensus among the teacher-tutor, heads of departments (maths and science), headteacher and assessor that Anna was a successful teacher, and would have no difficulty in establishing herself in the school. That seemed to satisfy their concerns. There was no discussion about extending competence or supporting her in the search for improvement. There was certainly support at the general oversight level, but the many issues which Anna raised did not find a forum in school. There was no time, little contact with colleagues, and a clear sense of teaching isolation. Our own discussions occurred during visits in the autumn and spring terms, and when Anna phoned in the evenings to talk things over. The range of discussion was summarized in my diary notes of February, which also indicate the way Anna was learning.

The next meeting took place during a non-teaching period. I had arranged that because I did not want to impose by observing classroom practice again, preferring to get a view from Anna of how things were developing. Following from the notes which I had made on previous visits and the discussions which I had had with Anna, I had worked out that I would want to talk in particular about the strategies that she was attempting to devise for teaching a wide range of pupils' abilities and achievements in maths, and also in science. Within that I had particularly to ask about mixed ability teaching and about whether she had been able to discuss those strategies with other staff in the school, or with other support staff from outside the school, including visits to other schools which she had said she would like to arrange.

Initially, I asked her to outline what strategies she had thought about. She elaborated the different range of groupings that she had to work with in maths, and that itself came as something of a surprise to me. First, she taught the fifth form low ability, the lower achievers (she called them 'special needs pupils') – those whom I had observed on my first visit. Secondly, she had a fourth-year Set 2 examination group. Those she declared were fairly level in terms of their achievements and progress, and she saw them as quite homo-geneous. The third-year group was what she called a 'middle mixture' with the top set creamed off, and a bottom set, residual group also taken for 'special needs' maths. The remaining bulk were the third year middle mixture. The

Form 2 class was a complete range of mixed ability, with no setting, creaming or banding at all. That range in itself, of age groups, of stages and of different mixes of ability, presented a considerable demand upon Anna's energies, since it meant that the different patterns in those groups in terms of pupil achievements had to be catered for differently in her teaching strategies.

This required some agility in terms of the development of teaching strategies, since it had to include alterations at the change of each lesson and different approaches to the marking of work, to the setting of work, and so on. The responses of the pupils in particular seemed to be a major influence on Anna's thinking. For example, she talked about the third-year middle mixture where she had thought at length about grouping the pupils around tables, but rejected it after advice from colleagues who said that they had tried to work this way but it had not succeeded. She reported that the children's responses had not been favourable in the view of those colleagues, though she did not say quite what that meant. However, in addition she reported that there was not a sufficient range of worksheets, work cards or resources available, that would allow flexible group work activity with different groups doing different things. At the same time, class teaching using textbooks and blackboard work, which had been the way she had operated, was not succeeding, and she had recognized that it was not fully effective because some pupils who found the work too easy needed to be stretched, while other pupils who found it too demanding tended to become relatively disturbed and difficult to handle. This different range of responses in terms of their motivation to the mathematics, their involvement in the activities and their tendency to be diverted into social misbehaviour, was of considerable concern. Anna reported that she had thought long and deep about the problem but had not yet resolved it, even after discussion with other colleagues.

There was not such a problem with the fourth year set. They were a well-motivated group, keen to achieve highly in their exams and able to cope with the demanding work which I had observed Anna setting on a previous visit. She nevertheless found it necessary with this group to expend considerable hours in terms of marking, feedback and preparation for moving them on to the next phase of their mathematical understanding. They were a demanding group in terms of the pace which she felt she needed to set for them in order that they should succeed in the exams.

The fifth-year low ability group, the special needs group, continued to pose a problem for Anna, but she was preparing to visit another school in the region where they had succeeded in developing work with such pupils which was more active and more motivating. Nevertheless, she believed that she had now developed a reasonably good relationship with the pupils, although Friday afternoon's last lesson for maths with these pupils was not the best time!

We did not discuss the total mixed ability second year group, but went on to talk about the first year science group in which the pupils were entirely mixed ability. However, Anna said that the nature of the activity made work very different. In maths, she said, much of the work was about testing mathematical ability, and about learning maths. In science, much more active participation was required from the pupils in the procedures of science and in understanding the concepts, and she found that this brought a different response from the pupils to their responses to maths. She felt that the pupils' responses were positive and constructive and she thoroughly enjoyed the work. Nevertheless, it meant a different pattern of working and different sorts of preparation, for a different age group of pupils in another subject in a mixed ability class. This range of experiences presented a considerable challenge to Anna and, as she put it, at the end of Monday after meeting all of them with no free periods, she was exhausted. Nevertheless, she felt that in most cases she had worked out suitable strategies for successful learning and teaching. Those strategies largely included formal class instruction. The pace at which Anna worked, judging by the observations which I had made on previous visits, meant that such instruction was 'successful'. This was the view of the senior maths adviser, who had visited Anna in the recent past. He had given a written report on his visit which Anna showed to me and which was constructive and positive in its comments. The report seemed to allay Anna's fears about whether or not she was succeeding in the induction year. I confirmed that in my view, and in the view of others that I had talked to, she need not have any deep concerns, as she was certainly seen to be succeeding. But that was not why I was there. She was casting me in the supervisor role.

We talked therefore about the general support that she had received. She said that it was of interest because a colleague, another new teacher in another area, had no visits at all, and had seen nobody. She had been discussing with him the number of visits she had received: two from the assistant area officer, two from myself – and this was the third, one from the headteacher and one from the senior maths adviser. She also agreed to visit other colleagues in the school as she had requested in the autumn term and they had worked out ways in which she would now be able to do that. Interestingly, she said that the colleague who had seen nobody had said to her, 'Well, what's wrong with your teaching, Anna? There must be something wrong with it.' It had disconcerted her to think that she was having so many visits because of perceived problems. However, she felt reassured, though no doubt a little nervous, and had said that it was because she was part of the project.

Two specific comments were made about the visits. First, that the assistant area officer and the senior maths adviser had visited respectively on the first and second Monday of the spring term. She said the headteacher had taken them to task about that, arguing that the last thing a new teacher needed was somebody to come in on the first Monday of term. Secondly, she said that she had received written comments from the adviser which she found helpful, but had not had written comments from the assistant area officer, and that, she thought, should be changed so that she had the written comments provided. I sensed that in asking for that, she was seeking reassurance that the comments would be positive and that she was not at risk. She was really concerned about formal assessment, and the written comments would, she implied, be an indication of that assessment.

She also commented that the verbal comments that she had received on the occasion of those visits had been, in her view, rather trivial. She gave some examples which were of the kind of advice about what she had done and might otherwise do in the classroom. Her concern was that these were minor matters, whereas she had rather major matters on her mind about the development of her teaching. I believed that the serious point she was making needed to be taken considerably further in terms of ways in which she could be supported in the development of those teaching strategies with that range of activities, of ages and teaching patterns, rather than the assessment procedures dominating. She was clearly able to see where her major problems lay and had attempted to find workable solutions which were effective in terms of the progress of the children in their learning. In the discussions at all of my visits, the major concern that Anna had expressed was about the progress of the pupils in their mathematical understanding, and ways in which that could be best effected. She was clearly thoughtful about that and determined that she should achieve the best possible learning for every pupil with whom she had contact.

During February to May we were in frequent contact. Anna often telephoned in the evenings to 'think things through'. In March I learned she had resigned, then withdrawn her resignation. She never discussed it with me. In May she had concluded her thinking about the fifth-form low-achievers. 'You won't like this,' she said, 'but the one thing they respond to is lots of blackboard work with no reading.' That was the instructional technique which she had settled on for that group. At the end of May she resigned to take up a post in a private girls' school, having been made 'an offer she couldn't refuse'!

Throughout the year Anna had worked in classroom contexts which were far from ideal, as did her maths department colleagues. There was little she could do about that. The teaching pattern was blocked into the administrative decisions of senior staff. So was the grouping of pupils. Given the range of demands and problems to be solved, Anna seemed to demonstrate considerable skill in her classroom practice as she orchestrated the variables of subject matter, class size, age and capabilities of pupils, and the resources available for teaching. Such was the range of combinations of these variables that it was difficult for her to pinpoint success (or failure) easily. The pace and demands of each lesson left, for her, only impressions of events. It was apparent to me as an observer that critical evidence of events within individual lessons eluded Anna. There was no surprise in that. Immediately after each lesson a quite different set of problems from the previous lesson was confronted and demanded practical action. There was barely time for impressionistic reflection, let alone systematic gathering of evidence. Judgements were made in good faith that the strategies adopted would 'succeed'. The corollary to that was that Anna was never sure. She constantly expressed doubt and reservations about her effectiveness. There were only others' supportive comments to reassure her, beyond the flimsy impressions of pupils' responses. Neither provided adequate evidence of whether she was meeting her intentions, satisfying her aims, and translating her beliefs into successful action. Neither school support, tutor support, nor her own reflections of practice could satisfactorily offer that evidence, given that range of problems.

DIANE

Diane telephoned me six days after the induction day, during the evening. She was clearly distressed and initially found it difficult to say why she had rung. She felt she could not carry on in the job; every day got worse than the previous one, and nothing which she did to try to improve the situation seemed to help. We met by arrangement in a local pub half an hour later, and she talked at length about the problems. She was in lodgings with a grandmother and her 17-year-old granddaughter. Diane had been there for nearly four weeks, since one week before the start of her new job. She had got to know the granddaughter a little and they got on quite well. Diane's family lived 200 miles away and she had no close friends in the school's locality, though she had 'acquaintances' in town with whom she intended to spend the weekend. She was teaching 31 6-year-olds in a four-teacher school which was built for 80 pupils but already housed 120 children. She operated a grouping arrangement whereby five groups of children each worked on different activities through the day, changing between maths, 'practical' maths, language, play (toys), and art/craft. There were not enough tables or chairs for all the children. Another table had been acquired from another classroom, but that caused crowding. There were still not enough work spaces for everyone. As a result she had devised five groups of six children around each table. Yet there were only 22 chairs and four uncomfortable stools. At best, five children had no seats and, since the stools were really unsuitable, nine children effectively had nowhere to sit. Diane explained that sitting was not part of the 'ethos' of the school. Only for music, story and PE did she teach a whole class. There was a carpeted area for a 'quiet corner' and story time.

Quite apart from the seating arrangements, Diane perceived problems in the classroom which were the result of her teaching. The children were not fully involved in the work which she was setting them. They were getting bored and inevitably finding their 'own amusements', talking, playing, making a noise and not paying attention when she expected them to. This did not apply to everyone. The majority of the children simply got on with their work because they knew that was expected of them. But there was enough noise to create a sense of disorder. It was not their fault, she said. It was her fault for not providing stimulating activities, but she did not know what else to do beyond what she was doing. An illustration of the problem was given. At assembly time, 10 o'clock, the children were asked to clear away. They had to do that themselves in order to learn classroom routines and to take responsibility for equipment and materials. Some inevitably cleared away more quickly than others. The command given was that as soon as they had put away their own things, they should line up near the classroom door ready to go to assembly. Diane was responsible for the music in that assembly, taking the whole school of 4–8-year-olds. I imagined that to be quite a worry in itself. Those first in line got restless and began to play, and Diane did not know how to solve this problem. We discussed alternatives, for instance, asking them to go to their places to wait. She said they did not have places; there was no allocation of places, space or chairs to individual children. I expressed some surprise at this; she repeated that there were in any case not enough chairs, but that such an idea did not fit the 'ethos' of the school. We talked about providing space on the carpet for some, and utilizing the few minutes with learning games, as well as introducing some competitiveness for speed in clearing away materials. This example was only one of a number of perceived problems. I suggested she tackle specific problems by looking for improvement at particular points in the day.

Diane talked about a different (but related) aspect of her problems. The head had told her off three times that day, and it had got to the point where she got a telling-off for something or other almost every day, often after being sent for from her classroom while she was teaching. She explained some of the background. The head was apparently unhappy about changing the grouping from four to five groups, and had said so the previous week. Diane had explained that it was necessary in order to accommodate the children at the table space available. The head's response had been, 'Oh well, if you can justify it ...' and had said no more, until this day, when the welfare assistant interrupted story time to say she had been sent to take over the class, because Diane was summoned to the head's office. She got a telling-off for not rearranging the tables. That would have to be the first task of tomorrow. 'It's got to the point where I apologize as I'm going in his office door before he's said what he wants me for.' The staff relationships were just emerging for Diane. It had taken some time to realize that the head and deputy head did not get on. The head was 'thick' with the other class teacher, and was not on speaking terms with the secretary. The welfare assistant was the only person who Diane felt she could talk to; it would be difficult to be seen making an alliance with the deputy; the other teacher was a confidant of the head; and the head was already well out of reach, even though he was the teacher-tutor for the induction year. The area education officer, who Diane had seen briefly at the induction day, was a 'man in a suit from the office'. In any case he formally assessed her, and that was already a major issue three weeks into the year.

Diane felt already that she was failing. There was no way she could talk to others in school about how she felt. She knew they would be seeing her as a problem, even as failing, but could not open up the question with them or seek their support. She felt she could not go into school the next day, Friday. She did not want to carry on; did not feel it was worth it. But the practical difficulties had already been thought through: terminating contracts, getting release immediately from contract, being unemployed, having no income, not knowing what else she would do; and the emotional difficulties of admitting failure had also been thought through. This situation was very different from her earlier encounters with teaching, which she had really enjoyed. But then she said she had only been a student and was not really held responsible for events. She was supported by everyone else, who recognized her as a student. Now she was fully responsible, and not carrying out those responsibilities well in her own estimation. But if she could get back to the feeling that she used to have, she knew she would enjoy teaching. If she did not go in on Friday, she could not go in on Monday either. It was obvious to everyone that she was not sick, so she couldn't use that excuse. We talked about the practicalities of providing support – of the need in the long term to have support from her teacher colleagues and headteacher, and how that might only come if she could open up dialogue. But in the short term – for Friday and Monday – we arranged that if she needed she could come over to my house, or ring, after she left her friends in town. The decisions were left with her. She said she felt much better than she had done earlier and that she would go in to school the following day.

Diane telephoned again two weeks later. Things had not improved; each day seemed to get worse rather than better. I went to meet her to discuss the problems further. 'I really, really, really hate it' were her opening remarks. She could not pin-point anything in particular: it seemed to be everything. She began to elaborate and distinguish. The main problem was that she felt she was doing nothing right. She thought she knew what good teaching looked like, but she certainly wasn't doing it. The group work activities left queues of children waiting for help, so she knew the work must be too hard for them. Yet the ideas she was using were what she thought were right for 6-year-olds. She had used the same ideas in teaching practice and it had worked then for the same age. She felt she was constantly nagging the children to be quiet, to sit down, to get on with their work, and did not have a good relationship with them. She had still not built a confident relationship with the staff – on the contrary, her relationship with the head had worsened. He had taken to talking to Diane after school each night. That was seen in negative terms, as was everything else. In trying to get a positive view of the good things, I asked Diane to pick out some aspects of her teaching which were working. She said she was unable to do so. What made things worse, she said, was that the headteacher was now raising the issue of formal assessment with her. A visit from the education officer was planned and the head had used this as a threat, telling Diane that the officer would want to see everything being done well. She was now terrified of the visit from the 'big man from the office'. She saw him as having a pure assessment function; I reassured her that he would also have a support function, and would respond if she sought help. We discussed the practicalities of how best I might assist her. I said I thought that a major difficulty for her was that she had no one in school to whom she felt she could turn. She agreed. I asked if there was any way I could help arbitrate, to open up the discussion (in the way, though I didn't say this to her, that the Principles of Procedure for the project said I should operate). She was adamant that the headteacher should not be approached. I asked if she would tell the officer how she was feeling. She said she would if he was a nice man. If he wasn't nice she would not be able to. If things got out of hand she might tell him that she intended to resign anyway. I suggested that a way in which I should proceed was to make a visit during the following week, after the head had attended the meeting for teacher-tutors. That would enable me then to discuss classroom events with Diane, and to support her teaching in more practical ways than I could through meetings out of school. It might, if she agreed, help me to open up the discussion with other staff, to try to generate the support she needed within school. Diane saw the logic of that, she said, and agreed it was a good idea, but didn't think it would actually resolve the problems. She could see no prospect of continuing: 'it simply isn't worth putting up with feeling this way'. However, she had gone in on the previous Friday and had not yet had a day off.

I visited Diane at school, by prior appointment, four weeks after term began, with two elements of action in view: to talk with Diane about her perceived teaching difficulties, and to try to open up constructive discussion for her with the head. Aims one and three of the project were very much in mind. Some detailed preparation had been done prior to the visit, through conversation first with Diane, and then with the head.

The school was a small, modern, single-storey building, with playground and recreation field alongside, set in the midst of a modern housing estate. The headteacher invited me into his office. He led the conversation immediately with comments about problems experienced with Diane. He said Diane had been rude and unprofessional during an inservice day with visitors from other schools. She had objected to being called 'dear' and 'treated like a child' by an older teacher she had never met before, and had said so publicly during an open discussion. The session had focused on relationships. The description of the event gave me the impression that such a comment would have been legitimate. The head clearly thought that it was not. Diane had been outspoken on other occasions with other members of staff and had had to be spoken to. The situation now was that the head recognized that his relationship with Diane had become so bad that it was now a 'personal thing' – he disliked Diane and found it impossible to say anything positive or constructive to her. If the head went into the staffroom for coffee and only Diane was there, he left immediately and went into his own office to avoid contact. Diane, he said, had a particularly peculiar way of staring at people without replying when they asked her something. That was said to be very disconcerting, and other people had commented on it. I pointed out that everything so far said about Diane was negative, and asked what was good about her teaching. He admitted that he was now almost unable to look for good things, but that music was a strength in practice and the factor on which she had been appointed. He said he would welcome help in resolving the breakdown in relationships. I said I would join Diane's classes for the afternoon and talk later to the head.

Music was being practised in the assembly hall. This was not Diane's own class, but the next class up — the 7-year-olds. The children were seated in a circle, each with an instrument. Diane was quietly instructing and conducting sequences of loudness/quietness, with group activities, paired, individual contributions, and whole-class performance in a well-managed series. After instrumental activity, there was singing accompanied by Diane on guitar and also on piano, according to particular songs. The children participated with enthusiasm, seeming to know most of the songs, though perhaps not fluently in all cases! Occasionally Diane had to insist on correct social behaviour or on rules for handling/not handling instruments. She did this quietly but clearly and firmly. The session was (apparently to me, and confirmed by Diane later) about encouraging co-ordination and controls in the sounds.

At changeover time I had listed seven brief comments on the high quality of the teaching. I later showed them to Diane, whose response was to ask 'but what about the bad things?' I said that there were none, in my view. She seemed unconvinced.

After changeover, Diane began group activities with her own class in the form base. There was minimal instruction from Diane about what was required. Trays with workbooks, paper, etc. were on the tables and the pupils started work on writing, drawing, reading or maths. Routines seemed well established, and individual children sought help as needed. I worked initially with a maths group, then for quite a long time with one girl on reading.

At break time we talked. She repeated that she felt dissatisfied with her teaching; that she was not doing enough for the children; and that they were not learning anything. We talked about how progress is judged in the short term with children at this age, the criteria used, and what kinds of knowledge, skills, attitudes and so on were included in her teaching intentions. She seemed to have some problems identifying these in this conversational context, though it was clear in the music lesson that she had no problem. We also talked about an evaluation strategy which would help her to judge whether the children were learning, and if she was doing enough for them. She said she was unable to identify what to do in order to improve teaching.

The children came in from play, took their milk, drank it and put the empty cartons in the bin provided. They settled in the story corner, crushed. Diane read a story and asked questions about it, then brought the guitar and led communal singing. Two children left to unload a bin full of sandwich boxes, ready for home time collection by individual children. At 3.15 p.m. the children departed, accompanied to the entrance by Diane to await collection by parents.

When they were all safely away she returned to the classroom, where we talked further about how best to develop her teaching. She said again that she could not work out how to do that and had difficulty identifying what aspects of her teaching needed developing; I suggested two areas which might be helpful, from my observations of the class-base session:

1. The organization and availability of resources for group activities; children did not have crayons, etc.

2. The development of stimulus material in the classroom; there were extensive displays of children's work which could be complemented by visual material on, say, number, colour, vocabularly, or on themes, using objects for display.

I also suggested that the development of systematic planning, preparation, implementation and evaluation techniques would help in identifying what was being done, what the children were learning, and what might follow. This, I proposed, might help to break through the general sense of 'not knowing'.

I also discussed the staff relationships problem, and said that the head would like to resolve the impasse. That seemed to me to be the best way to develop support for Diane within the school. She agreed. We met the head and opened up the possibility of getting dialogue going between them. I said that was only likely to work if the head could be positive toward the good work that Diane was doing. Diane said she felt no different after the meeting, and I said that it would take time and effort to build up a working relationship before she was likely to feel different — that I was not a miracle worker! I asked Diane to telephone me at home to let me know how things were working out. She agreed.

Eleven days later (Sunday mid-October) Diane telephoned to say that she had more or less made up her mind to resign from the job and to give up teaching. She did not see the point of continuing and realized that she would have to hand in her notice in the coming week to get out of the job at Christmas. I asked her what, out of the things we had discussed, lay behind the decision. In particular she felt that she was making no progress as a teacher and had realized that she had no idea what she was supposed to be doing in maths and language. Every day when she thought about what she was to do next with the children it seemed to be less clear. She said she seemed to have no sense of curriculum in these areas, and still no sense of how to go about learning what 'to do'. She was concerned to know what the procedures for resignation were. I suggested that she should talk with the head about how she felt. The head would then, I thought, take the matter up with the officer and I suggested Diane should take the chance to talk with him before acting decisively. Nevertheless, I said that if the decision was firm I would offer her support during the ensuing period of time, since she might be more in need of support than before. She said she thought the head would be glad to be rid of her, but she felt guilty about leaving the children after one term, since they had a disturbed year the previous year because of a maternity leave substitution. Diane would talk to the head on Monday morning, and would telephone me on Monday evening to say how things were. The events which followed were recorded in my diary:

Monday, 2.45 p.m.

The head rang me at the office. Diane had spoken to him of the intention to resign. The head had responded with a gut reaction 'Thank goodness' but on immediate reflection had considered the consequences of such a move for Diane. He spoke sympathetically about those consequences and how to avoid them. He had rung the officer who would go into the school Tuesday to talk to Diane. I said that Diane had rung me Sunday and reported in outline that conversation. The head said he had taken my view of being positive to Diane very seriously and had praised her work since my visit, particularly mentioning an assembly which Diane had conducted and been praised for. He went on to say that the school had been a happy and pleasant place before Diane arrived, that all the staff had felt so, but he had said to Diane that he thought Diane was not willing to give it a try in building good relationships. Even the deputy who was a most congenial fellow was finding difficulty with Diane. Here again the negative comments began to flow. I said that Diane needed time: that she is a particular individual with idiosyncracies which need to be accommodated. I was told that the staff had tried very hard and failed to make a relationship with Diane. I said that it would take hard work till the end of the year to support Diane in her difficulties; that from Diane's point of view, and despite outsiders' views of her teaching, she was unable to see where she was at with teaching. The head said that he would allow Diane to go beyond the deadline for resignations if that would help (but he had actually told Diane that resignations had to be in by Friday).

I was struck by an underlying query about the kinds of comments which the head himself had told me he had made or not made to Diane. There were contradictions — he was negative but said he was working hard on being positive; he emphasized a resignation deadline to Diane but privately told me he would be very lax. He told me that the cleaners had made negative comments to him about Diane. I wondered why he had taken them into account. Later the same day the officer phoned me. He would visit Diane the following day, Tuesday, because she said she was thinking of resigning. He knew I had been into school and was wondering what my impressions were. I told him the head had been on the telephone to me, that Diane had telephoned on Sunday and that there were deep and complex problems. I pointed out the lack of confidence in her own teaching, the uncertainties, not knowing where to begin in maths/language, etc., and how that had been compounded by lack of support in the school because of the relationships problem.

He said I may be aware that this was not the first case of its kind in the school. I said I was not. He revealed that there had been a recent case of a new teacher who had had a very rough ride, implying that it was the way that she had been treated by the head. He said that he would never place another new teacher there as long as he had control over appointments (presumably a reference to planned legislation and proposals?). I said that I was placed in a dilemma because I had had contacts from Diane which the head was not to know about, and that the content of the conversations was confidential. All I could say, because Diane had previously asked me not to talk to the officer, was that she had been in touch with me from the beginning of the project and had had a very bad time from the head. The officer had had the incident of the workshop related to him by the head, and he took the view that it was at worst youthful naivity. I said I thought the head was unforgiving of that and other incidents. He said that in his role he would have to be seen to support the headteacher; he would go in with a specific intention to dissuade Diane from resigning, and would point out the dire consequences for her career of doing so. He would have to say to her that if she did not resign she would have to work in the school, to stick it out and make the most of it.

The next diary entry was two days later.

> *8.30 p.m.* Diane phoned following the visit Tuesday by the officer. She reported what he had said about the implications of resignation for her career and asked her to consider the matter carefully over half-term – next week. He would go to see her the first day after half-term. She said that she was going to friends for a few days and would reconsider; that she felt better about classroom practice – 'I do feel better about what is going on in the classroom' – in the light of the comments which the officer and I had made. She had only spoken to him on a 'superficial level' recognizing that she 'had to be careful in what I say to him'. She reported that the head had spoken to her at length after school and seemed to have 'got things off his chest'. Diane had not responded – just listened.

Diane said she would ring me during half-term, after returning from friends, to say what she had decided about resignation. The following day the head rang me. I said that in my judgement Diane needed a few days away to think clearly. He agreed, yet said that the whole matter was preying on his mind and that Diane would have to make a decision soon about resignation because the parents were beginning to talk. He seemed to imply that pressure needed to be put on Diane, contradicting what had just been said about leaving Diane time to think and make her decision. I gained an impression – indeed he told me as much – that the head was having difficulty keeping a calm, rational sense of judgement in the case. There was no indication at all of a desire to support Diane or to consider the trauma which she was going through. The head said that he had developed the view that Diane was simply unwilling to try to do anything to improve the situation.

Diane telephoned eight days later having returned from her break away. She said she had definitely decided to resign. This was because she could not see any possibility of the relationship between herself and the head improving. It was clear that the head did not like her. When the head had given her a 'talking to' immediately before half-term, after the officer's visit, he had told Diane that he thought Diane was 'peculiar'. This left Diane with the view that there could be no retrieval of the situation, if that was the way the head felt about her, and that it would be impossible to work with the head after he had delivered such a 'put-down'. She had no idea what else she would do. She could not contemplate the idea of another school because it would mean waiting in the present situation for too long, and in any case there was no guarantee that she would find a better situation.

I suggested to Diane that she might phone the officer during Thursday or Friday whilst still on half-term holiday, to discuss matters with him before beginning back at school. She said she would try to contact him.

I was left with a serious dilemma, and a number of questions about the role I had accepted, its boundaries, and the moral obligations of it. First I felt a moral responsibility towards Diane, wanting to ensure that she should not suffer either short-term or long-term consequences because of the behaviour of the headteacher and the way he treated Diane. I had seen no evidence that Diane was a failure in classroom teaching and that had been confirmed by the head and the officer. Nor had I seen any evidence that Diane was 'peculiar'. Indeed she seemed to have some interesting views and talked openly and lucidly about her experiences in school, displaying all the doubts and uncertainties which I took to be very normal. I had reassured her over the telephone that what I saw was an individual with idiosyncrasies, such as we each have as individuals. The notion of being 'peculiar' in any case assumes some kind of norm, some collective identity from which she distinctly deviated. I thus regarded her as a victim who was in a relatively powerless position within employment, and whose major power was in the form of resignation from that employment. She was willing to use the power, and that in itself suggested to me a good deal of courage, given that it was likely to wreck her chosen career. While I wanted to intervene on her behalf, I knew that that power relationship was between her and her employer.

As a commissioned support tutor, my role was defined in the Principles of Procedure of the project as concerned with the development of classroom teaching skills and the capacity for reflective thinking about teaching. I had already moved beyond that in attempting to arbitrate the relationships problem at the request of the headteacher, and prompted by my own view that classroom practice could not be developed without solving the relationship problem. Since Diane took the view that she could not pursue the latter, and would terminate all efforts at both by resignation, there seemed little I could do. Yet I believed that the employer had a responsibility to Diane which was at least equal to their responsibility to other employees, including the headteacher. Indeed, in this case they were aware of a similar difficulty faced by a previous new teacher in this school. One might reasonably expect the officers to take the responsibility for Diane's future seriously by supporting and protecting her, maybe moving her to a different school. The dilemma of whether I had any justification for intervention on her behalf was strong. Formally I didn't think I had. Morally I felt I should. The cop-out was to trust the professional judgement of the officer, and hope that Diane was able to express to him the full picture and the reasons for her decision. I was not sure that she would feel able to do that, given her insecurity. On the other hand, that insecurity would in large part disappear once she had invoked the power of resignation.

My next diary entry read:

> *4 November*
> Diane phoned to let me know that she had resigned. I said I would wait to hear from the officer or the head, but would like to talk with Diane sometime soon after.

> *9 November*
> Diane phoned. I had had no contact from the officer or the head. Diane said she felt much better at school. For a few days the head had smiled at her, now he just ignored Diane mostly: 'I'd rather he ignored me than told me off.' She said that the secretary had prepared the letter of resignation, and that the head had come into the class in the middle of teaching recorder playing. 'He waved the letter under my nose and asked me to sign it, while I was trying to teach recorder. I said I would want to read anything I signed before signing it and said he would have to leave it for me to do later. Well I could hardly do that while I was in the middle of teaching recorders.'

Diane had not decided what else to do about her future. She had talked at half-term with her former college tutors and student friends about her intention to resign but had not told anyone else local to the school. I agreed to meet her to listen more fully to how she felt at that stage.

Chapter 4

Understanding Reflective Professional Practice:
Dave, Debbie, Kathy, Liz and Sue

I have attempted to show from the initial project's cases how the full complexity of the task of teaching was sometimes faced with inadequate opportunity for preparatory work from the start. That start occurred under variable quality and amount of support both within and from without the schools. A lack of shared professional enquiry characterized the nature and conduct of that support, which in any case formally carried the potentially punitive, summative monitoring associated with the assessment of teaching performance, often within hierarchical 'social-stranger' power relationships. This situation was exacerbated by the lack of a code of practice, both in teaching itself and in support tutoring, which left support agents and teachers alike to make it up on the hoof. This was further aggravated by a lack of material resources which might have enhanced the quality of experience for the teachers both in their teaching and the support relationships. The upshot was, given that context, that these new teachers learned largely in isolation and through self-reliance, based almost entirely on private practical experience. This state of affairs was shown to be similar to that of other new teachers by HMI's *The New Teacher in School* (DES, 1982a), and was also described well by Lortie. The learning conditions for each project teacher were remarkably similar. My adaptation of Lortie's (1975) portrayal of those conditions is thus:

- Abruptly assuming full responsibility
- Lack of systematic in-school support
- Supervision by imposed social-stranger hierarchy
- Learning anxieties exacerbated by status
- No accessible, crystallized or codified body of knowledge
- No shared or common occupational 'intellectual capital'
- Shortage of material resources, especially time.

Consequently I concluded that new teachers learn while doing, largely in isolation which assumes self-reliance, and in which individualized practical experience is paramount: 'I'm just in there on my own, it's sink or swim, just get on with it' (Sue, 4 November).

Sue was one of the research group of teachers who was not part of the project. As I have remarked at several points in the portraits of Pauline, Mike, Lesley, Richard, Anna and Diane, a detectable problem in my role was the difficulty of gaining an 'invitation' into that isolation and the reflective processes which, I have no doubt, went on within it. It seemed important in practice to see and get to know the work of the teachers in context. As it transpired I was able to record a good deal about these contexts, and something of the teachers' practice and ways of thinking about teaching. But the main point of those contacts had been to provide the 'common ground' for reflection on, discussion about, and development of the practice. It was these which proved much less easy to achieve in my neutral-tutor role. I felt I was gaining relatively superficial insights into the teachers' ideas, was not gaining much headway in promoting 'reflective practice', and that insights into how reflection occurred were largely eluding me. I will consider these aspects of new teachers' learning, based on data from the research group of teachers with whom my meetings proceeded during the same period as the project, but more frequently than did my contacts with the project teachers. They identified something of the complexity of exchanges which occurred with 'others', as well as how they thought about their teaching independently of others. In particular I will consider the nature of learning through reflection-in-action and reflection-on-practice (Schon, 1983). In their discussions these teachers recognized very clearly the principle and practice of reflection in- and on-action. Identifying what the practical knowledge was which attracted or prompted such reflection is relatively unproblematic, confirming classifications (or codifications) such as those of Elbaz (1983) and Wilson et al. (1987). These are identified in Table 4.1. The specific aspects of each of these categories which each teacher considered varied according to contexts, job specifications, idiosyncrasies of attention, and the flux of events in teaching. These issues were illustrated in conversation with the teachers and are described later in Chapter 7. How learning was achieved was much more problematic. It was clear from the project that the conditions of learning to teach during the first year produced or required frenetic pace and monumental amounts of learning, based largely on first-hand experience and reflection on events. But it was not clear what the nature and mode of this learning was. There was not sufficient time to explore it with the project teachers. It was therefore important, for the extension project and for our knowledge more generally about how new teachers learn, to gain greater depth of insight than was possible through my role as 'neutral tutor'.

Lortie observed that in their isolation it befalls teachers to 'discern problems, consider alternative solutions, make a selection, and after acting assess the outcome'. He noted that Jackson (1968) recognized that this occurred hundreds of times daily, leaving new teachers to work things out as best they could (Lortie, 1975, p. 72). We may presume such lonely decisions and solutions will be affected by personal qualities and predispositions such as confidence,

Table 4.1 Categories of teachers' knowledge

Elbaz	Wilson *et al.*	The teachers
Self		Self: • time management • emotions • self-concepts • self-respect • attitudes to teaching
Subject matter	Subject matter 'Pedagogical content'	Subject matter
School/curriculum	Curriculum Educational aims	School expectations/ Curriculum requirements
Resources		
Students	Learners	Individual Children: • learning needs/ achievements/emotions
Strategies	Pedagogy	Teaching strategies: • classroom management • pastoral care • instructional techniques
		Other: • Child abuse • Special needs • First aid • Organization • Report writing policies • Staff relationships
Self-appraisal (evaluation)		Evaluation: • Criteria for judging effectiveness, expectations of others

perceptiveness, energy, insight, commitment, perseverance, and will. I needed a sense of how these are brought to bear on the problems of teaching, and even how they might be developed. With an acknowledgement that self-reliance stands at the core of becoming a teacher I wanted to understand more fully what that process looked like from the new teachers' perspectives. Most of all, I wished to discern how these processes of learning could help me to understand the relationship between the development of skill, judgement, personal values and perspectives, and 'critical' capacities. The group of five teachers met with me as a research group throughout the year at two- or three-week intervals. The invitation to join the group was given in a letter circulated to new teachers starting in the area at the beginning of the school year. The research contract which was negotiated with the five teachers consisted of the following:

1. The research project will support teachers in conducting their own research into their teaching and learning.

2. Observation field notes, taped discussions, interviews and documentary information gathered during fieldwork will be the property of the teachers and available to them for their use, and of the researcher.

3. Both would have opportunities to use data for discussion, reports, or publication, subject to point 4 below.

4. Data will be treated as confidential to the research group or to the individual teacher, where that is specifically expected. Usually, it would be expected that data could be made available to the wider educational community, for 'open' discussion and the development of understanding about the experiences of new teachers.

5. For reports and publication anonymity will be ensured where that is appropriate.

Meetings were held as a discussion group, serving the teachers as peer-support activities as well as fulfilling the research project intentions. Those were, simply, to elucidate the educational experiences of new entrants to the profession. Matters for discussion were mainly decided by the teachers, sometimes by fixing a structured agenda, sometimes in unstructured and 'responsive' discourse. The teachers also accepted and responded to what they came to call my 'difficult questions' throughout. Each discussion was audio-taped, except when individuals occasionally requested total confidentiality. Transcripts were made immediately after each meeting, and copies given to the teachers at the following meeting. The regularity of and sustained attendance at 16 meetings allowed the teachers to present their views on aspects of life in schools, and on their learning and how it occurred, in ways which incorporated reports on developments and reflection back to earlier discussion. In that way a complex picture was built up through modifications and elaborations on the views expressed by the teachers. The picture was also enhanced, in my view, because each participant was free to ask questions of others. Many questions were asked, therefore, from the perspectives of new teachers.

In view of the assumptions in the initial project about reflective practice, and the research intention to test the application of principles of research-based teaching and their appropriateness for the induction year, my own questions in the discourse centred on the learning experiences of the teachers as researchers of their own practice. The data presented below were selected on that theme. Other themes were apparent in the extensive transcripts: for example, the effects of external constraints on teaching; staff support for new teachers; the power of assessment; taking on the identity of 'teacher'; the value of teaching practices as preparation for teaching; and the lack of impact of initial training and induction provision. Each of these could provide a focus for analysis and reflect features of the 'portraits' of the initial project teachers. However, the predominant concerns of discourse among the research group were twofold, and closely interrelated. The first was about how the teachers made professional judgements in their practice, and the handling of information on which those judgements were made. The second was about the emotional impact of events, and the ways in which the teachers learned to 'manage' the emotions. The emotional experiences were often directly linked with judgements in classroom teaching. In the reports which follow, the teachers have spoken for themselves in demonstrating the importance of these intertwined concerns.

The thematic bias of my interest with the group, and of my selection from the ensuing extensive transcripts of discussions, suggests how my interests were substantially influenced by Donald Schon's (1983) *The Reflective Practitioner*. I was not alone, it seems. His influence among teacher educators has recently been described as 'massive' (Zeichner and Tabachnick, 1991) and evidence of it can be found in numerous publications and research papers. Discussions about the relationship between 'professionalism' and the exercise of judgement in practice among my colleagues at the University of East Anglia were also influenced by Schon (MacDonald *et al.*, 1986; Sockett, 1986; Elliott, 1989). In the latter case, Schon's ideas were contributory to the elaboration of work in action research which had been extensively pursued since the late 1960s. In my own case I read the central ideas as a plausible (and perhaps even seductive) theory of professional practice, with clear implications for professional induction which Schon himself elaborated in *Educating the Reflective Practitioner* (Schon, 1987). Certainly the initial project's conception was influenced by Schon's (1983) analysis of how the relationship between practice and research can occur and its potential for professional development. Schon's theory of reflection-in-action is complex, yet it is based on a simple notion: that when a professional person reflects in action he/she becomes a researcher in a specific and particular practical situation. Because situations are complex and uncertain, and always unique because of the combination of variables which come together, practice problems are difficult to identify. They are also difficult to act upon, since judgement and action need to be taken to fit the particular characteristics of each case — 'selectively managing complex and extensive information'. The purpose of the action, in an activity like teaching, is to change the situation from what it was to a desired state, so that once action has been taken further management of information is required, to judge the effects of action and assess the newly created situation. According to Schon, this constant activity of appreciation, action, reappreciation, further action, leads to the development of a repertoire of experiences of unique cases, which are then available to draw upon in unfamiliar situations. Yet that repertoire is used by the recombination of elements of those other experiences, rather than as 'recipe knowledge', so that each new situation is dealt with through reflection-in-action, further enriching the repertoire of practice. The process of reflection-in-action, in this view, in the construction of each aspect of professional practice, involves experiment and enquiry. But the practitioner's experimenting is different to methods of controlled experiment: first, because the practitioner attempts to make a hypothesis come true; and second, because professionals do not control all the factors involved. The situation is therefore unstable and the outcome relatively unpredictable.

The first year of teaching is a period when practical experience is built perhaps more rapidly and more critically than at any other stage in a teacher's career because of the frenetic activity and learning which is required in meeting the full demands of teaching for the first time. I believed and asserted at the time that this is when the problematic nature of teaching is confronted in its most acute form, opening up the potential for educational experiences for new teachers to be developed constructively. I argued that it represents a particular and unique example of Schon's perspective in practice because there is no repertoire of experiences to draw upon in unfamiliar situations. Because of the nature of teacher induction, new teachers face almost entirely unfamiliar situations in which they must be self-reliant in making that repertoire of experience through trial and error judgements. The nature and circumstances of teaching, I contended, also represent a particular and unique example of Schon's view in practice because teaching is different from law, architecture, medicine, engineering and other professions which he considered in this sense. In teaching, the concept of 'case' is itself very complex so that when Schon refers to judgement and action taken to fit the particular characteristics of each case, that could mean each child at each point of intervention by a teacher. It could mean each group or class at each encounter, within which it is necessary to take some account of each pupil case. It could mean each event in corridor or playground, with the knowledge that action in that 'case' might affect the other cases, because of the interpretations and responses of pupils as they move from one situation to the other. In circumstances where much 'overlap' of cases is unavoidable, and where interpretation, inference and response in behaviour is inevitable, it is impossible always to judge the effects of action and to assess newly created situations. Even in the simplest sense of 'case' – an individual pupil's learning or behaviour – the availability and management of information is uncertain and unpredictable. The volatility of appreciation, action, reappreciation and further action, through 'selective management of complex and extensive information', is all the greater because usually numerous 'cases' have to be handled at the same time, and often immediately. The selection of information may be rapid and impressionistic, the likelihood of missed information or mis-information considerable, and the potential for misjudgement enormous.

Thus, I claimed, the problem faced by new entrants in attempting to become effective teachers, in Schon's terms, is that first and foremost they need to become effective researchers capable of enquiry, from which problems can be framed adequately; capable of constructing hypotheses as a basis for 'experiment'; capable of taking appropriate action to effect change; and capable of monitoring changes. Yet even that reflects a notion of a clinical, controlled case. In practice, information about the cause of a child's emotional state, the events of a previous lesson with another teacher, the micro-politics of peer groups in a class, and so on, may be the essential yet inaccessible information upon which all other acts depend for 'success'. Appropriate, effective action may depend upon the quality of that research, but as I said at the outset we know very little about how it occurs or develops during the early phases of teaching. Schon himself deliberated on the need for research in this field in the professions in general, and I had taken up that call in the design of the project, hence the action-research and interpretive case study elements associated with it. As a result, it seems to me now that there are problems in the notion of reflective practice which he posited, and which I pursued in the initial project. These problems emerged for me as I tried to make sense, simultaneously, of the data from the teachers, Schon's 'reflective practice', Zimpher and Howey's 'competences', and Lacey's 'social strategies' (as elaborated by Zeichner and Tabachnick). (Each of these were of course considered as I tried to extend my own views of action research and reflective practice, which had been the basis of my previous work with student-teachers.)

The essence of the problem with Schon's perspective is that his concerns (and those of MacDonald et al., 1986; Sockett, 1986 and my own in the initial project) centred on the way judgements are made in practical action, rather than on the values which underpin and direct the making of certain judgements rather than others. In terms of the conceptions of 'practical knowledge' defined earlier, the concern rests in the realms of the acquisition of 'pedagogical content', and of 'effective' teaching strategies, rather than in the realm of 'self' and the teachers' dispositions, values, and educational aims. In terms of Zimpher and Howey's 'competences' these are the areas of technical and clinical, rather than personal and critical conceptions. As I said earlier, my need was, and is, to explore the relationship between these conceptions (as well as the adequacy of the constructs), especially in the light of recent explorations in action research in Britain. An important question arising in this exploration is: does Schon's account of reflective practice constitute a 'technicist' conception of practical enquiry and thus equate closely with 'mere skills' which Stenhouse set out to subsume within the questioning of values and assumptions? And if it does, do we need a more extensive view of what constitutes research-based teaching than that which I held during the development project? These questions emerged as critical as the data from the research group was added to that from the initial project teachers.

DAVE, DEBBIE, KATHY, LIZ AND SUE

Dave age 26, taught science in a large 11–18 comprehensive school to a range of ages and ability groups, and was also a form tutor.

Debbie age 25, taught 11–12-year-olds mostly, with some other classes, in a middle school. She had a special interest in humanities/RE but taught all subjects.

Kathy age 23, taught reception class in a first school.

Liz age 26, taught 8–9-year-olds all subjects in a middle school.

Sue age 23, taught history in an 11–18 comprehensive school to a range of ages and ability groups. She became head of department at another school after the induction year.

The route to the range of knowledge required for teaching and to improved means of utilizing and developing it was a route of transformation, of status passage, for each of these teachers. The event of students coming into school for teaching practice pin-pointed how far the teachers had travelled, in their view, after two months in teaching. It also prompted some assessment of their identity *vis-à-vis* being a student and being a teacher:

> *Sue* I think they do see you [i.e. as a new teacher] as being more approachable, and more sympathetic towards them – you're not a threat, are you?
>
> *Debbie* No, you're half-way there.
>
> *Les (Tickle)* You're half-way there – it's a sort of metamorphosis which you're sharing with them, is it?
>
> *Debbie* I think it is. I mean, I don't feel, it was very strange right at the beginning, it's not quite so strange now, but right at the beginning I could feel myself I'd got into being a teacher and having this sort of idea of myself and as soon as the students came in on attachment I could feel myself becoming more of the student teacher again – quite peculiar because I then had somebody to relate...
>
> *Liz* I had someone to identify with ... and that was most peculiar, you know. (18 November)

Being half-way there, and presumably by implication, being all the way, was essentially a condition which appeared to depend centrally and crucially on the processing of events, on the nature and quality of the journey. It was a matter of experience, as Debbie's rhetorical question suggested:

> *Debbie*　Is that something somebody can actually tell you, or is it one of those things that it infiltrates through osmosis, and that eventually, through seeing a year's lot of work, you actually get an in-built knowledge? (18 November)

These 'infiltrations' were regarded as essential; they were seen as qualitatively different from being taught. There was a disregard for 'hypothetical' outsider knowledge in initial training as a means of preparation for 'very real practical issues'. There was a clear assertion, too, that the range of experience needed could not accrue from initial training:

> *Debbie*　I feel that it's maybe inherent in any post-graduate course there are things that may be they can't teach, may be it's absolutely impossible for you to be taught, but there are things that you come across, right, in the first week that I wasn't prepared for, that I hadn't been prepared for, only in theory ... not even a theoretical point of view. We've talked about various ways of classroom management, and very hypothetical situations, that in no way prepared me for having this classroom that was mine, and I had to organize it – that no way prepared me – the shock to my system for having to do that. It didn't prepare me for my first parents' evening. It hasn't prepared me for the on-going stress and knowledge how to cope with stress.
>
> *Liz*　I mean, an awful lot of real practical day-to-day things we weren't taught, but then, you know, it was a year course and it taught me from being really, really raw to somebody who could go into the classroom. (18 November)

This journey into practical experience included the acquisition of additional curriculum-subject knowledge, especially for the primary teachers, and pedagogical expertise, about which the teachers were self-conscious. They actively pursued such knowledge, seen as directly pertinent to teaching tasks which they were required to undertake:

> *Debbie*　I'm teaching a class maths, doing co-ordinates – and you think, 'well, where do I go about finding this information?' and you have to literally go and find out for yourself. I'm teaching hockey, I didn't even like hockey at school – now I'm teaching it, and I've had to go and find out the

rules – and then I go ahead and start teaching and I
suddenly think 'yes, that's how I did it' and I'm actually
thinking out techniques and skills as I'm doing it, because
it doesn't tell you in any books and it's not until you
actually start teaching you think 'I should be telling them
to do that and do that'. (2 December)

Equivalent aspects of academic knowledge were identified by each teacher:
particular periods of history for Sue; aspects of science for Dave; music for
Kathy. Most of these and others were largely available in forms of information
which did not depend on colleagues or on experience of teaching. They were
preparatory matters, prerequisite to translation into pedagogical forms suitable for the pupils. They were the know-what of teaching. Much more problematic was the know-how of a thousand elements, demands which could only
be met by fulfilling tasks directly with the children. These were far wider than
pedagogical strategies:

> Liz   Well, I suppose it's things like having to take the children
> swimming on a Thursday and having to leave 14 behind.
> So you have to make sure, they have to walk to another
> school, across the roads, get them ... make sure, I,
> myself, have to do all this, I've never taken 20 children on
> my own before until I became a teacher having to do all
> that sort of stuff, plus keeping the others occupied,
> thinking of things for them to do. We had a priest in
> today, I had to organize the class around that, that sort
> of thing I've never done before and wasn't used to – um,
> what else, I'm sure there's loads – like having to get the
> Christmas card, well, my art group did, having to get that
> done by a certain time – hand out letters, remembering to
> do – just hundreds of things, little things like that,
> nothing very big, nothing I can't really cope with, but
> when it all seems to come in at once. (2 December)

These reflections on the problematic nature of teaching, and on the self in terms
of confidence and competence, often intuitively detected gaps, or problems,
but could not easily determine or analyse their nature or what to do about
them, because they were so extensive:

> Liz   You were talking about our own note-taking and record
> keeping, it's very difficult to keep up on it, I've got my
> mark book and you can mark homework, but there's only
> so much you can do, a tick or perhaps a star if it's good,
> or whatever your code is. At half-term I took in all their

books and went through and wrote two or three lines, perhaps a few more if I needed to, perhaps less if I didn't need to, in each subject, but it took ages and it gave me such a headache, and I don't really know how much I achieved from it, so that wasn't very satisfactory. I confined it because I told you about these five boys with their maths, it's very difficult to do it on my own really, to know, I don't feel experienced enough, or perhaps, I could if I sat down and really worked at it, but I haven't got myself together enough to think systematically, I need to find out how their language is going, has it progressed, are there still basic flaws with certain children that they need to pick up on. What about their maths? and eight, nine, ten subjects, it's ever so difficult to – and that's one thing I do feel I ought to work more on.

Les Does that mean that you think about the need to do that all the time, but haven't actually ...?

Liz I think about it a lot and feel guilty, and then it's very haphazard. I go in and I might pick out one child and spend an awful lot of time with that one child, but again that isn't satisfactory, again I haven't quite sussed it out, and then I'll say 'I'll do it at the weekend,' or 'I'll work it out at Christmas' and it still hasn't really happened ... and even to know who to go to. I mean, it's not like a problem where you can say 'I'm having difficulties with this child, I'll go and speak to so-and-so about it,' or 'I don't know where to take my subject area from here, I'll go and speak to the specialist,' you know, it's not even those, where you can go and seek advice. (16 December)

At other times the know-how existed 'in principle' but there was a failing in its applications, and reflection-on-practice resulted in some feeling of inadequacy, or recognition of the practical limitations to doing the 'best possible'. Dave had realized that he was not ensuring that the laboratory was tidied after each lesson. He knew well enough how to manage lesson time and to organize pupils to improve that, and to act accordingly. He compared that evaluation and action with a different problem, where resolution was restricted by the limitations of time resources, and where less than the ideal was accepted as inevitable:

Dave I would say that most of the problems are that line, probably more organizational – that sometimes it's 'well, I've only got half an hour to do this worksheet so I'll have to get one out which will at least be functional,

rather than brilliant', so that sort of thing. Now
sometimes ... it's not the best way of doing it, but I don't
want to spend all the time planning that worksheet when
you've got two or three others to get out, and which I've
found some of the groups have got more worksheet thirst
than others. So, it's just one of those things.
(16 December)

Much of what the teachers discussed were 'problems' of this order:
technical know-how which had to be applied within the constraints of time,
resources and expectations but which, once identified and acted upon were
readily routinized; academic knowledge which, once researched and assimilated,
was readily accommodated into teaching programmes. The more problematic
realms of knowing were associated with the making of judgements during
teaching, and what Debbie had called 'knowledge how to cope with stress' –
handling all the variables in particular 'cases', and handling one's own responses
and reactions in the face of the unpredictable and uncertain. Each of the
teachers saw the need to learn by personal experience, with and without
support from others. Their curriculum was in some senses self-determined
though unpredictable, a programme but not programmable. Its extent and
volatility left little scope for systematic, selected 'study'. What seemed to
matter was to develop the ability to cope with the anarchy of learning/
experience, and gradually to control, tame and manage it to best advantage
for improving one's teaching. At these stages in the first half of the year, the
teachers certainly saw themselves as being *en route*, enjoying status passage
into 'experience'. The route was not an established, metalled road so much as
a route through uncertain topography, the main features of which were
dominated by three elements: the technical knowledge of subject matter,
pedagogy, and management of those 'hundreds of little things'; the handling
of information and making of judgements about the curriculum progress of
pupils; and the relationship between one's ideals for teaching and pupils'
learning and one's emotional capacities and sense of self while travelling the
route.

The main characteristic of the journey through this topography appeared
to be the processing of 'experience' which would mentally map the route, for
reference and source of ease for future occasions. It seemed necessary to the
teachers that such processing should be done first hand, on their own account.
Lortie (1975) recognized that the teachers he studied selected from and adapted
the ideas of other teachers about 'what to do and how to do it' matters for the
classroom, converting the ideas through personal perspectives and application
to their situations, and judging them by the criterion of whether 'it works ...
for me'. He thus formulated a view of each teacher as 'self-made', even where
opportunities for observation and discussion occurred. Confirming this,
the research group teachers reported that where colleagues observed their

teaching, or offered advice, they judged the information provided, determining its validity or its value for them in informing their own practice, and gauging whether it might be applicable to future situations. Alternatively they sought advice from trusted colleagues, though there were conditions to its 'acceptability'. Debbie could adopt some advice provided it came from a close colleague with similar 'personality' and 'approach' and provided 'I can see that applying to me'. By that, Debbie meant if she had solicited advice, if she had reflected 'should I have done it like this?' or 'should I do it like that?' Sometimes these questions were prompted by measuring consequences after events; sometimes predicting possibilities to inform potential courses of action; and sometimes in trying to check actions against such intentions. The questions sometimes arose because of a difficulty in proposing any course of action. In each case the key referent was 'experience':

> *Debbie* taking on board his [colleague] advice because he's
> obviously been there, he's obviously been there, he's
> taught fourth years, he knows those particular children ...
> which is the type of knowledge that I haven't got.
> (18 November)

It was not sufficient simply to defer to the experience of others, but to establish it for oneself. Having a guide to the route was not enough; travelling it was essential. Liz identified clearly the need for 'ownership' of the knowledge:

> *Liz* I think it's something we've got to go through and find
> our own method − I know teachers have talked to me
> about what they do and I haven't been able to take it in
> because it's not my way, and I think I can only find out
> my way by trying what works and what doesn't.
> (18 November)

The delicacy of the advisory dialogue was rehearsed at some length by Liz, who argued cogently that advice after 'failing' an event was stressful and inadequate as a means of support, no matter how well meaning, extensive, and eventually effective such advice might be. The crucial feature for her effective learning was to be 'given the right question' in identifying problems in her teaching. She noted the similarity between inadequate principles of learning for her pupils and for herself:

> *Liz* I had I suppose constructive comments made after my
> adviser came in because he assessed the lesson, he's the
> maths specialist and he assessed the maths lesson which
> didn't go too well, investigating, which didn't work out
> too well, and so he felt able to give me advice and I

suppose at the time I found it quite difficult – I mean, nobody likes being criticized and everybody would rather be told beforehand and then helped over the problem than having to do it and fail and be seen to fail and then get help, which is what happened. I obviously didn't do too well and he went and talked to the head about it and after that I was given a whole lot of support in maths, I went to visit classrooms and the head came into my class and took over and had a special group going out to another teacher and the teacher – you know, a lot of support this way, that he did care about me. But I couldn't help thinking at the time that it was a lot of stress and bother when it would have been nice to have had a chance to talk about it beforehand, and sorted that out ... 'worried about my maths, and I'd like a bit of help' before I actually had to fail ... and I'd talked to the deputy head about it, but again I wasn't given the right opportunity, I mean, you answer, you speak to people and give them what you think they might be wanting to hear. I mean, the conversation I had with the deputy head wasn't 'what are the problems you are having at the moment? Tell me how I can help you?' More very general – 'How are things going?' It wasn't that I want to get into a deep discussion about this – it's 'I want to know generally how things are going.' So, I wasn't really specific about it – I hadn't been given the right question really, I hadn't been fed the right vibes to answer it. I mean, I know this in class, the SMP system is very much a one-way – children have to fail before you can help them – they have to work through the card and get it wrong before you see the problem. You don't teach a topic to the class, explaining the possible problems and then letting them get on with it. (23 February)

Here Liz was able to articulate an educational theory about the importance of success in practice, and the importance of prior opportunities, through prompts presented within conditions of dialogue and 'shared' problems. For herself and her pupils she was seeking to avoid failure in trying what works and what doesn't, by having the chance to establish in advance more 'secure' principles for teaching (in this case mathematics). What she identified was the way in which such opportunities to establish theories before testing them were missed. The realms of technical knowledge and the making of judgement, she seemed to be saying, got into crisis because of the 'glossing over' of problems by the deputy head, and her own inability to articulate her ideas in the conditions which pertained. Being given the right question and the right vibes to answer it was in this self-reflective theory about her own learning crucial for ownership as well as for the development of understanding and experience of success. Dave also recognized the after-the-eventness of learning from advice – in this case commissioned comment which might help him to understand events better as a means of developing practice for the future:

> Dave I was fortunate on the one occasion because it is a
> remedial group and you have one of the teachers in to
> help with writing and stuff, and he could actually be my
> evaluator on the situation. [I could say], 'well, this is what
> happened' or 'you saw that happen now what could I have
> done?' Sometimes the answer is nothing more, that's it,
> sometimes you get extra advice. But you know that little
> tip is useful when the situation occurs; you can store up
> in your mind for the next occasion – that comes out of
> something else – somebody else's experiences.... And
> sometimes in that situation you give replies, but think,
> 'OK, but I can't do that', which is an evaluation on
> evaluation, if you like. You come to a point and say, 'no,
> that's not me.' I find usually, being new, it's always in
> the, sort of, post event that you seek advice, you're never
> really told where some of the problems are unless you
> have gross problems, so you're continually seeking advice
> after the event, which would be better to have that
> information beforehand, but it doesn't seem to be
> happening that way, so far. (16 December)

Sue regarded herself as confident in the classroom and self-sufficient as a learner, though she discussed details of teaching with the head of department in what she described as a dialogue where they shared ideas. The contrast between being supervised as a student and independent learning as a teacher was a marked one, with an explicit preference for the latter.

> Sue Yes, 'cos this is what interests me, because I feel that
> what I've partly liked about this is that I've been left on
> my own, and if I've learnt, I've learnt on my own terms
> and not on somebody else imposing ideas and strategies
> and everything upon me – you've learned yourself whether
> it's going in the right direction or the wrong direction. So,
> that is independence – that's self-sufficiency maybe.
> (2 December)

While independent self-sufficiency in classroom matters was Sue's preferred mode of learning, the others wanted to assert that confidence in framing problems, and in setting the agenda for commissioning advice and support in testing strategies in their teaching. Even within that framework Liz acknowledged the need to be 'asked the right questions' to unlock her concerns about specific teaching problems, because of a lack of confidence in 'revealing herself'. It was at this point of reflection-in-anticipation of events, at the predictive, planning stage of teaching where a sense of *going through it* began alone. For Liz, Dave and Debbie it was here where support and advice might have been most effective, subject to their own interpretations and predispositions, in helping them to clarify their aims and proposals. Beyond that stage the implementation of ideas and conduct of practice added to the sense of going through it, alone, as a means of gaining 'experience'. From the point of view of the research, the question was whether the evaluative judgements of 'what works for me' were limited to the manifestations of aims and theories represented in technical proficiency and clinical judgements, or whether the aims themselves were the subject of introspection and debate.

For Sue, *going through it* had a much more traumatic meaning outside the classroom. While supremely confident in classroom matters, she was not independent and self-sufficient emotionally in social – and wider professional – relationships. A stranger to the locality, she had anticipated making friends among what turned out to be an unfriendly though superficially pleasant staff, many of whom conveyed to her their disaffection from teaching, and actively tried to undermine her enthusiasm. This was exacerbated by 'the woman who is in charge of new teachers' telling her that she 'had her spies out' listening in the corridors and staffroom. Sue interpreted such surveillance as assessment-related, and experienced inhibition and depression during the first term.

> *Sue*   You see, I want a good reference when I leave there, and
>   I don't want people to know how I really feel and if I can
>   sort of, if they think I'm doing fine, if they think I'm
>   really happy – I don't want them to know how I feel,
>   exactly, I don't want it to go down on my reference that
>   maybe I haven't quite settled in.

This provided a different sense to the question of reflection – reflecting on the possible consequences of revealing oneself in the sense of the emotions, as well as aspects of one's teaching. Each of the teachers revealed within the group that they regularly engaged in reflection on revealing or not revealing details of their teaching, of classroom events, of their 'personal' ideas and philosophies, and the ways they felt. They asserted how it was necessary to judge how much to reveal of the rationales (or the uncertainties or vagueness) in their thinking, and whether or not to expose their practice, or their evaluations of practice, let alone their emotions, to the scrutiny of others. So here was a kind of double-bind circumstance. The need to learn self-sufficiently was important for reasons of self-esteem which affected interpersonal relationships with colleagues, and also for micro-political reasons. Yet this was also a denial of the aspiration for dialogue about principles, aims and practice. The power of 'going through it' on the route to 'experience' was strong:

> *Sue* Maybe people aren't that concerned about it [the problem] but you are, and you've got nobody to talk to about it.
>
> *Liz* I've got to get through as well as I can without bothering people [and] you can't bare your soul, can you, because it gets trodden all over. (18 November)

Yet the bright side of that, certainly for Liz, was the development of confidence, a greater sense of independence and self-sufficiency both in the classroom and in the staffroom. In parts, however, the world remained a private one:

> *Liz* But there's quite a few things I do and I − it's still because I'm not quite confident about where I stand in the school, I suppose, that I think I'm sneaking in the odd lesson. Today we watched a video version of the book we've been reading, and I feel that's a very good thing to do, to contrast the cartoon version of the story, but again, I kept quite quiet about it, I didn't tell everyone − although I'd be happy to justify why I was doing it, if anyone asked and happy to tell them, but it's just one of those things, I think perhaps when I'm more confident in the school and feel more confident in myself, this is the sort of thing I will go and talk about − do you see the difference? (16 December)

Given this private world, the conversation in the group was much less about how the teachers learned from colleagues and more about how they learned alone, by *going through it*. This had a number of notable features. In particular the unpredictability of events made direct experience perpetually problematic, since the combination of variables affecting any specific circumstance was complex. The information needed to predict and manage events was often elusive. Even the teachers' own ideas were sometimes unclear and uncertain. It was these factors which made 'second-hand' learning either irrelevant or at best subject to testing and firsthand experience. But given the instability of situations and volatility of personal responses to events, what were the guiding procedures for gaining experience? Initially it was to treat events as a practice-ground, and to store them in memory.

> *Sue* The make-up of a particular group is different every year, so problems with one particular exam group are different

> every year, so experience is there for you to draw on, and,
> say in a couple of years time when you have the same
> kind of problem — 'oh, yes, I remember that group, I did
> this with them'. (18 November)

This confirms Schon's notion that what was important was the construction of a repertoire of such experience, from whatever source it might come, to provide firsthand knowledge. That, in Dave's terms, meant maintaining (healthy) distrust of knowledge from all sources, on the road to becoming experienced.

> *Dave* I think it's important to distrust what you're doing. I
> think it's building up a body of experience that is your
> experience rather than second-hand information, and once
> you start doing that then perhaps you become, with a
> capital T 'Teacher'. (18 November)

The notion of the capital T teacher as someone imbued with a body of practical experience was shared by each of the teachers. However, acquisition of that body was not in itself sufficient, especially in the realm of practice beyond classroom techniques. The teachers recognized the need not only for firsthand experience, but also to develop perceptiveness during classroom events in particular by monitoring the responses of pupils to one's teaching. This was the means of evaluation toward the most effective teaching and learning. This amounted to reflection in the immediate post-action situation, and required rapid processing of data.

> *Debbie* You've still got to be watching out the whole time for
> their eyes and for their attitude and for the way they are
> or what they are doing, as to whether they are lapsing or
> not. (2 February)

Going through it by testing out initial judgements made in planning and implementation of those plans in teaching against pupils' responses incorporated such reflection as the central feature of formative evaluation. Those evaluations were perceived with the same 'distrust' as were actions when it came to considering their value for future events:

> *Debbie* I think this year is for very much trying out these things,
> and then next year looking back and thinking, 'well, that
> one worked reasonably well but I would improve it in this
> way, and that way and another way to make it a little bit
> more slick, and it will actually work a little bit better, and
> it was a bit hit or miss in that place or that place'. I find

> very much I'm ... on my feet in some situations reacting
> to how they are reacting. I think, well, next year there is
> a distant possibility that they will react in the same way
> and therefore you can plan for it in advance. So you will
> be a bit more prepared for their reactions and their
> responses, it actually makes the lesson more valuable
> because you can go that step further. (2 February)

In the practice-ground for now, however, it was largely a case of hit or miss, especially in the immediate and medium term. Recognizing the pupils' immediate responses meant that the teachers also reflected on practice in the less immediate afterward. The process certainly included immediate responses to the implementation of their own planning decisions, judgements, and performance, selecting information to feed the reflections in the immediate, and responding or adjusting on the basis of that information on the spot. On-the-spot reflection also fed later reflecting-back on events. These in turn were seen as feeding the capacity to predict and anticipate future events in a way which they saw as meeting their aim to improve teaching. At this stage the lack of experience was a self-conscious phenomenon that left most judgements and actions in a position to be 'distrusted'. The teachers were self-conscious about their own inability to make sound dependable judgements or to take assured action. These considerations were not about teaching technique, but about making 'effective' judgements. Developing such judgements was, for them, an important element of practical proficiency which was closely coupled with growing independence and self-sufficiency. The way in which this capacity could be realized was thought to be through self-criticism, again in private:

> *Liz* Having to learn to be able to judge my lessons for myself,
> being self-critical, to work out am I going along the right
> roads? Why am I teaching this lesson – is it leading to
> anything? Having to do that the whole time I think.
> (2 December)

The immediate, on-the-spot judgements raised questions for the teachers about how to gauge a situation when immediate action was required so as to know how to act appropriately in the circumstances. Dave identified clearly the dilemmas involved in making judgements on the spot, and located recurrent examples of his practice when different judgements over superficially similar events were needed. For example treating different children's social behaviour differently in what might appear to be similar situations, in order to achieve the best results from action for each particular child, was crucial to the development of good relationships with pupils – a major priority for each teacher.

> *Dave* I just find this big dilemma of when to come on the
> heavy, authoritarian figure: 'stop doing that', when

> another child is doing the same thing and you know that's
> not going to work, it's going to upset them, stop them
> working entirely. [It's] difficult to gauge the situation
> before you act so you can act appropriately. [That's]
> something that has happened quite often in the past
> couple of weeks. (16 December)

Dave exemplified a specific resolution to this dilemma from a classroom incident. A child had put down a pair of safety goggles, having completed part of a chemistry experiment, and another child had picked them up to use. The first child reacted harshly, resulting in a classroom 'scene' in which the child packed his books and refused to continue working. Dave had to decide how to act with both children. Taking account of what he knew of each, he provided a second pair of goggles, but still had to restore the first child to working normally:

> Dave I could have shouted at him but it would have done no
> good ... [with] another child [I could have said] 'Now look
> you're being a bit of an idiot now, pick up those goggles
> and do it.' It would have worked better for that child that
> way, and a more soft approach for the other child, and
> when to gauge the difference, that's the difficulty.
> (16 December)

Such an apparently minor event contains complex features, all of which influence the judgement and action – legal health and safety requirements and ethical concerns for safety; social justice; motivation of pupils; concern for feelings of others; maintenance of order; establishing an image as a teacher; the availability of resources; desire to complete a lesson successfully; and a wish to develop good professional relationships with pupils, could each play their part in creating this 'difficulty' or dilemma. Each might need an exchange of information – why did the pupil react as he did? What will the others think?, etc. Yet there is little time for such information processing. There is even less time for exploring the underlying principles, or theories, which guide the individual teacher's responses in such circumstances. These are calls for action.

In any case, some information is not available until after action has been taken. There are also inherent tensions within intentions, which are determined in part by professional perspectives and ideals. But it was not clear from the teachers' deliberations whether, for example, Liz could gain and sustain opportunities to address such questions as 'why am I teaching this lesson – is it leading to anything?' Such 'deeper' problems appeared to be submerged by concerns about information processing and the rigours of the route to experience.

What was the nature of these rigours? Was the pace of events such that they submerged any view of the reason for being on the route in the first place?

Let us consider these in relation to just one element of teaching. The problem of judgement had to incorporate appropriate means of relating 'well' to individuals, within appropriate ways of responding to the corporate body of a group or class. And the solution needed to offer both short- and long-term 'benefit', in the context of the aim to achieve the best learning for all pupils, when each of these may also require different responses. This was a feature of the route to be trodden with caution, yet which had to be crossed quickly:

> *Debbie* Getting to know the children is so difficult to describe
> because your relationship changes so much. It's also so
> difficult to know where is the balance that is needed
> between them working for you because they'd like to work
> for you and actually working for you because they've got
> to work for you. And sometimes you think, shall I just
> ignore that and treat it with kindness and just treat it as
> a bit of a joke, or do I go and be really hard with them,
> which is going to be the best as a short-term solution and
> which is going to be beneficial in our long-term working
> relationship? And it's very, very difficult to walk that
> tightrope, and several conversations I've had and I've
> thought, maybe I should have reacted this way and there
> have been several recently because I hope I'm quite
> friendly to them and you think, well, is the way that I
> dealt with that the best way that I should have dealt
> with it and I'm constantly turning over in my mind
> situations – should I have done that in that situation, or
> said that, or dealt with it in that way. Because it is all to
> do with the building of those relationships. (2 December)

A desire to ensure that such judgements take full account of the circumstances in which they are 'embedded' recurred in those hundreds of events each day. The specific considerations were extremely varied. For instance, judging the language appropriate for explaining concepts to different children, or particular teaching tactics appropriate to individuals, was also exemplified:

> *Dave* Well it comes more in explanation of concepts, we've just
> been going through them in chemistry ... [it's finding] the
> best approach, the learning for the individual child ...
> you've got to be very much different with each child.
> Some you can just say 'well here's the information, get on
> and just do it', and they learn better that way, others
> you've got to go through it over and over again. (8 March)

The need to conduct teaching in a way which was perceptive and also receptive to the 'messages' of classroom events was part of the trial and error of experience. Yet the elusiveness of information was a feature of events which heightened the need for perceptual activity but maintained a sense of groping and grappling with uncertainty. This was discussed with regard to pupils' academic achievements. Dave had undertaken a prediction of exam scores for a class, which he compared with actual scores, as an investigation. Reporting it led Debbie to reflect on the problematic nature of information handling:

Debbie   I think one thing about what Dave is saying is important in that it is important for the teacher to try and predict and have these exercises because it shows you how – well, all of us as teachers are making value judgements about the children, the work that they are capable of and able to do, we feel based on certain aspects that we have seen of them, when you actually analyse it we don't really know and that can be dangerous. It came up today with one of the girls in my class who – her parents are very, very worried about her spelling, in fact they have been all year, and I've spent an awful long time with Clare, giving her extra work to do, talking to her mum, mum's come into my class about three times as well as a long time at parents' evening. They are very worried that she is not working hard enough, her spelling is very bad, her writing is very bad, all this sort of thing. My impression of Clare is that she is a little bit lazy, she is about average, she can be dull, but often I think it's because she is lazy rather than is stupid, she can do good work, you know, it's all these sort of things. Well, today the parents had phoned the deputy head about it, and so Clare was actually tested and there through the test today we realized that although she had a comprehension age which was about a year above her actual age, her reading age is about a year below. I was totally flabbergasted about this ... I thought, helping her, working with her, talking to her parents about her, I'd missed something really basic. That's quite bad, and in fact I wasn't the only one who had missed it, she was missed out last year and the year before and the year before. That's why it is really important for us to try and predict what we feel children can do – not only children who miss things, but also children who are really bright, who are missing out in that way. (8 March)

The combination of searching, selecting, assimilating, rejecting, monitoring and modifying engaged the teachers constantly on the route to becoming a 'capital T Teacher'. The management of individual 'cases' for these teachers was a search for 'appropriate' action, in the sense of action which solved problems and was 'effective', within the values which underlay their aims for the best possible learning for every child.

> *Debbie*   It feels a continuing puzzle. The only thing I think I've learnt is to treat each child differently: it will work a certain amount, it will work with one person, but it won't work with another, and when you've got 30 of your own children, and I take, not only my class, but I take another fourth year class and I take a third year class, a first year class, occasionally a second year class, and then my two different lots of games group in the third year, a games group in the fourth year, each of which change every two weeks, so, my relationship with my class is obviously different from my relationship with the other classes ...
>
> *Liz*   I think it is a bit of a continuing puzzle ...
>
> *Debbie*   I'm glad I'm not the only one ... (laughs)
>
> *Liz*   There are children that you don't know whether they are having real difficulties with the work, that's why they are not doing it, or they are just messing around, and I'm certainly finding that: have I been setting the work too hard for some of them? ... I didn't know how much to tell them off, how much was my fault in not gauging their work properly, and how much was it their fault.
> (16 December)

Debbie described the deliberations as 'constantly turning situations over in my mind'. That occurred prior to events in anticipation, during the conduct of events, and in reflection after them. Perhaps the most difficult pieces of the puzzle were those with blurred images or no picture at all – where a lack of information or its inaccessibility formed an internal puzzle in itself. Difficulty in diagnosis led in such instances to uncertainty in trying out solutions – *playing it by ear* in talking 'maturely' with the children, testing their reactions, and proceeding step by step to balance motivation, good relationships, and effective learning. The notion of *playing it by ear* appeared to form a central response to the acknowledgement that 'you can't say that that (i.e. any particular action) will work'. Nevertheless, within this insecurity, this healthy 'distrust' of one's judgements, decisions were made, had to be made, and actions taken. So what strategies were invoked in this gathering of experience?

Playing it by ear (and eye, of course) represented part of the exploratory process; the eliciting and receiving of impressions and information; its selection and interpretation; and the formation of plans based upon that process. But the elusiveness of the information, its complexity, its lack of dependability, meant taking action on the basis of *playing the hunch*.

Les   Debbie raised this question about judging whether somebody was not pulling their weight, or whether they weren't quite capable.

Debbie   Yes, 'cos I've had that in a few instances. The one that really showed it up to me so clearly was a lass in my class who really wasn't doing particularly well in maths, and she didn't do very much, she kept on making mistakes, and was obviously very frustrated and very bored with it, and I was thinking is it because she doesn't understand what she is doing, or is it because she is actually more capable than where she is in the SMP scheme, and therefore she is bored and therefore making mistakes. And just having talked to her and found that she had moved to the area and had found changing into the SMP scheme difficult, I sort of kept getting this hunch, it was very much playing the hunch, that there was something or other, there was no evidence, you know, no written evidence from her past teacher to say, 'yes it was boredom', and 'yes she was more able', 'cos the teacher before (I'd talked to her) said she hardly did any work. I just couldn't get through to her, she just wasn't interested. And so I talked to her and suggested that she started taking some maths home and she has literally gone sky high, she enjoys her maths now, she hardly makes mistakes, she knows she's going to get them right second time, and at the beginning of the year she was at the start of Level 3 SMP, which for fourth years is fairly low, and she is now half-way through Level 4. (8 March)

Playing the hunch with regard to choice of curriculum topic was also a recurrent feature of planning and practice. Debbie had introduced ecology as a concept in humanities, without knowing how the children would respond in terms of interest or handling concepts. It was introduced:

Debbie   [T]o see how the children reacted, and the mere fact that the project that I thought we would do in a week then took four weeks because the children latched onto it. I just thought, well, great. ...

Kathy   I think a lot of it is trial and error, well, it is with me –

> if the topic is not working we drop it, bring it to a close, and start something else.

Liz And the longer you get to know your class then you build up the relationship, get to know what they like, what will go down well.

Kathy I suppose there is some sort of intuition in it, if you think it will work then you try it and you do sense what they might enjoy. (8 March)

Playing it by ear and playing the hunch (or vice versa) combined elements of underlying educational aims and ideals with managerial judgement. Achieving motivation, good relationships, and the most effective learning for every individual pupil were common referents. These were contextualized by the uncertainties of situations and dependence on 'intuition' for determining action. Other purposes and judgements such as gaining and maintaining credibility as a teacher, being consistent, not being able to plan and prepare alternatives rapidly if 'error' of judgement was detected, trying to do what is 'best for the children', by controlling uncertainty, were also evident in the conversations. Sometimes such considerations were not easy to reconcile, and learning to play the hunch meant learning to manage inconsistency, tension and conflict as a persistent feature of the route to 'experience':

Dave What makes it most difficult to me is learning all the time, you can go through a situation and you are half-way through it and you know you should do something else but because you are committed along a course, to seem consistent you have to carry it out, and that sort of conflict between the learning experience and the consistency, I think that is probably one of the most difficult things to communicate to anyone, and actually is probably the most tiring thing.

Les Give us an example there of ... where you stuck to your guns.

Dave There was this ... class ... and I said what I was going to do with them ... and half-way through I thought, this is wrong, I thought, well I've said I'm going to do it so I've got to. So you know, this conflict was built up. If you are going to do it differently you've got to start all over again to — this could have been done better using these illustrations, and then, sort of, you have the right decision, do I go back to the beginning and might confuse them doubly or leave it for a couple of terms and then come back to it, so it is something fresh. These sort of

conflicts and decisions which you make and you learn
while you're doing it, which may come half-way through
teaching that subject. Surprising and very, very tiring,
constantly wanting to do something, that you can't do ...
it seems to be best for the children to stick it out, and
then come back later.

Les But have you ever been in a situation where you've said
'hold on a minute, I'm not going to continue'?

Dave Yes ... [I might think] well that way of delivering it is
totally wrong – it won't get anywhere and it's just
confusing them so just stop then – so put a guillotine
motion on it, say, right, let's think about it, let's go right
back to the beginning, and start all over again.

Les So it's not always a case of sticking to your guns?

Dave No, sometimes it is best to change, but there's always
conflict whether or not. (21 June)

Handling that conflict and improving on the judgements seemed to depend
on the frequency of hunch-playing and the intuitive handling of evaluative
evidence – the evidence of what 'worked' in specific teaching episodes and
particular circumstances:

Debbie You find that a lot actually, especially in subjects that
keep cropping up, with a scheme of maths like we have,
you'll get the same problems coming time and time again,
and the first time you encounter a problem like that you
think, try and explain it one way, and gradually every
time your explanation becomes more honed into a good
way of explaining it to the children so they understand,
without causing unnecessary confusion, and without losing
them. I noticed my explanations of things like that have
definitely improved over the year, almost by trial and
error, when you see the blank face you think I've got to
re-explain this because they still don't understand, and
eventually you can get to a point when you say, 'look,
just watch out for ...' and being a bit more explicit in the
instructions.

Les In both instances you talk about seeing the blank faces, is
that the evidence for evaluating most of the time,
watching the responses conveyed by facial expression?

Dave Sometimes I get a feeling, it's not something that you can
see, but you feel that they are not understanding it, you
feel there is something wrong. I don't know how that is

129

actually communicated, but maybe it's just the way they sit, but it's not facial expression, there's a difference. It's almost as if we've got this far, yes, you know, they look interested but you know they haven't grasped the idea. I think it comes to the point where they think they've got it, but you know they've got the wrong idea and you try to sort of unravel where the wrong idea is because they don't know themselves. (21 June)

Such on-the-spot judgements were compounded by the complexity of decisions and information-processing. Instructional aspirations were central to the discourse among the teachers, and underlying them was the concern for social and professional relationships with pupils to be established in such a way as to make instruction 'effective'. Achieving these aspirations depended on the ability to manage multiple elements of information and events at one time:

Debbie It is so difficult when you've got the classroom management, the organization, the marking, the problems, you're dealing with everything from SMP Level 2 to SMP Level 6 in my class and you all know that is a ... so wide-ranging from very remedial right to high-flying stuff, and its mental gymnastics. And then trying to talk to the children and deal with them as people – plus interruptions.

Les So what you're learning is mental gymnastics?

Debbie Most definitely.

Les That's a skill in which you're becoming proficient?

Debbie Plus, yes, being able to not only do mental gymnastics within the content of SMP but having your brain on ten different things all at once.

Liz That was the teaching practice, wasn't it, you had the one thing to concentrate on, and you did it, that's the real difference, you've got so many things to think about.

Debbie And all the unexpected things.

Les Like what?

Liz Well, visitors into your classroom and ...

Debbie Something going wrong with the computer (laughs). (2 December)

Like gymnasts, however, there was a possibility of learning particular sequences, of routinization, of becoming 'honed in', as Debbie put it, to particular tactics and strategies in teaching, especially where 'problems' were recurrent and solutions tested to a point of removing the problematic. However, while this was regarded as a desirable state of certainty, it was also seen as an undesirable removal of thrill and challenge. There was a desire to remove risk by mastery and achieve proficiency through practice, yet when that was done in some areas it was supplemented by consciously introducing new ventures, which were known to entail risk and the same sort of uncertainty in learning. During the first term most aspects of teaching carried risk of failure as well as promise of success until it had been demonstrated that they 'worked'. Not all, however. Some carried such promise of success that they offered little stimulus or opportunity to learn. For the two secondary teachers teaching some lessons repeatedly, the search for stimulus was under way during that term as 'boredom' was experienced:

> Dave 'woke up one day – [thought to myself] – 'these lessons have been boring, they've just become boring because you are just doing the routine.' After a while you have to start inventing your own challenges.

> Sue My main thing is that ... it [level of subject knowledge] is just not very intellectually challenging. (4 November)

Both the search for and the willingness to initiate and undertake 'intellectually challenging' ventures in the classroom ran parallel with responding to the many 'ready-made' challenges, and the 'honing' and routinizing of 'solutions'. This can be explained by Dave's concern to identify not just 'what works' but 'what is best'. That was also Debbie's concern as she mounted a major risky operation: conducting a simulation exercise as a new teaching strategy:

> Debbie Trying to teach twentieth-century history is not exactly my forte, and trying to get them not only from an academic, intellectual point of view to understand how the women who became suffragettes, why they became suffragettes, it came over that we really needed to get over the emotional aspects of it as well, how frustrated and angry the women felt, and that's why they did it, not just because they intellectually wanted the vote. So, I decided I'd try something by, for a whole of a lesson, actually put the boys down the whole of the time. The girls were raised up, they did all the experiments, they did all the interesting work, the boys had to set up the equipment, they did all the boring writing, they did all the clearing away, which, is, if you've got a mixed group it's more likely that the boys would have taken the lead and the girls would have done those things, and then the ultimate insult was to send the boys off to do the

cleaning of all the equipment, while me and the girls sat in front of the computer and put in the computer programme, and the boys felt very degraded, very hurt, insulted, and used, felt like they were slaves, they felt I was being incredibly sexist because they saw my actions as being in favour of the girls because I was female. And it got over to them the point. Now that sort of social experiment and dabbling with their feelings, I would never have tried last term...

Liz No, I wouldn't, you need real confidence to do something like that because they could have rebelled, and said 'get lost, we're not doing this' (laughing) ... taking a risk.

Les How did you then help them to talk about the point that you were making?

Debbie Well, when I got them back together again, and I just asked them how they felt and they were very reluctant to say anything, and then I told them that I'd done it quite deliberately, in fact that made them even more angry to know that they'd been totally duped by the teacher (laughs) and then I introduced why I had done it, I tried to explain why I had done it, and they still were just totally flummoxed, flabbergasted that I could have done such a thing to them. Then one or two of them started putting their hands up, and I said 'honestly, I want to know how you feel at the moment?' So we started getting their reactions, a few at a time, and then all hands sort of came up with the lads, they all wanted to chip in because they all felt the same, but in fact I found out that they'd actually been talking about it while they were clearing up – they wanted to walk out of school and go home, they felt that bad [laughs] and angry, and then I said that those are the feelings, and I related it to the subject, then I asked the girls how they had felt, and they genuinely felt elated, they just couldn't believe it, they just felt so relieved, so excited – then they started to feel they were glad they weren't in the boys' shoes, and I got them then to write down their feelings. But still that wasn't enough, they still couldn't relate it, they couldn't relate the two ideas, nor had they released all their feelings yet, so I went round, each of the groups, and talked it over, because there are three boys on each of the tables, roughly, and talked it over with them in small groups, while the rest were writing down their feelings.

> And I think over the week, now we've talked about it
> again a week later, they certainly remember it, because
> they keep saying, 'when are we going to get our own back
> on the girls?' They remember it and we've done some more
> work on the suffragettes and they can understand, so it
> worked, and I'm very pleased [laughs]. But my adrenalin
> was so high ... 'cos I didn't know how they were going to
> react – I really didn't know whether it was going to work,
> nobody knew because it hadn't been done before.

Les   So you had no way of predicting anything about their
responses?

Debbie   No. And I didn't know how they were going to react over
a longer time, either. Whether I'd get feedback from home
or anything, nothing like that, but certainly it's had a big
impact on them.

In the everyday demands for decisions, judgement and action, and the
information-processing through perceptiveness and the receptivity to ideas and
possibilities which accompanied practice, the skills of *mental gymnastics*
seemed essential. Like the physical gymnast, they entailed a range of routines
(in the sense of movements and sequences) from the mastery of 'basic' actions,
through tried and tested repertoire elements, and new developments. However,
there were considerable differences. Even some 'basic' elements eluded mastery
because of the elusiveness of information, the unpredictability of events,
and the relative anarchy of human responses and interactions. Others were
mastered. Certainly, as with the initial project teachers, there was a sense of
mastery and confidence in the technical 'skills' of teaching, with some minor
exceptions. What was problematic, and also deliberately problematized (I use
deliberate in terms of conscious intention and thoughtful action), were teaching
strategies which would enable the objectives of teaching to be realized. So
far those objectives themselves, and the underlying aims of education, were
not the subject of deliberation among these teachers. Their thoughts, like
this detailed description of Debbie's teaching, were focused on the means of
realizing predetermined goals which in themselves were treated as unproblematic in discussions. It was the instructional role's conduct, rather than its
purposes, which raised problems. Once again I would suggest that the volatility
of events surrounding the teachers' instructional role was in some respects
responsible for this focus of their attention because of their *unpredictability*.
Dave raised the issue of dealing with a sudden unexpected event when a child
fainted, and the tension between providing for the child and managing the rest
of the class. The discussion flowed:

Debbie   I've had to deal with children being sick, children injuring
themselves, and to stay calm yourself, when you are

thinking, 'oh, my god, what am I going to do?' and not to panic the child who's obviously done whatever it is, to make them feel at ease, plus you've got this sudden management problem.

Sue   It's something teaching practice didn't prepare you for, that, or your course or anything.

Debbie   No, no. 'Cos there was always somebody else who was more in charge than you were.

Liz   I had an experience of the same sort of thing – not somebody being ill but last week I was on bus duty and sent the first bus off and this girl came running up to me crying, saying she's missed her bus, and on teaching practice we'd say, 'Oh go and find Mr so and so'. Of course, I couldn't do that, and I had to really think, and stop this girl from being upset and calm her down, do you know what I mean, I hadn't a clue really. I've only got a bike – go charging up the road after the bus, I was waving and all the children were waving back, eventually they stopped, we went over the road – I don't know what I'd have done, but I was very proud of myself for not panicking and not, saying, 'ohh ...

Debbie   And dealing with unexpected situations like that – that's something that we've had to learn how to do. Like in the middle of yesterday's – totally different – I'll make it brief – yesterday's video, the sound disappeared half-way through it, completely, television's broken – 'OK, folks, we can't watch this video any more, let's do something else' – what am I going to do, this is supposed to last until the end of ... (19 January)

The nature and impact of such events provided a major theme in discussion around a plethora of examples of the unpredictable: a child bringing in a map to show the class; a visit from an irate parent; or a host of events which surround the progress of the curriculum and teaching, punctuating and sometimes puncturing planning:

Sue   (to Kathy) can I ask about the social thing? You've got kids in your class who burst into tears?

Kathy   Yes. Even wet themselves. (loud laughter)

Dave   I haven't had one do that yet ...

Sue   I find it very difficult to be sympathetic towards a child who bursts into tears in my lesson.

Such unpredictability in children's responses was a 'normal' event for Kathy with her reception class:

> *Kathy* We were showing a film today about giraffes, and I said, 'we are going to show a film now'. And one little boy said, 'oh, is it going to be *Ghostbusters*?' And I said, 'no, it's not, it's about giraffes'. And his little face fell. That would have been exciting for him, seeing something like that, not giraffes.

But there were many equivalents with all age groups. It was not only children's responses or external events which were unpredictable, but one's own ideas and actions too. Spontaneous judgement deriving out of concern to improve the effectiveness of teaching was reported by Sue.

> *Sue* Yesterday I was doing a very traditional lesson, then I thought as I was — that would be a good idea, it just came to me, just as I was about to start teaching them that particular topic, so I just changed the strategy of the lesson.
>
> *Les* What was it, Sue, can you describe it?
>
> *Sue* I was going to get them to — well, they were learning about the Aztecs and Incas, I'd just introduced the topic and I set them some questions to try and find out as much information about the Aztecs and Incas as possible, and as I was doing it, I thought why don't I get them to work in twos or threes and produce a sketch or something like a Two Ronnies sketch or a documentary, or a news report, like News at Ten and get them to work on it as a script, rather than just as a series of set questions. So, then I've arranged to bring a video camera in and actually video them, and that all just stemmed from inspiration in the lesson, I'm trying to think of new ways, new techniques, secret dossiers and files and everything, it was just the standard question and answer technique I was going to use with them, but at the moment about two minutes before I was due to teach the topic, it just came to me, so in the middle of the lesson, I said, 'oh, I think we'll do this', and it has worked really well, they really enjoyed it, concentration from them was fantastic. Just in the lesson, I don't know why it happened, but it just did. You see, I think — this is the thing you can plan meticulously a lesson, and it can just go so wrong and

> you can spend ages planning it, I'll do this, I'll do this,
> sometimes it just doesn't work, and then something what
> is planned say, ten minutes before the lesson, goes down a
> treat. So the whole combination of facts as to why that is,
> obviously the children, yourself, situation in the classroom
> at the time — you know that's why all this planning,
> sometimes is to no avail. Obviously you need the material,
> you need to prepare lessons but . . .

It was in this sense that anticipation and prediction were important features of decision-making, despite the unpredictability of events. Indeed, it was in efforts to curtail the unpredictable that the practice of discerning the possible consequences of judgements was engaged. This had the characteristic of gazing into a crystal ball; a kind of predictive reflection on how what is done or not done now may affect future events:

> *Debbie* Then you think if you let them do that, and perhaps you
> don't stamp on something, well, what will that do — [will]
> the way that I'm treating them now affect how they treat
> me when it comes to the final term? I can't know that. . . .
> That is very difficult because you can't know the
> consequences really. (18 November)

Gaining insight in such cases depended, it seemed, on 'picking up on' concerns or issues, or information, which was often gained from 'a sort of feeling' which helped to 'fill in some of the gaps' in knowledge that may be critical for making sound judgements and taking effective action: to enable the teacher to proceed *en route*. The elusiveness of information made the topography around the route very uneven and rather precarious:

> *Debbie* One of the things that always amazes me is that the
> children's views of situations, often they are very different
> from your own. You may make certain decisions or
> instigate certain actions, that in fact you do it from a
> very different motive than the children actually pick up.
> Let me just illustrate something that has just happened
> during the last few weeks. I thought my relationship with
> one particular boy was fine, I mean, I sort of stopped him
> mucking around when he was mucking around, but I can
> think of many other children who I have sort of pulled up
> far more often than I would he, and to my knowledge I
> was treating him exactly the same as anybody else, and
> yet his mum asked to come and see the Head because he

was not liking coming to school because he thought I was picking on him, and did not like him whatsoever. And I was just totally shocked that he was even thinking like that, and I couldn't think of any particular instances where I had treated him in an unfair way. To my mind what I was doing was treating him in the same way, but it just really pulled me up that the children's perceptions of your actions, the decisions you make and how you handle a certain situation may indeed be very much different from [your own] perceptions.

Les   So you can't even predict what the immediate response would be because you can't predict what the interpretations will be that they put on anything you do?

Debbie   'Cos that must have been a – that wasn't so much a one incident but that must have been a build-up of several incidents that gave him the impression of me, which I didn't intend giving him and it certainly was not in my mind to be giving him – it was in fact the complete opposite to the impression I was giving him – hopefully he's the only one. He was the most unlikely one of the ones that you would have thought – which shocked me even more. (2 February)

What these reports indicate is that the lack of control over events, the unavailability of sense data, even to the perceptive teacher engaged in constant surveillance, ensured that proceeding *en route* was intrinsically problematic. Handling such events could not be achieved through an apprenticeship in skills training in the view of these teachers, nor did the events themselves constitute a body of knowledge to be transmitted by experts and applied by novices. In that respect, *going through it* was a rational description of what was seen as necessary for the acquisition of practical experience. *Playing it by ear* and *playing the hunch* could be regarded as creative strategies in that acquisition, using mental agility in that playing to try to ensure 'satisfactory' practice in the face of inherent instability and unpredictability in situations. For the teachers, the call upon that mental agility continued beyond the immediacy of events. The need to interpret sense data, whether it was flimsy like Dave's 'feeling' or substantive like Debbie's contacts with parents, succeeded the acquisition of the data itself. The implementation of teaching plans and on-the-spot judgements, applied in trial-and-error experience, led to further reflective evaluation on the events which ensued. Judgement, action and outcome were considered, providing a different kind of perception of a situation. This involved questions such as 'did I do the right thing in that situation?' It was an evaluation of role performance, as well as further reflection on the circumstances surrounding that performance, and it was another form of mental gymnastics, conducted in less immediate circumstances:

> *Liz* [T]he same day, I think about everything – you know, cycling home from the school, the whole day goes through my mind, just relationships with children ... every single aspect of the day goes through my mind. (16 December)

But it was a form quite different from on-the-spot reflection, as the comments below from Liz indicated. She had to 'sit in' on another class; she didn't know the children; and she didn't know whether to be 'friendly' or more strict, especially since it was 'near Christmas'. This first encounter with a new class, Liz concluded, was not handled in a satisfactory way. It was only a five-minute caretaking event, but she minded deeply about it:

> *Liz* They were going to watch a video, but it's an awkward five minutes – five minutes is a long time when you come in and you settle them down, and then there's nothing else for them to do – you know, they are not your class, you can't tell them to get their reading books out, or whatever, and so I said that while we're waiting I'll go round and ask your names, I don't know any of them, so of course this gave a few of the bright sparks a chance to pretend they were somebody different, or have a little joke, and I passed it off as a joke but then I thought this is just giving them a chance to get one up, and I don't like being put in a position where I'm being got one up – whatever the phrase is, you know, where that's happening – perhaps I should have come down a bit harder.

There is an interesting difference in the kind of thinking as she cycled to the teachers' centre after the event, evaluating her own behaviour in that situation, to making the decisions and applying her judgement at a moment in time.

> *Liz* It is, it's quite different, you're there in the classroom and you've got five different things happening all at once that need your attention, you've got to make a snap decision and you're turning it over in your mind after the event, you can be a lot more perceptive. I'm sure we've talked about this before, haven't we, learning by experience that this is the thinking that's been hammered home to me all the time that I am a new teacher however confident I feel about my teaching, I'm going to have new experiences

every day, nobody could ever have taught me these
things, we've talked about it before, and how satisfactory
our courses were. But how could somebody teach you:
'well, when you go into the fourth year class a few days
before Christmas, you want to behave this way' – of
course they can't – it's something that you learn and
apply. (2 February)

The central question arising from this data for me was: what was it that
Liz was learning and applying? How not to be in a position where pupils can
'get one up', it seems. The concern in this instance is a management strategy,
based on a belief that the teacher must always be 'one up' in social relations,
a matter of self-esteem, dignity and honour. But the teachers' main concerns
seemed to be about the effectiveness of instructional strategies, and the power
of impressionistic evaluation of this kind was often much more concerned with
such effectiveness as Debbie described:

Debbie I find that in games because we have a circuit, so I'm
teaching the next house the same thing, so by the end
I've done four lots of the same thing and I know the ones
towards the end were getting much further on than were
the first ones because my presentation was much clearer
and much slicker and therefore we were getting much
more valuable learning. (2 February)

The conscientiousness of Liz's concern, even about a minor performance with
another class, was possibly kindled because it was an unfamiliar situation. The
possibility of complacency and the dangers of accepting superficial impressions
of events in familiar circumstances became evident to her when her practice
was 'challenged' by a pupil. Again it was the unanticipated and unpredictable
incident which rekindled her conscientiousness:

Liz I had a surprising incident, a revelation from the children.
Some of the children were doing stream of consciousness
writing, writing down all the things that come into their
mind, and I was reading Thomas's and he'd written 'Miss
C is reading out Joanne's work again to the class – she
always chooses the girls, she really likes the girls – she
never chooses the boys – I bet Joanne has got a house
point for that.' And this was just written – this was what
he was thinking, obviously, at the time. And that was
surprising, and I talked to him about it, and I said do
you really think that I always favour the girls, because
I'm pretty sure I don't, in fact, most evidence would

139

suggest that it is the boys who get favoured rather than the girls, the boys get spoken to more than the girls and praised and so on — or even told off more, but whatever, you know, often you would praise a boy hoping that that would prevent any [mis]behaviour, but according to Thomas I was, and I found that incident made me generally question everything, you know, like if Thomas was thinking that, who else might be — was I really favouring the girls? I watched what I was saying, and that led me on to think 'why is Danny behaving this way?' — you know, different things, it certainly shook me up completely because before then I had just been drifting along accepting things.

Les So it made you watch more carefully for, not only for your actions, but for any responses to those?

Liz Yes, and not only in that particular thing, like favouring girls more than boys but also in behaviour — like picking on, like you were saying — I've got this feeling, he's not actually said anything, but I've got this feeling that Danny doesn't like me or feels that I don't like him, which I've picked up, which I probably wouldn't have thought about unless Tom had started me thinking along the lines of the girl/boy thing — that just made me more sensitive to the children in the class — that they are all individuals, and I haven't been treating — you know, it's been going quite quietly and quite calmly and people have been getting their work done, so I've not really thought about things, just accepted it. So, I think it's a good thing every now and then to have a bit of a shake-up and to think about things. (2 February)

This resurrection to consciousness of the problematic nature of teaching's many facets may not have been such a shake-up as Liz claimed. The data show clearly that none of the teachers were complacent in general. What the data do indicate is how complacency and assumption about specific features occurred, exacerbated perhaps by the inaccessibility of evidence within human interactions. What these reports also reflected was that underlying their actions were aims and values which were themselves largely taken for granted. The treatment of all pupils as individual persons of equal worth, especially irrespective of gender, was a matter about which Liz minded deeply. A realization that she had apparently not translated these values into practice caused her considerable anguish. She acknowledged that 'drifting along generally accepting things' in a period of quiet and calm characterized her disposition. Turbulence which led her back to generally questioning everything was sparked by recognition that her practice in this instance was not consistent with her values. But it seemed at this point that what mattered was to review the practice, to ensure that 'effective' strategies were invoked to realize her aims in practice. There was no discussion about the aims or about the personal theories which underlay teaching; these were only inferred in the discussions within the group, and only in relation to 'critical incidents' which provoked turbulence. At such times *minding* about the quality of practice was characteristic of the teachers. Minding focused on the acquisition of subject knowledge by the pupils (mathematical and scientific concepts, historical events, the rules and skills of sport, communication skills in language, etc. were cited examples), teaching strategies for effecting this acquisition, and the motivational and ethical questions which might ensure success for the strategies. Minding led to a search for indications of success in constantly turning things over mentally, but also in the longer-term accumulation of 'indicators'.

In particular, the latter part of the year offered some indicators of the successes or otherwise of teaching. Earlier anticipations could now be checked against events – if only impressionistically or on the basis of restricted evidence. As well as seeking the evidence of pupils' learning achievements from the pupils themselves, the teachers reflected on just what those achievements should be, or were. The way in which they learned criteria by which to judge the effectiveness of teaching was another experience of soliciting, assimilating and managing the largely intangible.

> *Liz* By last term I was realizing that there were children who
> had slipped through, their spelling ages were really low
> and I hadn't noticed until we did the tests, and there were
> children I hadn't heard read, or who I hadn't noticed with
> a reading book, a non-fiction book, and suddenly I
> stopped and realized that I was so keen on getting all my
> writing projects done, I hadn't stopped and done the
> bread and butter things that all teachers do, and I think I
> stopped and sat back. I was so used to talking to my
> friends about a really good idea for science, or we tried
> this in maths, here's a good investigation, and you don't
> talk about how you teach 'o u g h' spellings, word family,
> or, how are your children getting on with their reading,
> are you checking it? And we hadn't talked about those
> things, and I think it was last term that I suddenly
> started to realize that I needed to do much more – not
> just exciting lessons each week.
>
> *Les* And you realized that because of the performances of the
> children, you noticed?
>
> *Liz* Well, a combination, certainly the performances of the
> children, the results of the tests, concerns from parents

who came in, making a fuss. I think probably talking to
other teachers, finding out what they were doing. What
other factors? I mean, a lot of factors building up, rather
than suddenly waking up and having an insight. (26 April)

Levels, standards, achievements and progress were 'picked up' from other
teachers, and derived from 'common sense', as well as more objective measures:

Kathy I'm very aware of things that they don't know, that they
should know, like, I was absolutely horrified to find that
some child didn't know his colours properly, and things
that I know they should really know by now, and they
keep coming up and I keep having a panic about colours
or shapes or something, so at the moment there is quite a
lot of things running in my mind that I must get them
to do.

Les So that comes to you from the evidence that the children
convey, the things they don't know, you're picking up?

Kathy Yes.

Les And that's being measured against some mental check-list
that you have really?

Kathy Yes, I don't know really where I get my check-list from, I
suppose other teachers say things like 'goodness me, so
and so in the third year still doesn't know what a rec-
tangle is' and you think, oh goodness, I wonder if mine
do, and then you start checking up on it. But there's also
things like the maths scheme that's been laid down by the
school ... and that does help in the vague areas, but
obviously you can't say why by such and such an age
they have to know, and then tick off everything, it doesn't
work like that, but you do have a general idea of what the
child could achieve if you know the child well enough.
(17 May)

The importance of this *monitoring* was in part to ensure that colleagues,
especially those who would next teach the same children, would recognize the
quality of teaching. It is a matter of achieving professional credibility and
respect. But it is also a matter of improving teaching on the basis of evidence,
especially through classroom assessments:

Debbie So they are testing the skills that they have acquired and
it's quite good to see things that have worked, but then
you see these glaring misunderstandings, and you think,

crumbs, that means that next year I will look out to make sure I'm not enhancing these misunderstandings that this lot have had. It has been quite useful for that, I think, well, that was right at the beginning of the year, they understood that concept and have been able to interpret that information, great, the next question, roughly the same time, that obviously wasn't put forward effectively because they have misunderstood that technique, and therefore I will pay particular attention to examining the way I put that across next year. (21 June)

With other aspects of teaching competence, however, there was a lack of concern to seek evidence. With regard to the technical skills, it seemed there was an assumption that such skills had been learned long ago and that they could now be taken for granted, with some exceptions where specific teaching behaviours were conducted self-consciously:

Les   But there are other things about your teaching which would not show through in achievements of the pupils – the way you speak, the way you ask questions, the way you discipline the children, and whether it is effective or not.

Kathy   The sort of things you were always told about by your tutor on teaching practice.

Liz   It seems so long ago, doesn't it.

Kathy   'Your ... control is coming along nicely, dear' (laughs).

Les   Are those sorts of things irrelevant now?

Liz   I think they almost are because I've not really thought about that. Seeing the poor student in our school and seeing the worries that she's got, it seems so long ago that I had the same worries. I mean, I can go into other years now and talk to them, talking in the corridors....

Kathy   I tell you one thing I do notice about myself, is that I often say to myself, 'you really must listen when the children talk to you' because it is so easy when you've got about 20 children asking you a question all at the same time, to just say 'yes, no, no you can't, yes, you can' – to really listen. I often hear myself saying – 'Miss ..., yesterday I did so and so' – 'did you, dear' and you sound really like Joyce Grenfell and you think, I don't know, it's so awful, I often think I must be just like Joyce Grenfell because I always try and sound so interested but half the time your mind is totally somewhere else, and it's very rarely that you actually sit down and talk to a child properly, and I really wish I did that more often, but I'm not very good at that.

Liz   It's suddenly something that has got so much easier because it is not a worry any more, I just accept, I know I've improved, I know I've progressed. When I think back to the teaching practice and my first term at this school, the children's work I can see does need improvement – I'm sure really if you'd come in you'd say, 'well, you should have moved around the classroom more', or whatever – improvement, but that's not a major worry or concern any more.

Les   Or is it even, you're implying earlier, it isn't even a consideration.

Liz   No, it probably isn't because that's the first time I've thought about it since you mentioned it.

Kathy   I do think about some things that we've done. Like I often think, where shall I sit? Because if I'm sitting with a group, the tutor always used to tell me it's obviously stupid to sit with your back to the rest of the class, because they'll just run riot and you won't notice, so I consciously seat myself somewhere where even if I'm right at the other end of the classroom I can see everybody, and I consciously ...

Liz   Don't you think you do that because you tutor told you when you were a student, or – I mean, that's the sort of thing as an experienced teacher I would do.

Kathy   Yes, but I still think about it, I don't just do it automatically, and I consciously make myself look around the room a lot because that was one thing I was very bad about on teaching practice, and I still don't do it naturally. I have to make myself do that. (17 May)

It was clear that, while technique was often relegated to the subconscious, some techniques remained subject to constant reflection in action. But even then they seemed to be momentary (if persistent) and minor compared to other concerns which occupied the reflective consciousness. Some of these were major concerns which reflected the problematics of teaching being tackled by senior professionals at national level. Debbie, for example, was wrestling with records of achievement, in addition to 'knowing the right things to say when telling pupils off' and 'to what extent you should suppress their personalities to get them to conform, or to deal with it by giving them responsibility', and other 'major' issues. Debbie wanted to improve her record-keeping, partly because she had written reports and relied on her record-keeping and seen inadequacies within it, but also because she felt that she had not given the children much opportunity to be self-critical of their own performances, and so was thinking of introducing some sort of self-evaluation for next year. She regarded just marking off whether they had got the work in as not good enough for building a picture for her own purposes of reporting to parents, but also aspired to find a strategy which would help her to realize an underlying educational aim – engaging pupils more actively in critical appraisal of their learning achievements.

Debbie   I really hadn't conquered this problem of children analysing their own work and being self-critical and being able to learn from their own mistakes, long before I had to write the reports, but the lack of information that I suddenly found myself with from my mark book was as a result of having to write the reports.

Les   So that element of getting the pupils to do self-evaluation, you were trying to resolve that, [yes] as a teaching strategy.

Debbie   Yes, I've been thinking about it for quite a long time, since about Easter, or even before, and mulling it over, thinking would it be a good idea, or wouldn't it? What sort of questions would I have to ...? (5 July)

Such deliberations can be regarded as intentions to change practice in order to reflect educational aims which the teachers themselves held. The notion of *mirroring* such aims in practice was apparent at points in the discussions in the latter part of the year. Technical competence was still on the agenda, but it had been relegated. The way in which it became relegated seemed to be partly through routinization; partly through being overshadowed by more problematic aspects of teaching; perhaps because external supervision did not occur; and possibly because the search for challenge led the teachers to other creative considerations. In an attempt to describe how that challenge had become more complex, Dave identified the shift from assumed technical competence to problem-awareness and self-evaluation as he broke out of a 'confidence of ignorance'. And Debbie highlighted how that state of awareness was born of the passage of time and looking back on events which had fermented and matured with experience and reflection. However, these concerns rested predominantly within the realm of classroom technique and instructional strategies:

Dave   People have said my lessons are better now than they used to be, I think, because of things I've learnt they are worse because I know I now can see the mistakes I was making and the mistakes I am making. I'm now beginning to see the problem, so instead of me appreciating that there has been an improvement it's almost as if my self-evaluation is beyond my improvement, so I can turn round and say, 'well, they [lessons] could be better' whereas I think sometimes you are in a position when you are first starting off of 'I don't know how anybody can do this better' — almost the sort of confidence of ignorance.

Debbie I think also because we are no longer, I say, no longer, dealing with the basics of standing in front of the children and actually taking lessons, now we are thinking in more detail, more carefully about the details and about how things are phrased, ways you can present it, a better way of tackling the subject, and you can see, I've been thinking, 'well, I did it that way, now that worked reasonably well, but I certainly won't do it that way again and I would certainly change the way that I approached that for various reasons'. Make it clear to the children, make it more interesting for the children, and again that's only come with reflection on the way something did or didn't work. (5 July)

Most of these forms of reflection in and upon action were part of the process of determining future classroom action. Using the experience of events as perceived in reflection, potential action was constructed in that constant mental turning-things-over approach. The development of practice appeared to be dependent on the development of the capacity to gauge situations and to apply professional judgement, in specific circumstances, and through their own professional enterprise. Throughout the discussions the major theme of uncertainty and unpredictability was paramount. It was the sustenance of learning; for in the problematic elements lay the potential for discovering not just what worked, but what worked best, as Dave put it. As the 'routines' were established, teaching day to day brought the myriad minor experiences, adding to the accretion, potentially for routinization of some things — administration, resource storage and distribution, aspects of classroom management, and so on. Other 'one-off' events were 'stored' for future reference, but remained a feature of the unpredictable and were the topics of conversation throughout the year.

The data confirmed and consolidated the notions of being *en route* to 'capital T Teaching' by means of going through it; playing it by ear; playing the hunch; and conducting mental gymnastics. The experiences *en route* were often unforeseen, but the focus of attention was guided by *minding* about the quality of judgements and actions. That disposition led to surveillance and monitoring, through whatever means possible, as a feature of learning teaching in those worlds of often intangible evidence and anarchic information handling. By February the group began to reflect upon their earlier conversations, identifying aspects of their teaching and learning which they began to pursue as themes of reflection. During the sixth meeting some of these themes were clarified, and the group sought to explore them more deeply in later meetings. These were listed in notes:

- managing the unpredictable;
- predicting the outcome of actions;
- making decisions in unfamiliar situations;
- considering options for actions;
- planning more exciting teaching;
- using 'alien' teaching strategies (those you don't agree with);
- developing new teaching strategies;
- learning unfamiliar knowledge;
- judging what children are capable of:
  - what we do/might expect them to do/learn
  - how we do/might expect them to do/learn;
- judging the quality of learning and work produced.

These were themes in more than one sense. They were broad categories of recurrent 'problems' illustrated by specific events which raised the same types of questions over and over again and which members of the group discussed and elaborated on as they came to share the series of conversations. They were group themes, illuminating teaching technique and especially instructional strategies based on sound judgement as the main features of topography along the route. Each member had specific concerns to follow within these themes in developing their individual teaching. But they were also themes about the experience of learning, about how experiences were met or created by deliberate intention, and then reviewed, interpreted and incorporated into the realm of practical experience. Throughout the discussions there was also a quite different kind of theme, one which centred on more 'personal' responses to being a teacher, and especially on emotional reactions and responses to particular circumstances and events, and to their own judgements and actions. The explorations by the teachers of the emotions of learning teaching were as prominent as the substantive concerns about teaching competence. They were directly related to the experience of being 'half-way there' and 'going through it', and can be seen in the wider context of literature about new teachers. Much of the literature presents an image of emotional trauma and highlights the 'difficulties' of induction by concentrating largely on this realm of response to the experiences of the first year. Consider some of the titles:

Lifeboat Ethics and the First Year Teacher (Brown and Willems, undated).

Transition Shock: The Beginning Teacher's Paradox (Corcoran, 1981).

Reality Shock: A Problem Among First Year Teachers (Gaede, 1978).

'Lion tamers and baby sitters' (O'Rourke, 1983).

Don't Smile Until Christmas (Ryan, 1970).

Hangman or Victim? (Cormon, 1970).

'X is for the unknown' (Richardson, 1970).

In the case of the research group, however, emotional responses were not all negative or aversive. Being 'half-way there' and 'going through it' included excitement and elation as well as anxiety and anger. Specific emotions were aroused by the experience of classroom events, staffroom relationships, contacts with parents or employer personnel, and social circumstances outside the school. They fluctuated erratically, sometimes coexisted, at times were controllable and controlled, yet at other times seemed unstable and explosive. This element of the experience of the first year was perhaps as prominent in the discussions as were comments about how teaching in the more 'technical' and 'clinical' senses was learned. As the discussion proceeded, the relationship between the emotions and the competences of teaching appeared to be of considerable import, and worthy of analysis in itself.

The impact upon one's sense of 'self' of the early stages of the first year had been described by the initial project teachers, and was discussed earlier in this book (see page 51). Most notably, and unsurprisingly, individual emotional responses varied considerably. The particular emotions invoked by different influences and at different times were as unpredictable as the sense data, judgements, and events of teaching. The research group teachers were no different. But there was sufficient opportunity to explore the emotional experiences with them both immediately through the group support discussions and in the longer term by reflecting back on the experiences. It was their considerations about how they learned to manage the emotions that became the focus of attention in the second half of the year, and which I want to explore here. This provides a picture of the longer-term dynamic of the emotions within which, I believe, the immediate, reactive, dynamic heat of the moment of specific events can be better understood. Half-way through the year the world seemed very different for Liz, compared with how it looked at the start:

> *Liz* I think the Christmas term really does seem such a long
> time ago — all those problems and hassles — I remember
> that all happened in a week — Jason's dad phoning up and
> the inspector coming in — it was such a horrible week,
> and having to get through it, whereas now things seem so
> much more stable and secure. (23 February)

For Sue, on the other hand, there was a continuing tension between the class-room world and the school world:

> *Sue* Half-way through the year. Well, it feels very established, I suppose, I feel very confident, but I always did feel very confident ... it's when I get to school, look around and I think is this what life is come to, you know. Gets fairly disillusioned at times. But that's just when I think about it. Once I get in the classroom with the children and I do the teaching – it's fine – I'm fairly happy, and sometimes confident about it – and they can lift me up. But it's sometimes going through the door, passing the sixth formers, and thinking I wish I was one of those, and I wish I hadn't made myself in a state that I'm in right now – teaching – I wish I had my time again I'd do things differently.... I feel very similar to the way that I felt at the beginning, you know, confident, fairly happy in the teaching, but not sure if it is the right thing to do.
> (23 February)

For Debbie and Kathy, there was a rather unexpected downward turn as relationships with the pupils seemed to decline:

> *Debbie* I feel it's a bit of a battle at the moment, it probably doesn't come over like that but I feel quite tense inside, which is something that I hadn't come across last term. ... Some days it's better than others, but at the moment I'm just feeling this is my sticky patch. We've all got to go through them, and as a result I don't know whether it's my lessons that are causing the problem, or is it just their attitude, which it could be.

> *Kathy* I think it just makes me feel more positive. My disastrous week was the one before half-term. I had terrible trouble with discipline – it all came to a head one day and went to the head and four children got severely told off. He came down to the classroom, and really gave them such a talking to, I was practically in tears as well – made me feel really awful. He kept saying things like, 'you've really upset Miss ...' because I'd been going to him saying that I just can't cope with this any more. I was practically giving up because they were just absolutely dreadful.
> (23 February)

However, these events went against the general trend of increasing confidence which Liz had described, which is why they seemed so traumatic. There was a direct link. The more stable and secure teaching became, the greater the impact of each 'sticky patch' or 'bad week', which meant that, at times, 'basic things' — classroom technique and relationships with pupils — were unsatisfactory. Gaining competence in those basic management skills was the earlier priority. Once gained, such competence offered a clearer view of events, and opportunities to analyse situations more fully in order to predict and plan with less confusion. The growing confidence enabled the teachers to put 'difficulties' into a broader perspective of their teaching, even though the dips and troughs could still be met along the route. The sense of being able to 'see' teaching in a more holistic way, with a sense of overview to complement attention to fine detail, was important half-way through the year:

Kathy I've stopped panicking about sort of basic things, and I can see things in a better perspective, everything is much clearer and I can start looking ahead to the rest of the year and, you know, thinking I'd quite like to cover this and they really should learn this by the end of the year. Whereas before it was just sort of a mass of worries and you couldn't pick one out to start off with. Now everything is much easier to look at.

Liz My diary used to be filled with notes, every single little thing I'd have to think about during the day, or questions to ask people or things to get the children to do, all written down, whereas now I can go and I don't need to have written something down about the lesson I'm going to teach, I need to just sort it out in my mind, and that's enough. I will still, for most lessons, write it down, but I never, ever would have believed I could have got to that stage, where I could go in and teach quite confidently without having a guide in front of me, and, as you say, now what I'm looking forward to is the things I've planned. I've planned nice things for this half-term, whereas this is the first term I've really done that. (23 February)

A critical element in this development appeared to be the relationships with colleagues. Liz had established herself among a friendly, supportive staff who had encouraged her to 'open up' and discuss her teaching when she needed to. Kathy's headteacher encouraged the staff to 'communicate more' in order to build a 'proper team atmosphere' of colleagial support and professional discussion. Initially, Debbie and Dave had experienced such support from year-tutors and subject team respectively, but that waned in the second term.

Debbie   But I felt more isolated this term than I did last term, I
have been left to get on with it right from the beginning,
but now it's more just being left to get on with it, and
therefore I don't see very many people and they don't
come enquiring after me. So, may be I am beginning to
feel a little bit isolated as well.

For Sue, the isolation was constant; the emotional response to it changed in
a way which made it bearable:

Sue   I feel incredibly isolated. When I first started it was
terrible, it was something I just hated every minute of,
now I've just come to terms with it — I've just accepted
it. (23 February)

The condition of isolation was not just physical separation caused by working
alone in a classroom, but also a matter of how colleagues related to the teachers
and vice versa — or didn't — in the few opportunities when they met. From
the teachers' point of view allowing feelings to be seen by colleagues seemed
even more risky than discussing practical matters with them. Usually, the
emotional states were generated by those practical matters, providing a double-
disincentive sometimes to 'open up' with colleagues:

Debbie   I don't feel fed-up I just feel internally panicking
sometimes, not even the word 'panic' — that's too strong,
just anxious inside, yes. But it doesn't come — it probably
does come out — I'm not sure whether it does or not, you
can't tell what you look like from inside — you can't tell
how you are reacting.

Les   Do you talk about it with anyone?

Debbie   No, I haven't, maybe it's taken me to sort of now-ish to
actually admit it to anybody (laughs).

Les   You mean like tonight?

Debbie   Like tonight. I mean, I've been thinking it, but it's just a
case of actually admitting it, which is a quite hard thing
to do.

Les   Yes. But that's not unlike the sort of anxieties that Liz
described — wanting to find a solution to a problem but
not being able to talk about it, not being able to ask the
right questions. You said, when you talked with the
deputy head he didn't ask the right questions, to unlock
your anxiety?

>   *Liz* That's right. It is that you want somebody to ask it, it's
>   so difficult to go and you to start spilling it out because
>   it will come out wrong, it will sound a lot more than, you
>   know — they'll probably think 'oh, Deb's got a real
>   problem' because it isn't that, you just need somebody to
>   be sensitive and to ask the right question, to be
>   supportive in the right way. (23 February)

That relationship between practical judgement and emotional state, and the relationship between self-reliance and colleagial support, was characterized in a report by Sue of a 'critical event'. The incident is one of the 'hundreds each day', but for Sue — confident in the classroom — it was a challenge to that confidence. It also highlighted the fickleness of the momentary judgement and the teacher's emotions, and the depth of professional isolation.

>   *Sue* I had an incident about three weeks ago when I had, what
>   I'd call a very naughty pupil, who'd missed one of my
>   lessons. So I chased her up, got her form teacher to send
>   her into my registration group, she came in and I said
>   'why didn't you come to my lesson?' She told me that
>   she'd missed the bus, or something, so I said, 'OK, I'll
>   give you all the homework that you've got to catch up on.'
>   So there she was stood in front of the desk, I was saying
>   'you've got to do this, this' and I was looking down at the
>   work that I was giving her, and I looked up and I
>   noticed, I mean, I felt so bad about this, I noticed that as
>   she was stood there at the front of the desk, she was
>   beginning to sway a little bit, and it all happened so
>   quickly and I said to her 'are you all right?' and with that
>   she fell backwards, her head hit a desk with an enormous
>   thud, and she fell on the floor, and it was all over so
>   quickly that I can see it now — all happening in slow
>   motion. So, I thought what can I do, my registration
>   group went deathly quiet, so I just went, immediately this
>   had happened ... sort of sat up straight away, so I just
>   said to them 'now, just stay where you are' — very calmly,
>   I was obviously very shaken up by this, 'go and see
>   Mr so and so', the form tutor, and he came in and picked
>   her up and put her down on the chair, and all this blood
>   was streaming out of her head, and I said, 'oh, God'. And
>   we sorted it all out and we sent her home, and I was free
>   fortunately, so I had to go and sit down in the staffroom,
>   just sit there, 'oh, my God, why didn't I see this was
>   happening?' You see, my thoughts I looked at her and I

saw her sway, she is so naughty, this is why I felt so guilty, I thought that she was having me on, you see, 'are you sure you're all right?' 'No, I don't think so' – bang over, and if it had been any other pupil I would have noticed it, but because it was her I just ignored it and I think in another situation now I would try and relate better to the pupils perhaps, not prejudge them like I was judging that girl. And obviously it was the guilt, I had to speak to somebody else in the staffroom because I felt I really just needed to talk about it. They were very good about it, and said don't worry, it's not because it's you and you are young and inexperienced, anybody would have not noticed it – because I couldn't catch her or anything – she was too far away. But it was this thought in my mind that I didn't believe her when she said, in that brief moment, that she didn't feel very well, I just didn't believe her. So if I had that situation again I wouldn't judge her so harshly as I was doing at that time. She hasn't been to any of my lessons since. But that's quite frightening.

Les Yes. Do you think it was especially frightening because it was the first ever incident?

Sue Yes, first ever. I still think if it happened again, I would hope that I would have the foresight for it not to happen again because I was just so wrapped up in giving this girl her homework and not letting her get away with it – she was going to do the homework just like everybody else – and I was reading it out to there, and may be if I'd have just looked at her and been more concerned about her as a pupil, rather than just as a lesson, may be I would have noticed that. And I think in future I would perhaps be a little bit more sympathetic. I should have noticed really when she walked in the door, shouldn't I, that she wasn't really, but you know. I don't know, I really don't know, it's difficult. But that fact that she actually said to me that she wasn't feeling well, and I didn't believe her, you know, that was terrible. I haven't told anybody at school about that, I just said that she just said 'I don't feel very well' or I said 'Do you feel all right?' and she said, 'No'. But she'd actually said she didn't feel very well.... All very sympathetic when she was on the floor, I thought, 'How do I get out of this one?' (laughs) Get somebody else. (24 March)

The third term brought further fluctuations in emotions. Debbie expressed 'awe and wonderment' that she had got so far so quickly, through so much change in herself and her teaching. Dave went through 'a sort of a low' — his enjoyment and satisfaction working with the pupils was sustained as it had been throughout, but assessment of his teaching by staff who 'don't know how to communicate with me' and who 'think the ways I see [things] are totally eccentric and wrong' adversely affected his desire to stay in teaching. At best he wanted the year completed so that he could say 'great, now I'm on your side of the fence' to those teachers. Kathy had by now learned how to manage her expressions of emotions within the classroom:

Kathy Something that I'm learning even when I'm tired, and I know I'm tired, is to try and not be really ratty with the children and to try to physically relax and think 'you're getting paid so just relax, just don't — because the timetable seems to take everything at such a pace, just hang in, just relax . . . go slowly.' (24 March)

It was these fluctuations and realization that managing oneself was as important as, and an intrinsic part of, managing the pupils' learning, that were at one and the same time very individualistic in detail, but common to each teacher in their trends and patterns. Individualism and commonality were reconciled by Liz.

Liz It's a very individual problem, we can all understand and sympathize with because we are going through it.

This notion was elaborated by Debbie and Sue in a way which raised questions about the experiences of new teachers who do not have a 'support group' to express and explore their emotional experiences. It was clear to them and to Dave that the educational experiences of the first year of teaching were about the growth of 'self'. Being on the road, half-way there, performing emotional gymnastics, in states of unpredictability which went hand in hand with the learning experiences of practical teaching, meant that their reflections and deliberations were about life as teachers in the broadest sense, about the quality of 'being' in the specific events which arose.

Debbie It's the fact that all of us have gone through times when we've felt, the first term or so, when we've been quite confident that things were going well, but there was also at different times when we felt — all of us — really down in the dumps. Now that happened to every single one of us, for different reasons, we just felt 'crumbs, we can't cope — can't hack it'. But for very different reasons, but we all felt those same feelings, because that was the one thing we all felt that this [the meetings] was good, that we said 'well, I'm not the only one'. And I know that's certainly been true of other new teachers that I know of, as well. So, that certainly is a common experience. Feeling isolated, I think, is a common experience. Feeling there is a barrier, even if it has been broken down over the year, between ourselves and other members of staff, trying to infiltrate existing groups, and existing cliques. That, I think, is a common experience to us all.

Les   What did you have in mind, Sue, when you said there were common experiences.

Sue   Well, this is something that Liz and I were talking about today, just saying that there were certain times, we mentioned that time when Deb felt quite down at one stage and yet she'd been super-confident, and then, you know, well – Liz had been through that at another time – and we were able to give each other support, there were times when I'd been through that, right at the beginning when I really felt down, and isolated, and so every single one of us had been through that kind of experience.

Debbie   Even if you can't find things that you have in common, we've found a great deal of common experiences, common feelings.

Sue   Yes. The feelings are caused by different things, but we have been able to identify, I mean, I've been able to identify with the feelings you have had, and with Kathy, although with very different situations.

There seems to be a direct connection here between the developing overview of teaching, the capacity to put incidents and events into a perspective of growing confidence, a sense of being in control of the technical aspects of teaching, and a sense of managing personal (emotional) responses to particular events and to life as a teacher. The management of these responses was not, according to the teachers, a preordained personal capacity. Rather it was learned from a complementary and parallel set of experiences to those related to teaching 'skills'.

Debbie   I think you learn to cope with your own emotions, as well. You learn to deal with those things that caused emotional upheaval to start. (7 June)

The identification of that relationship by the group provided a turning point in my understanding of the education of new teachers, and perceptions of how to provide for it. At the start of year the plethora of practical problems produced extensive ranges of anxieties, most of which seemed to be minor in themselves – 'nothing I couldn't cope with'. They seemed to be contained within the normal bounds of conscientious learning, as new tasks were undertaken, new experiences encountered, new relationships built, new knowledge assimilated and, in particular, new judgements made and evaluated through reflection on the quality of those judgements. The extent of the new learning made analysis difficult, and anxieties were experienced as an agglomeration. Although Debbie talked of emotional upheaval in a negative way, the fluctuations included many high points of excitement, satisfaction and pleasure – attested to by the data presented earlier. These too were often based on many minor accomplishments, too many to identify individually and analyse, as myriad tasks pressed for attention and further judgements were required, each in turn to be added to the repertoire of experience. The events themselves were idiosyncratic and individualized. Although they fell within the realms of practical knowledge discussed earlier, the 'programme' of events for each teacher differed widely. Yet the ways in which events related to emotional responses, the nature of the feelings, and their fluctuations, were very similar. Learning how to handle the emotional responses was as important as learning how to conduct tasks, meet new experiences, make judgements, build relationships or assimilate new knowledge. The educative processes of going through it, playing it by ear, playing the hunch, mental gymnastics, experiencing unpredictability, monitoring, and mirroring, were as evident in learning about one's emotional self and developing that aspect of teaching as they were in the more conventionally defined practical knowledge of teaching. In the case of these five teachers a *de facto* curriculum for the emotions emerged, intertwined with their curriculum for technical and clinical competences in the tasks of teaching. It was largely self-determined, depending for support on the goodwill and sensitivities of colleagues in schools, and on other members of the research group.

As the 'basic things' (technical competences) were mastered, and day-to-day tasks were remembered easily and routinized and some aspects of classroom management became established, so the emotional responses towards these matters stabilized. Where judgements about pupils' learning, or dealing with behaviour (clinical competences) were made, the uncertainties and unpredictability of events and consequences sustained the fluidity of the emotions. Furthermore, where new ventures were initiated risks were deliberately taken in order to test potential improvements in the quality of teaching and learning. Those developments were consciously undertaken in the knowledge that they would test the emotions. They could potentially enhance confidence and improve the ability to handle other emotions at other times – or of course, undermine it. Either way, such initiatives provided source material for the curriculum of the emotions. The emotions, then, were also the subject of attempts to manage them as well as being subject to the unexpected and uncontrollable.

The picture was complicated, and raises questions which I was not fully able to pursue with the group. There is a need for further exploration of the relationship between the emotions attached to becoming proficient in the technical details of teaching's hundreds of tasks; those attached to decision-making and judgements which carry ethical dimensions and reside in the realm of clinical competence; those associated with how one feels as a person engaged in a social practice; those associated with being ignorant of, and acquiring, new teaching knowledge; those attached to minding deeply about mirroring teaching aims in practice; those attached to status and changes in status; and those which concern one's sense of direction as a person having embarked on a particular career route. Each of these 'sources' of emotional turbulence, much of it reflected in positive feelings as well as negative, could be detected in the teachers' discussions. Sometimes different 'causes' meant positive and negative feelings coexisting. A particular question in this complex picture is: in learning to 'cope with their own emotions' by learning to 'deal with those things that caused emotional upheaval to start', were the teachers seeking comfort and security in practical proficiency and the routinization of teaching? The data suggest that to be partly so. But there was also risk-taking and the initiation of problematic ventures. Perhaps, if the relationship between the emotions and these realms of teaching experience were understood more fully, it would be possible to provide a *de jure* curriculum for the emotions which would enable constructive developments of this dimension of personal competence.

Chapter 5

Induction Support for New Teachers:
A Search for Principles and Practices

Several main, related sets of questions arose from the review of policy on teacher induction; my practice in the initial project; the research of the teachers' working contexts; and the research group conversations. One set grew out of concern about which conceptions of induction, and of teacher education more broadly, pertained within the 'culture' of teaching, in the disputes which emerged in the late 1980s and early 1990s, and among those with whom I worked in the initial project. A second set concerned my capacity to conduct practice in such a way as to effect my own educational aims, especially given the social and material contexts in which the teachers and I worked. A third concerned the nature of those aims themselves, especially the central feature of developing reflective practice. In the latter especially, I was aware of emerging doubt and growing self-consciousness about conceptions of research-based teaching, reflective practice and action research, terms which I had tended to use interchangeably. It was from these deliberations that I began to gain a sense of a set of constellations of concepts as my initial ideas about research-based teaching interacted with the policy analysis and review of research; as both interacted with reflections on my experience with the new teachers; as those reflections were further informed by interpretations of data from the research group; and as I attempted to relate all of these thoughts to the theoretical constructs of competence (as defined by Zimpher and Howey, 1987), social strategy (as defined by Lacey, 1977), and reflective practice (as defined by Schon, 1983).

The constellations of concepts did not develop in a simple chronology. Indeed, chronologically in the progress of the development project and the research, the summer period of the first year was a particularly puzzling time as these ideas were juxtaposed in the face of demands for practical action. The initial project was not concluded, and its evaluation not reported, until the early autumn. Data from the project and from the research group were extensive but still growing and being transcribed, sorted and stored through the summer. Analysis was partial and provisional. Yet proposals, policy decisions, publicity and planning for the extension project were being executed jointly with staff of the employing authorities throughout the same period. (That included coming to terms with and working within the reallocation of responsibilities for induction as policy for induction support changed, including its funding through the new arrangements of the Grant for Education Support and Training (GEST) budgeting mechanism.) At that point, those concepts which had particularly influenced my thinking – the distinctions of kinds of teaching competence and of social strategies, and the notion of reflective practice as an aspiration of professional development – maintained a definite impetus in my rationalization of aims for the extension project. The policy analysis and research review, my experience of working with the initial project teachers, and the extensiveness of the next phase of the project provided a different impetus for the way in which the latter was conceived and organized.

Prior to the initiative provision for new teachers' support had been made separately in each of several administrative areas. In its first year a co-ordinated 'programme' of induction for new teachers was introduced in all but one area, where the initial project was devised separately. Both were developed knowing that the employing authority intended to make fully co-ordinated provision the following year. Liaison between the initial project and the programme occurred throughout the year in order to blend the experiences, with the extension project in mind. Major differences between the initial project and the programme were:

1. Bringing teachers together to consider topics general to teaching (e.g. authority and discipline in classrooms; personal relationships; teaching strategies) was a feature of the programme. The development of classroom skills which were the concern of individual teachers, and of reflective thinking about specific aspects of teaching, were key aims of the initial project.

2. School-based tutor support was left to the schools in the programme. In the initial project external staff took an active tutoring role, independent of the assessment of the teachers, in liaison with teacher-tutors in schools, providing out-of-school pastoral support in addition.

3. The programme involved a series of half-day and whole-day meetings with visiting speakers, and with opportunities to meet colleagues from other schools. Initial project teachers met only once at the beginning of the year. Other contacts were made in schools in order to minimize disruption of teaching programmes.

4. The number of teachers involved: over 100 in the programme; 16 in the initial project.

The evaluations of both argued that effective induction might be better achieved where a range of elements in support of new teachers were successfully provided. These included the following:

- The conditions and nature of appointment set by the employer/school:
  - temporary/permanent, part-time/full-time contracts;
  - clarity of job description, responsibilities and tasks;
  - timing of the appointment to allow visits and preparation;
  - matching candidates to specific posts.
- Provision of employment information and induction support:
  - the structure of the school system; support services; professional development opportunities;
  - assessment procedures;
  - out-of-school induction to complement school support.
- 'Job-embedded' support and school information:
  - appropriate conditions – timetabling, rooms, resources;
  - curriculum information and school routines.
- Regular contact with a skilled teacher-tutor to:
  - provide information and advice;
  - offer counselling support;
  - develop classroom practice with the teachers.

The evaluations showed that the commitment and energy of the new teachers was not always matched by effective support. While they generally felt welcomed, schools had usually been supportive, and employer initiatives helpful, this was not consistent. The cases of Mike, Lesley, Richard, Anna and Diane described earlier provided some detail of the teachers' varied experiences. In the programme new teachers in primary schools felt that their needs were not satisfactorily met. Some initial project teachers found too many support personnel were involved. School support was reported to be variable, ranging from minimum and *ad hoc* to extensive and well planned. There was a tendency for support to cease early in the academic year. The assessment of the teachers' performance and the provision of assessment reports to them, although not part of the projects as such, revealed varied procedures, some of which left teachers uncertain about how progress was perceived by assessors. A number of key recommendations emerged, upon which much of the planning for the extension project was based. These included the following:

- Appointments of new entrants to temporary/part-time posts should be avoided.
- Clear job descriptions including the teaching to be undertaken and the timetable arrangements in which it will occur should be provided in advance.
- Support information should be provided by the employer.
- Assessment procedures should be made explicit, identifying when visits will be made and explaining in which parts of the

year new teachers will be informed of their progress and how this will be done.

- Appropriate conditions of work for new entrants should be assured, especially with regard to teaching load, teaching bases and resources.

- Information about the school should be provided well in advance of the start of the appointment. This should deal with the essential information for the teaching needs and arrangements for support of the teacher.

- A teacher-tutor should be appointed/identified in each school as soon as a new entrant is appointed. The task of the teacher-tutor should be clearly set out for all schools.

- Teacher-tutors should be selected for commitment to professional development of teachers and willingness to attend meetings to improve the complex skills involved in such work.

- Regular systematic contact with one skilled teacher-tutor should be the basis of an in-school induction programme.

- A programme dealing with aspects of professional development should be introduced for teacher-tutors.

- A programme of induction outside the school (at each teachers' centre or other appropriate location) should be provided.

- This programme should operate through the establishment of support groups.

- Separate groups for primary and secondary teachers should be arranged, to take account of different school worlds which they inhabit.

The aims and design of the extension project, co-ordinated by myself and an officer of the employing authority, took into account the perspectives on new entrants' support needs developed during that first year. Although the experience provided a large amount of information about the needs of new teachers, the extension project sought to achieve a better understanding of those needs. The project also had the instrumental aim of co-ordinating provision for the first time and involved 150 new teachers from 90 schools. It was important to gain the co-operation and agreement of teacher-tutors in order to ensure consistency of good quality school support. The base-line for that was to identify a teacher-tutor from each school with a new entrant. It was recognized that in many cases teacher-tutors might not have worked with new teachers before, or not for a long time, and that in-school support would need to be developed. In particular the project aimed to provide learning experiences for the new teachers based on the observation of classroom practice – including both observation of their teaching by a trusted colleague, and observation of colleagues' practice by the new teachers. It was intended that observation of colleagues would also extend to other schools where appropriate 'good practice' could be seen. In both cases it was intended that observation would be complemented by discussion. From the start it was assumed that central to such observation and discussion, and to the development of teaching whether it was observed and discussed or not, was the notion of critical reflection. The aim to extend and improve the quality of such reflection, as teachers sought to solve practical problems, had been the central aim of the initial project and it was transferred to the extension project before the analysis of the research data was done. The establishment and support of such reflective practice was maintained as a main assumption and principle for successful induction. That characteristic was seen as potentially providing a basis during the induction year for longer-term inservice professional development. In short, it was asserted that induction would not necessarily provide 'answers', but would equip teachers with the support and the skills of enquiry and discussion with which to seek and gain their 'own' answers to their particular and school-specific needs. This view reflected my own aspirations for the project.

The assessment of individual teachers' progress was conducted formally by headteachers (in practice sometimes by teacher-tutors or other senior colleagues) and by advisers or officers who were 'named assessors' by the employers. The activities of the project did not include direct involvement in assessment. Indeed, its aims set out to avoid such involvement and to offer tutorial and counselling support to the teachers which could operate independently of the assessment role. However, the experience of the initial project demonstrated the benefits to the teachers of opportunities to be informed about, and to discuss together that assessment. The criteria which applied to all new teachers were discussed with them, from the start of the year, by an officer of the employing authority. Information was also provided on developments in the National Curriculum and assessment as these emerged. Further, the long-established and widespread recognition that the induction year can be traumatic for some new teachers, and is certainly an intensive and potentially lonely learning experience, was provided for. Informal gatherings with other teachers during lunch, prior to formal meetings, were a deliberate part of the programme. Other informal meetings, after school hours, were arranged by myself in a role which both formally and informally was independent of assessment.

The aims of the Project were summarized as follows:

Information-seeking

1. To understand the support needs of new teachers better;
2. To understand the support needs of teacher-tutors.

Support-providing

3. To ensure all new teachers have a teacher-tutor in school;

4. To provide information about the education service and national developments;

5. To offer peer networking and counselling support independent of the school and assessment of teaching.

Support-development

6. To establish in-school support procedure and practices, agreed by the teacher-tutors;

7. To make observation of and discussion about teaching 'work' effectively for the teachers' learning.

Teacher-development

8. To establish and support reflective practice as a main principle of induction;

9. To make the induction year a basis for longer-term inservice professional development.

Taking direct action with regard to the conditions and nature of appointment was outside the jurisdiction of the project co-ordinators. Whether posts were permanent or temporary, full-time or part-time; whether clear job descriptions were provided; whether appointments were made in time to allow preparatory visits; whether candidates were suitably 'matched' to posts; and whether appropriate conditions were provided for the teachers; each of these and related questions were in the power of the employer's staffing and schools' personnel. On these issues the recommendations of the initial project could be implemented only to the extent that teacher-tutors had the power and will to act within the project activities. Information was collected across the schools on these features of new teachers' work. That information was discussed with teacher-tutors as representatives of their schools, in a collated form which anonymized individuals' schools but which allowed them to address the issues in relation to their own institutions.

The design of the project established meetings at five teachers' centres for new entrants, and separately for teacher-tutors. In both cases teachers could attend any centre, according to which place and dates were most convenient. An initial 'Welcome' meeting for the new teachers in late September at each centre after school allowed the senior secondary adviser, area officers, teachers' centre co-ordinators, education welfare officers, psychological services staff, and project tutor to be introduced. The teachers were able to briefly meet each other for the first time. Information about the induction programme was provided, and also sent to teachers who could not attend. A pattern of half-day meetings during the autumn and spring terms was designed to 'leap-frog' so

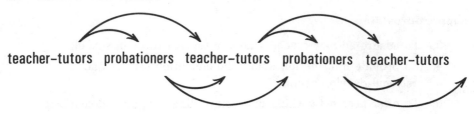

teacher–tutors   probationers   teacher–tutors   probationers   teacher–tutors

Figure 5.1

that information and ideas from development activities with teacher-tutors and new teachers could be made available to each other (see Figure 5.1).

The gathering, collation, and presentation of information from the groups was done in such a way that it was anonymized and 'collective' from across all five centres. In that way it was intended to establish a sense of collegiality and co-operation across the schools, and to provide opportunities to contribute to the development of the project, both from what they did in their schools and from participation in the meetings.

The meetings dealt with the following:

- the qualities needed by the teacher-tutor;
- appointment and induction arrangements for new entrants;
- tasks of the teacher-tutor;
- circumstances of work for new teachers;
- in-school support programmes provided by teacher-tutors;
- observation of teaching for professional development;
- assessing the need for classroom observation skills;
- identifying opportunities for observation;
- recognizing contributions made by new teachers to the school;
- identifying aspects of teaching to be developed;
- reviewing potential contributions and constraints;
- formulating procedures for effective longer-term induction;
- the nature and qualities of professional development experiences.

The second HMI report on *The New Teacher in School* (DES, 1988a) provided matters for discussion within the project. It also stimulated my own thoughts about the project's aims in a way which linked to the wider political context of teacher education. Aspects of those thoughts, taken together with the emerging constellations of concepts (competences, social strategies and reflective practice) form important background to understanding the way in which the project was devised and implemented.

The HMI report said nothing about research on teacher induction. It referred only to its own predecessor (DES, 1982a). However, it added to that earlier report, albeit that both presented Her Majesty's Inspectors' perspective based on their methods of survey. From that perspective it aimed to judge how well 297 teachers were equipped for their first job, including the quality of their training and their teaching. It also asked whether schools made the best use of their talents, and examined the contexts in which those talents were deployed and the ways in which those contexts affected the work of the teachers.

In this latter aim it brought up to date, and took further, the national survey (Taylor and Dale, 1971) and various earlier assertions about the lives of new teachers. It addressed those perceived basic prerequisites and conditions of employment which had been widely proposed since McNair and reported by Taylor and Dale. It also sought to make qualitative judgements about the consequences of different conditions for the teachers' experiences, performance, and opportunities for learning. In doing so it exposed some of the assumptions of what HMI expected of new teachers and from support colleagues in the schools where they worked, in terms of new teachers' professional development.

The report also acknowledged the rapidly changing educational context into which the teachers entered. Among the changes HMI recognized that the expectation that teachers should be more involved in the evaluation of their performance (and presumably its subsequent development) had widened the role for which new teachers needed to be prepared (as well as GCSE, Certificate of Pre-Vocational Education, Technical and Vocational Education Initiative, Special Educational Needs, links with industry, contact with parents, assessment and records of achievement, multicultural awareness, information technology, etc.). It did not explicitly anticipate the dramatic changes impending for all schools with the advent of the Education Reform Act. Nevertheless, it did assume a more dynamic relationship between the talents of new entrants and those of experienced teachers than a simple apprenticeship view could assume. Hence its concern to judge preparedness for a first job was only partly in terms of minimum technical competence in the classroom. It argued that even the most competent (i.e. in classroom skills) were entitled to structured discussion and evaluative support for developing their teaching. It also argued that schools need to make provision for the best use of new teachers' special expertise and wider experience of work other than teaching, as contributions to the development of schools (DES, 1988a, para 1.45). On first impressions those assertions reflect, albeit unwittingly, the range of competences in Zimpher and Howey's analysis and the different kinds of social strategies identified in Zeichner and Tabachnick's study of new teachers, as well as my own arguments for extending the concepts of social strategy to professional self-development strategies. This appeared to be encouraging support for the aims of the induction project. However, that may have been somewhat seductive, and my interpretation at the time may have been governed by what I hoped to read, in this sense. The views aired by HMI of pro-active new teachers engaged in professional self-development and in school development within supportive environments are a marked contrast to some earlier perspectives about assessment of new teachers. Even the DES *Teachers Regulations 1989* (DES, 1989a) focus on failure and institute procedures for dealing with incompetents at the earliest points in a new career. In contrast, HMI appeared to reinforce the aspirations they set out in *Quality in Schools: The Initial Training of Teachers* (DES, 1987) towards extended professionalism, questioning, debate, analysis of and argument from evidence, and the examination of assumptions. In *The New Teacher in School* emphasis on selection was thus in some respects displaced by a focus on support; quality control by quality assurance; monitoring by mentoring. Each of these was set within a clear view of what were deemed appropriate environments for beginning teaching in terms of reduced demands of the teaching situation encountered and smaller workloads, compared with experienced colleagues. 'Matched' deployment of expertise and teaching responsibilities, and sufficient opportunities to question, debate, analyse and argue, were also demanded by HMI's view of the new teacher as novice. However, with regard to this shift of focus the most interesting feature was the implicit denial of new teachers as learners and contributors to professional self-development, which was encased in the judgement of the quality of teaching among the survey's 297 teachers.

First, it must be said, the judgements were based on inexplicit criteria. For example, 'good relationships with pupils', 'adequate planning and preparation', 'over-directed work' and 'mastery of the subject' were judged without saying quite what these meant, and measured in terms of 'the vast majority', 'most', 'many', 'much', and 'often'. Furthermore, the focus was almost entirely on performance in teaching. The HMI impression of the quality of new teachers provided the view that in their judgement against a range of criteria for classroom practice, three-quarters of the lessons observed were at least satisfactory. Forty per cent were good or excellent. In making their judgements, HMI made *no allowances* for inexperience and judged the teachers as if they were experienced. Given that, the overall impression of 40 per cent good or excellent and 75 per cent at least satisfactory, might demonstrate clearly the calibre of new teachers in such realms of practical proficiency as HMI took into account. If we allow for inexperience and assume that the induction period with effective support will bring improvements in learning teaching and in performance, then the quality of new teachers, by HMI criteria, must signal extensive potential excellence.

Most crucially, however, from the point of view of my present arguments, despite HMI aspirations for new teachers to be continuous learners, they did not address the processes of learning teaching, nor how much, nor what kind of learning occurred among the sample during their first year. We were offered no idea of how the quality of teaching might be improved, the directions it might take, the pace which its learning could sustain, or the substance of it. Nor did HMI say what the actual or potential contributions of the new teachers would be, either to their own learning, or through that learning to the schools in which they worked or to the profession at large.

The kinds of criteria invoked in judging quality read as 'output' measures following initial training. They were located in the realms of technical and clinical aspects of practice: observable behaviours, and measurable performance. The implied potential contributions related to the implementation of policy initiatives and their related practices from locations beyond the educational ideas of individual teachers and particular schools. In short, the teachers' qualities favoured by HMI for consideration could be read as those of technicians. The qualities of questioning, debating, analysing and arguing from evidences, the qualities of educational *tacticians*, appear to have been no more than rhetoric. However, in the fields of technical expertise and competence in making professional judgements, it is also clear from *The New Teacher in School* that such potential of new teachers may not be fulfilled. The most severe constraint they faced was said to be an absence of clear guidelines or schemes of work within departments and schools. In addition, some schools were unable to offer them a system of support and guidance, even though they saw the need for it. Such a system, 'involving a designated colleague or colleagues, regular meetings, observation [of the new teacher while teaching], open and frank evaluation, the opportunity to see experienced colleagues teaching, and time for discussion, preparation and thinking' was 'less than adequately' provided in 25 per cent of schools. Only 37 per cent provided such support 'substantially' and only 9 per cent 'fully' (DES, 1982a, para 1.30).

A further area of concern identified by HMI (which will be considered later in this report in relation to the extension project) is that of the conditions which encourage or facilitate the full professional development of the new teacher. They regarded less than half of the schools as providing suitable conditions for such development – particularly in terms of 'job-embedded' support. According to HMI, constraints on the content of lessons or on teaching methods imposed by the school or department adversely affected 25 per cent of lessons in primary/middle schools, and 30 per cent in secondary schools. The same proportions were affected by the lack of availability of teaching materials. Inadequate accommodation was a further constraint. While HMI took a step out of the deficit view of new teachers, and looked at the deficiencies in structures which prevented these teachers being even better than they judged them to be, they revealed a certain contradiction in their views. While acknowledging that some new teachers were constrained by their more experienced colleagues, one premiss on which HMI aspirations for supported professional development lay was the role of the teacher-tutor and the place of classroom observation. Even here however, they had little to say which was helpful. After the first six months of teaching, 63 per cent of primary/middle school teachers had been observed teaching, and 87 per cent in secondary schools; there is no indication of how many times or how frequently this happened, by whom observations were conducted, what the quality of the experience was, or its benefits. Even if such details had been spelled out there remained a problem about the purpose, nature and effects of such 'mentoring'. The place of observation by new teachers of colleagues and of themselves by colleagues has been a prop of teacher induction practice, proposals and aspirations since pupil-teachers, through McNair and James, and is endemic in the most recent debate on routes to qualified teacher status. The nineteenth-century and recent Hillgate proposals carry clear tones of craft apprenticeship, with teachers learning the technical skills of a fixed and steady trade, mentored and monitored by a master craftsperson. And so the 'technicist' view of teaching and of learning to teach was sustained by HMI without critical acclaim. It is implied that the novice would be inducted into a serving, stable system of schooling. Yet it was made clear that such stability did not exist.

In the induction project pursuing my own aims for 'partnership' and collegial debate about education within a context of educational flux and a perspective of plural (and sometimes conflicting) educational values, there was undoubtedly a commitment to that side of HMI's view of the new teacher as 'agent' rather than mere instrument of educational change. That view had implications for the relationship between new teachers and their teacher-tutors, which were reflected in the Socratic images used by Jerome Bruner in his proposals for developing the intellectual curiosity of pupils:

> all forms of assisted learning ... depend massively upon
> participation in a dialogue carefully stabilized by the adult
> partner. So much of learning depends on the need to achieve
> joint attention, to conduct enterprises jointly, to honour the
> social relationship that exists between learner and tutor.
> (Bruner, 1977, Preface)

On that side of their view it was quite clear in the judgement of HMI that the idea of a craft apprenticeship into 'received' knowledge was inappropriate for achieving educational change, but also that the conditions did not pertain whereby new teachers could benefit fully from carefully stabilized support in terms of their practical performance, learning, and contributions to their schools (DES, 1988a, paras 1.29–1.35). I saw it as incumbent upon me to pursue these matters with the new teachers and teacher-tutors in the project, in order to establish what I saw as pre-conditions for the development of reflective practice. The initial project had detected major failings in support, not only for acquitting the responsibilities of teaching, but also for learning from the experience of doing so. Failings existed in the work of teacher-tutors, in my own support-tutor role and in the work of advisers and officers of the employer. Perhaps most of all it was in the combinations of so many personnel that the support failed most. As many as seven 'tutors' — subject adviser, officer,

headteacher, head of department, project tutor, and other colleagues –
operated at one time. That clearly abrogated carefully stabilized approaches to
learning through supported, reflective dialogue.

As a consequence of their 'findings' HMI made the following
recommendations:

> Local authorities and schools should review their practice [of
> appointments and support for new teachers] to ensure that
> induction is effectively arranged and delivered.
> At the very least all schools with newly trained teachers should
> have a plan for their induction and should make arrangements
> for the close monitoring of progress including the observation
> of, and feedback on, lessons taught.
> Schools also need to consider what special expertise new
> teachers have to offer and how this might best be used.

These recommendations were 'adopted' within the aims of the extension project
as a basis for part of its research and development, particularly since such
'structural' needs had been identified among the initial project teachers. A
major feature of proposals in favour of establishing such collective support for
new teachers has consistently been the observation of teaching, in order to
facilitate discussion about and development of classroom practice. Some of the
assumptions which underlay that feature in the initial project, and which were
transferred to thinking about the extension, were that observation and discussion can:

- ensure that teaching is treated as problematic and subject to
  constant enquiry and potential improvement;
- encourage positive attitudes in learning teaching, while
  reducing the feelings of deficiency which are common among
  teachers;
- bring teachers 'out in the open' in sharing and solving
  difficulties and in seeking improvements in practice generally.

The establishment of such openness in learning teaching may depend upon
conditions of trust and principles of procedure for the conduct of observation,
the use of criteria in judging teaching, the communication of judgments about
teaching, and implementation of action for developing it where that is
appropriate: Schon's 'essential pre-conditions' for the development of professional knowledge and an epistemology of practice. Of course, those assumptions are not the only ones which might underlie proposals for observing new
teachers at work.

In the recent past the political climate in which teachers have worked has
represented teachers in general as being in some measure deficient and in need
of being 'managed' and 'monitored'. This climate has not been one which

recognized the problematic nature of teaching. Rather it has portrayed teaching as if it is a matter of technique to be performed, in any circumstance. It has not addressed issues about learning teaching. Rather it has assumed that its performance can be quickly and easily assessed, especially if the teacher is observed at work. These different assumptions about the place of observation can be seen as conflicting and creating a tension for teachers.

New teachers in schools, encountering what is probably the most intensive period of 'learning while doing' of their careers, and teachers who work closely with them, face the tensions of mentoring and monitoring, of advice and assessment, of support and report. Statutory requirements and advice relating to the assessment of new teachers for confirmation of qualified teacher status have regularly been laid out for employers (DES, 1983, 1990, 1991b, 1992b, 1992c). Expectations for the employer and schools to support the learning of teaching during this time were also clear. By and large, however, there was little evidence for the 'need' to weed out incompetence at this stage. There was evidence of the need to develop effective learning conditions and appropriate procedures to enable and sustain learning, so that initial teaching competence could be developed to its full potential. How could that potential be fulfilled? If teaching was in a 'stable' and single state it might occur through effective mechanisms for training new entrants in the tricks of the trade. New teachers might adjust compliantly to the demands of a job which would be predetermined. That, however, would seriously misrepresent teaching and the kinds of professional action required of teachers. It was (and is) my own belief that teaching depends substantially for its effectiveness on the purposes, intentions, actions and initiatives of individual teachers. I also acknowledged at the time (and even more so now) that schools, employers and governments seek compliance and adjustment to their policies and curriculum designs. But they also demand the adoption of responsibilities, initiative and leadership qualities which presume participation in institutional change. The new criteria for initial teacher training require that by the end of their ITT course student teachers should recognize that part of their role involves leading their colleagues (DES, 1989b, Appendix A, para 6.8 (ii)). Teachers' pay and conditions of service require similar responsibilities. In general terms, the work of the Council for the Accreditation of Teacher Education (CATE) was based on an implicit assumption that 'a new generation of teachers [which] is now beginning to emerge' will have an impact on teaching quality in schools. What constitutes quality is a matter of contention and controversy. It was (and is) my contention that the kinds of contributions teachers make will depend upon the characteristics of the teachers and the opportunities they encounter in their schools, and that those characteristics should include the dispositions and skills to research their own practices. Highlighting these particular criteria is deliberately hyperselective in order to fit my own arguments for an educated profession capable of engaging in 'personal reconstruction' and 'social reconstruction'. It was in pursuit of those aspirations that I drew together threads from *The New*

Teacher in School, in particular the notion of maximizing the potential of new entrants; from social theory in the concepts of competence and strategy; and from epistemology in the ideas of Schon's reflective practitioner. Together, I saw these as forming a basis of aims for teacher induction appropriate to the changing educational context.

Within that context, secondary school teachers had engaged in the rapid introduction of the GCSE examination, the development of the Technical and Vocational Education Initiative, the introduction of records of achievement, and other innovations. These tensions and changes, following as they did on the growth of comprehensive schooling, provided only a foretaste of the impact of the changes being brought about by the 1988 Education Reform Act in all age-phases and types of state schools. The teachers in the extension project were among the first to enter the profession under the new law. Its provisions for a national curriculum, local management of schools, teacher appraisal, increased powers for school governors and inservice teacher education, provided quite different working contexts for these new teachers to begin their careers. It was a context to which their senior colleagues were seeking or obliged to make adjustments as changes were implemented.

Such a period of institutional change provided a different perspective on teacher induction from that which Lacey and Lortie studied. It was a period where institutional change invoked by law was being pursued in all state schools around those new teachers as well as with them and by them. They were not entering 'stable state' institutions. Nor, for the most part, might they (or their senior colleagues) assume passive compliance with a worked out and tested set of institutional requirements (except in some respects with regard to material resources until LMS is fully implemented). It was unlikely that new teachers would experience a 'match' between their perspectives on schooling and those held within institutions, for it was not likely that institutional perspectives would be held consensually during a dynamic response to external demands, even if they might have been previously. The possibility to engage in strategic redefinition was more likely to be transformed into a requirement, along with other colleagues, as institutional structures were transformed and mechanisms devised by groups and individuals as they responded to new pressures and constraints. Not least, that would be likely to occur with regard to curriculum aims, content, teaching methods and assessment of pupil performance as these were (re)formulated and implemented with the Education Reform Act.

There was also an invigorated professional context to consider, which was partly related to the political, educational and demographic contexts. The requirement/duty to ensure implementation of the National Curriculum rests with the Secretary of State for Education, local education authorities, governors of schools and headteachers. Success depends upon an adequate supply of motivated teachers of 'quality'. Unlike a decade previously, teachers were in short supply, and the 'climate' which once denigrated them had begun to change. Perhaps more importantly, teacher appraisal (which stemmed from that denigration) had incorporated a 'professional development' view of the teacher as learner, as well as a punitive view of the teacher as failure. Inservice teacher education displayed an increasing interest in teacher research, with recognition on the one hand of the importance of the development of individual professional practice within specific school contexts. On the other hand, the benefits of whole-school review, school development plans, and school curriculum policies increased the need for institutionally-collective research and development skills. The latter, with review and renewal assumptions built into them, confirmed the view that 'redefinition' might become/has become an integral part of the professional strategies needed by all teachers. That situation, with the possibility at the time of teacher appraisal led by teachers through research-based teaching, suggested that the concept of strategic redefinition might also be applied to introspective activity in the individual teachers' perspectives and practices.

As project co-ordinator, I believed that there would be at most only a few cases where new teachers were still striving to reach basic teaching competences; that the majority would be engaged in consolidating their expertise while applying it to the new situations in which they worked; and that most would be actively engaged in developing their teaching through constant reflection on classroom events. It was also assumed that many would have contributions to offer to their schools in the way of particular qualities, strengths and expertise, which went well beyond basic teaching competence. In all aspects of teaching, at whatever level of 'quality' it was judged by the new teachers themselves or their colleagues, my optimism inferred that the evidence of the initial project had shown that critical self-reflection and constant striving for improvements was a feature of new teachers' lives. The project set out to recognize and to build upon such reflective self-development through the provision of support which would suit the invigorated professional context which the new teachers were entering.

This chapter will show how the development of in-school support was approached in the extension project; how the project sought to capitalize on the expertise which new teachers had to offer; and how liaison between schools and employers was effected. It will also show, through evidence gathered during the project, where further development was deemed to be needed in the support structures for new teachers. The numbers involved and the logistics of the programme of meetings are set out in Tables 5.1 and 5.2. In addition 11 part-time teachers appointed during the previous year or full-timers appointed later in the academic year, continued their induction period into the following academic year. In January of the second year an additional 17 teachers joined the project. Each half-day meeting was supported by the cost of supply cover from the project.

In addition to the formal programmes of meetings, provision was also made for voluntary, informal support group meetings for new teachers at each

Table 5.1 Programme of meetings and visits

New teachers	Teacher-tutors
September	
November (early)	October
February	November (late)
April–May (visits)	March
June (early)	June (late)

Table 5.2 Number of participants

Meeting centre	Number of schools/ teacher-tutors		Number of new teachers	
	Primary*	Secondary	Primary	Secondary
1	20	15	22	37
2	10	8	11	12
3	7	6	8	9
4	6	9	8	21
5	1	6	1	10
Totals	44	44	50	89
	88		139	

* 'Primary' includes nursery, infant, first, primary, junior, first and middle, and middle schools.

of the teachers' centres, co-ordinated by myself. In order to provide a forum disconnected from the assessment of the first year there was no participation by teacher-tutors or employer personnel. The meetings were on dates which fell midway between formal sessions, but were held after school.

The aim to understand the support needs of the teachers better, and in turn to establish consistency in support procedures, depended upon knowing the patterns of experience of the teachers in the early stages of their appointments. Those patterns were later used (in generalized and anonymized forms) to raise issues with officers of the employers and teacher-tutors, in order, where necessary, to improve initial induction arrangements. The establishment of an agreed 'standard' of provision was sought through consultation with the teacher-tutors. Individuals were encouraged to examine practices in their schools accordingly, and to take action to amend practices appropriately where they could. The details of some aspects of the appointment and induction arrangements are presented in Table 5.3a–d. The adequacies of the various aspects were discussed at length with the new teachers. In particular the

Table 5.3 Some aspects of appointment and induction

(a) Type of contract	Number of teachers	
	Primary	Secondary
Permanent	25	59
Temporary	19	22
Don't know	–	3
No return	6	5
Full-time	38	78
Part-time	6	6
No return	6	5

(b) Preparatory visits made	Number of teachers	
	Primary	Secondary
None	6	13
One	14	33
Two or more	17	20
Supply teaching	1	2
Teaching practice	6	8
No return	6	13

(c) Provision of school handbook	Number of teachers	
	Primary	Secondary
None	8	3
Timetable only	2	–
Prospectus/brochure	13	–
'Very little'	–	7
Full file/handbook	20	74
No return	7	5

(d) Provision of curriculum guidelines	Number of teachers	
	Primary	Secondary
None	12	14
Some	8	12
Full	26	58
No return	4	5

number of temporary contracts raised serious concern. Almost a third of the teachers were in temporary posts, presenting overriding insecurity during a period which is anyway potentially fraught with professional uncertainties. Those teachers did not know which school, if any, they might be employed in during the following term or following year. That inevitably presented questions of commitment to the school – an important feature of teachers' work. This was an issue which related to the development of aspects of professional practice in relation to particular contexts. It also had implications for the ideals of professional learning in general. That is, given the ideals of professional self-development, undertaken in co-operation with colleagues in schools, working on short-term temporary contracts may adversely affect the teachers' learning or the tutors' commitments to that learning. This was seen as a denial of the pre-condition of the maintenance of continuity over the learning process.

It is difficult to ooo how teachers can be adequately prepared for their new posts without making preparatory visits, yet some made none and many made only one. This was contrasted by one teacher-tutor with the visits arranged for student-teachers in advance of conducting 'blocks' of teaching practice – a substantial number of day visits in preparation for a few weeks' teaching. At best, new teachers who were previously resident locally, who were positively invited into school for numerous visits, and who were able to give the time, said that they benefited most (along with those who had had initial teaching practice in the school prior to appointment, or had done some supply teaching). It was clear from discussions with both teachers and tutors that clear invitations were needed from the school, with commitment of staff time, to ensure that new appointees felt welcome. Even then there were limitations of time and travel costs for those who resided (and perhaps also had temporary jobs) outside the region. In relation to these appointees the (contentious) possibility was discussed of providing travelling expenses, and using the first few days of September (prior to school term but during the first salaried month) to provide access to schools. That proposal highlighted the question of existing staff resources and how best to arrange and provide induction visits. Constructive proposals included the practice of new teachers attending on the same day as induction visits for pupils from feeder schools, and joining the same arrangements to get a 'pupil's-eye view'. Another was to 'attach' a new teacher to two or three pupils to be conducted through the routines and the buildings of the school.

The provision (or lack of it) of school handbooks and curriculum guidelines was not as straightforward as it might at first have seemed. It was clear that in many cases there was a serious lack of provision of information. That was discussed with teacher-tutors with a view to rectifying the policies and practices of the schools where necessary. The new teachers had a morass of detail to record and recall, and written guidance would seem to be essential as part of it. On the other hand, long, detailed and over-elaborate documents such as those intended for experienced teachers already established in the school were said to be unhelpful. Between the two (i.e. sparsity and plethora), some new teachers reported that they received sufficiently full and very helpful detail of those aspects of school life and the curriculum which were essential for effectively starting their new jobs. Often where those practices worked best, the information used was suitable for any teacher newly appointed to the school.

The range of circumstances in which the teachers worked was very wide with respect to school type, size and location. Primary schools included nursery (3–5 years); infant (4–7); first (5–9); primary (4–11); junior (7–11); middle (8–12); and first and middle (5–12). These ranged in size from 54 pupils/three teachers to 550 pupils/19 teachers. They were located in isolated rural villages, suburban communities, city and town urban centres, and 'London overspill' development areas. Secondary schools located mainly in the towns ranged from 360 pupils/25 teachers to 1,800 pupils/120 teachers, with varied age ranges: 11–16, 11–18, 12–16, 12–18, and 16–18. Some secondary schools had 'split' intake at both 11 and 12; one school was a boarding school. That information was a superficial indicator, for example, not showing the kind of buildings, extent of resources, size of department (in secondary schools), specific location of the schools, or 'human factors' such as the age-profiles of staff. Table 5.3 adds other dimensions to the information about circumstances – contract arrangements and school induction. Further indicators which show the variations of working circumstances experienced were the amount of non-teaching time available to, and the number of rooms used by, the teachers. These are shown in Table 5.4.

Again these were in one sense superficial. Little of the non-teaching time was specifically provided for new teachers; it largely reflected the time available to all teachers in the schools where it was provided. Nor does the table show 'protected' non-teaching time. Comments from the teachers showed that often the time was 'taken' for covering the lessons of absent colleagues. However, it does show the considerable variations in starting point, especially highlighting the discrepancy between the primary and secondary sectors.

The number of rooms used, and the opportunities to develop teaching within the 'stability' of a main base or few bases, also indicated the considerable variations experienced by the teachers. This too was a superficial indicator in some senses – it did not show where different gymnasia or laboratories were used with different classes for different purposes, for example. However, it did indicate where, say, three or more rooms were used on a transient basis, shared with other teachers and used by numerous classes, so that some aspects of resourcing, organizing and managing learning might be less than ideal. Where six or more rooms were used and, say, the same groups of pupils met in different rooms at different times, those matters could be very problematic. Although superficial, this information signalled the kinds of issues highlighted in more detail in the initial project, and reported in the HMI Reports, about the difficulties (on the one hand) and the opportunities (on the other) which working circumstances created. Evidence from the initial project showed how the

Table 5.4 Further variations of working circumstances

(a) Non-teaching time per week	Number of teachers	
	Primary	Secondary
None	25	
Up to 1 hour	13	
Up to 2 hours	5	
No return	7	
Total	50	
10–15%		30
16–20%		41
21–25%		7
26–30%		3
No return		8
Total		89

(b) Number of rooms used	Number of teachers	
	Primary	Secondary
Mostly main base (plus hall in primaries) (plus one other in secondaries)	32	36
3	7	20
4	2	8
5	3	7
6		5
7		1
8		1
9		2
10		2
No return	6	7
Total	50	89

teacher-tutor appointment could either make or break a positive approach to professional development. A letter to schools from the Chief Inspector expressed the view that the prime responsibility for successful induction rested on the work of an appropriate teacher-tutor. This was an indication not only of the need to appoint one (where none existed) but to ensure the 'right' one was appointed.

Table 5.5, taken from data provided by the new teachers, shows that

Table 5.5 Teacher-tutors' appointment/status

	Primary	Secondary
Head	8	2
Deputy head	15	35
Senior teacher	–	3
Head of department	–	2
Main professional grade teacher	12	1
Appointment not known	3	–
Status not known	1	–
Item on questionnaire not completed	5	1
Total	44	44

almost all were aware that a tutor had been appointed by the school and that contact had been established by November. Over 70 per cent of teacher-tutors held senior positions in their school.

However, who would be the right teacher-tutor? Were the necessary qualities for establishing a dialogue of learning carefully stabilized by the experienced partner to be assumed as a pre-condition or to be developed? Given that many teacher-tutors had not previously done the job, that some might be reluctant appointees, and that in any case there was not a clear or consensus view of the necessary qualities, the teacher-tutors were asked to define, discuss and if necessary seek to develop and apply those qualities. These were arrived at by inviting the teacher-tutors to answer the question 'What qualities does the teacher-tutor need?' The tutors worked in small groups (three or four in each). The proposals of 17 groups were collated (48 items in all) and returned for further discussion. They were also shared with the new teachers, to gain their views of the proposals and to gain a perspective on whether the perceived necessary qualities were in evidence in their experiences of working with teacher-tutors. The qualities were grouped for further discussion under subheadings in order to make the list manageable, and to suggest that the items fell into a number of categories of quality and skill which could be used as a framework for discussion.

Discussion about the full list indicated an obvious problem: for each teacher-tutor to attend to the whole range may be desirable but quite impractical. However, the majority of the qualities were initially identified by only one group. Others were selected by several groups of teacher-tutors. A working short-list under the subheadings was constructed from those offered by several groups, with a view that these should be regarded as the basic, necessary qualities. These, then, would be regarded as the qualities which a new teacher might expect to find in his or her teacher-tutor, or at least to find the teacher-tutor striving to develop them within his or her work with new teachers. They

Table 5.6 Essential qualities of the teacher-tutor

Professional standing
Credibility as a teacher
Experience

Pastoral
Empathy
Sympathy
Sensitivity

Personal/Relational
Approachability
Sense of humour
Good listener
Calm manner

Tutorial
Accessibility/availability
Positive constructive nature
Supportive/encouraging
Honesty
Reliability

are qualities which may not all be universally well-developed or easy to display in the hectic work of senior and experienced teachers. Table 5.6 sets out the final short-list arrived at.

In the development of the teacher-tutors' role the following issue was also brought to each group:

> Some schools have new teachers year by year, have
> long-standing support programmes, and teacher-tutors with
> increasing experience of working with new teachers. Other
> schools have received their first new entrant in years (some
> others may do so in future years) and are working on 'intuition'
> in support of the new teacher.

In discussions it became clear that the majority of schools did not have an identifiable support programme. They were more common in secondary/high schools than in primary/middle, where what one teacher-tutor described as 'corridor induction' was more commonly reported. Those who already had substantial support programmes were invited to work with those who did not in workshop activities, setting out what they did, where the successes were, and where improvements might be made. The purposes, content, and structure/ timing of support programmes were considered, and co-operative planning established to set in motion the task of implementing a programme in every school, and writing down their main features for use with the new teachers. Where programmes did not exist (as well as where they did) the value of having one was overwhelmingly agreed by teacher-tutors, with an equally overwhelming proviso that programmes needed to be flexible because of:

- Size, type and organizational structure of individual schools;
- Number of new entrants at any one time;
- Frequency of employing new entrants in the school;
- Maturity and previous experience of new teachers;
- Date of appointment;
- Contract, e.g. part-time/full-time; temporary/permanent;
- Range of teaching responsibilities of new teacher(s);
- Opportunities for conducting support meetings;
- Negotiations with new teachers to accommodate their needs;
- Preferred 'styles' of implementation of teacher-tutors.

From the examples of 'good practice' reported and the experiences of the new teachers, and in recognition of these variables, the following broad framework was devised in order to guide schools in ensuring that key aspects of professional knowledge and practice were dealt with in a systematic way for all new teachers.

A FRAMEWORK FOR IN-SCHOOL SUPPORT PROGRAMMES

Information Provision School handbook and supplementary material, curriculum guidelines, timetable, calendar of events, duties, rules and routines, procedures, INSET activities.

Meeting Teaching and Support Staff Understanding the roles, responsibilities and duties of staff − knowing who to turn to for what − as well as establishing personal rapport with colleagues.

Resource Provision Explaining and enabling areas of responsibility and control over resources for teaching, including sources, location, ordering and purchasing.

Induction Opportunities Ensuring appropriate conditions of work, levels of responsibility, and opportunities to gain knowledge, skills and understanding within a supportive environment. This includes establishing and protecting non-contact time, assured meetings with teacher-tutor, head of department, etc., opportunities to observe teaching and to be observed.

Locality Residential areas, link schools, and the locality as a learning resource.

School as a Community The place of individuals, groups and inter-relationships; pastoral systems, parental links, governors, educational support services, LEA personnel.

School as a Centre of Learning Core values of the school, other subjects/year groups, pupil grouping, assessment/examination arrangements, record-keeping/reporting,

Quality of Teaching Examining the purposes, implementation, and outcome of teaching – planning, preparation, classroom management, practical skills, and evaluation.

The qualities of teacher-tutors' work and the provision of initial induction arrangements within the 'framework' related directly to the 'tasks' which were undertaken in supporting new teachers. The conduct of those tasks also depended upon opportunities to work with the new entrants, and those opportunities were affected by the circumstances in which teacher-tutors themselves worked. In some circumstances it is a misrepresentation to talk of teacher-tutor tasks, since many support functions were carried out in practice by other colleagues, in particular headteachers and heads of departments. Thus the teachers established a view of the tasks to be co-ordinated by the teacher-tutor. That was begun by inviting the teacher-tutors to identify and define what they (or colleagues) did (or thought they should do) in that role for the new teachers. A set of 'prompt' tasks was then used, to identify additional items seen as desirable in the role. Collated responses were returned to the teacher-tutors, in consultation about how to refine and represent the 'collective view' of the tasks to be co-ordinated. The result is presented in Box 5.1 and Box 5.1a–e, and was reproduced for all schools as part of the guidelines for in-school induction.

A central assumption held by the project co-ordinators (in common with many teachers, teacher educators, teacher appraisers, HMI, and others) was that the observation of teaching and discussion about it constitute an important mode of professional development. A related assumption was that there was a need for the development of expertise in conducting such observations and discussions, since they involve complex and difficult skills. In the project it was assumed that the observations of new entrants' teaching (which were deemed necessary for the assessment arrangements) could be developed within in-school support programmes to enhance new teachers' learning. It was also assumed that this could and should be complemented by the observation by new teachers of their senior colleagues' teaching, with follow-up discussions. Those assumptions and aspirations were shared by the teacher-tutors and by the new entrants, especially at the start of the year. Discussions among both

Box 5.1 In-school support for new teachers: tasks to be co-ordinated by the teacher-tutor

These guidelines were devised by more than 70 teachers from a wide range of schools, as they sought to develop their role as teacher-tutors.

The guidelines assume that where a new teacher is appointed the school will identify one member of staff to act as teacher-tutor, to co-ordinate the support provided within school.

The guidelines are a summary of many ideas about basic support needed by new teachers. They are not a prescription, but a statement of the kinds of support which new teachers might expect. Other teacher-tutors and new teachers may choose to amend the guidelines to suit specific circumstances. Further support may be part of a school's organized support programme.

The 'tasks' are of two main types:

1. *Specific, identifiable actions to be taken* are arranged as a check-list. Against the list the teacher-tutor may identify members of staff who have agreed to take responsibility for specific tasks. A copy of the document can then be provided for each support teacher and for the new teacher.

2. *General professional support to be communicated* is applicable to all staff who contribute to the support of new teachers. This section highlights the professional *care* which can support learning during induction into teaching. It also identifies activities which will *encourage* effective learning in the early stages of professional development.

The sections are devised according to a time-scale, from the time of appointment. This assumes the most common arrangement of appointment prior to the start of the academic year. Variation and adaptation will be needed for new teachers appointed at other times.

Teacher-tutors may also prefer to carry out some tasks at different points in the time-scale, or to review, extend or repeat some tasks at later stages.

The guidelines are intended to be used with flexibility.

Box 5.1a After appointment

Actions	*To be undertaken by:*
Introduce oneself, congratulate, welcome to the team	
Explain the teacher-tutor role	
Introduce teacher to other teaching staff	
Arrange for time to be spent with colleagues	
Tour school (in action)	
Outline ethos and expectations of school	
Provide school handbook, curriculum policy/guidelines	
Provide schemes of work	
Outline teaching responsibilities/classes to be taught	
Provide class lists (if possible at this stage)	
Survey resources	
Invite to visit school/arrange dates if possible	
Assist with residence, contract, salary matters	
Provide dates of terms and pre-school meetings	
General support	
Encourage questions	
Act as friend and get to know teacher	
Help to feel at home in school	
Provide contact telephone number	

groups centred upon how to realize the aim of making the observation of teaching 'work' effectively for the teachers' learning.

In some cases an underlying question was critical – how to obtain the opportunity to observe or be observed. That question was raised with the new teachers and an assessment made of their experience of observation in the early part of the autumn term (Table 5.7a and b). Substantial majorities of both primary and secondary teachers had not, by November, undertaken any observation of more experienced colleagues' teaching. About half of the secondary teachers, and a large majority of the primary teachers, had not been observed teaching. The question was also raised with teacher-tutors, and assessment made (during the spring term) of the need for opportunities to

Box 5.1b Prior to start of term

Actions	To be undertaken by:
Provide school routines	
Discuss curriculum policy guidelines	
Help work out timetable	
Ensure pupil records are obtained and understood	
Discuss planning/forecasts/schemes of work	
Allow time to select/prepare resources	
Instruct on use of audio-visual, computer, photocopier, etc.	
Arrange meeting with children (where possible)	
Provide maps and staff lists	
Discuss support available from other staff	
Provide information about school and locality	
Tour catchment area	
Provide information on school/LEA induction programme	
Advise on teachers' centres, libraries, other support	
Advise on professional societies and associations	
Examine college reports for/gain information about strengths and weaknesses	
Discuss special talents/weaknesses of teacher	

General Support

Be available

observe new entrants' teaching and for discussion based on observations. Seventy-one teacher-tutors recorded the opportunities which they had for observing new teachers and for discussing those observations and other teaching with them. A summary is given in Table 5.8a and b. On the assumption that observation and discussion constitutes an important mode of professional development, the evidence showed a generally unsatisfactory state of affairs. The views of the new teachers demonstrated that lack of opportunity rather than lack of will was often the reason why no observation occurred. The

Box 5.1c At start of term

Actions	*To be undertaken by:*
Ensure teacher knows school building	
Help with classroom layout	
Ensure administration/routine/duty procedures understood	
Check timetable and forecasts of work	
Ensure resources to hand	
Advise on assessment/record keeping/exams	
Inform about events in school calendar	
Ensure contact with main school personnel	
Advise on pastoral system/discipline/relationships	
Discuss parent–teacher contacts	
Discuss support and assessment	

General support

Meet before/after school – help settle in

Monitor workload/advise on time management

Ensure support from staff is seen to be available

Provide 'space' for settling in

importance of providing and using opportunities for observation at the early stages was discussed by them and they were generally keen that the advantages of such early supported learning should be gained. Later might be too late, they argued. Perhaps more importantly, the sharing of experiences with teacher-tutors (or other colleagues) would be more meaningful for them when based on lessons observed. The establishment of a 'common agenda' based on observations was seen to have considerable potential, which was not being realized for most of the teachers.

Some teacher-tutors expressed a view that new entrants should be left alone to 'settle in' at the early stages; others that once they were settled and had no 'problems' (i.e. were not in difficulty) they could be left alone. The isolationism of teaching was evident in such attitudes and ran contrary to the assumptions and aspirations of the project. However, the majority in principle saw value of engaging in observation of and discussion about teaching – either their own or the new teachers'. For them, the issue centred on the question of

Box 5.1d As first term unfolds

Actions	To be undertaken by:
Ensure regular contact/weekly dialogue	
Implement support programme in school	
Begin observation of teaching/help in classroom	
Enable observation of colleagues by new teacher	
Discuss classroom organization and display	
Discuss classroom management and discipline	
Advise on children's learning and practical skills	
Advise on support services	
Liaise with headteacher and other staff involved	
Liaise with assessor/appraiser	
Review progress	

General support

Check teacher has settled/offer general support

Give encouragement and communicate success

Encourage reflection on teaching

Listen, and respond with advice when appropriate

Encourage trying out ideas

Encourage contributions to staff meetings

opportunities and the development of expertise which would enable them to make the most of observation. Almost three-quarters of the teacher-tutors had none or only casual/occasional opportunities for observing their new colleagues. Among primary teacher-tutors that figure was almost 90 per cent. Forty-five per cent of primary tutors had no opportunities at all, because they 'carried' full teaching timetables. This was in a context where a substantial proportion of tutors were either headteachers or deputy heads – itself a situation which the project co-ordinators tried to avoid because of the assessment responsibilities which heads had in relation to new entrants.

Opportunities to conduct observation and discussion obviously related closely to previous experience in those activities, which in turn could be seen to underlie the development of expertise. Information from the teacher-tutors showed that such experience was varied, and absent in the case of 39 per cent

Box 5.1e After first term/throughout

Actions	To be undertaken by:
Continue support programme in school	
Communicate success and offer advice on weaknesses	
Distinguish and discuss formal assessment of teaching	
Discuss lesson plans	
Ensure timetable and record keeping satisfactory	
Help arrange visits to other schools	
Help arrange attendance at INSET courses	
Raise awareness of national developments	
Encourage contributions to extra-curricular activities	
General support	
Ensure confidentiality in first instance	
Engender self-appraisal	
Encourage reflection on practice	
Encourage taking more responsibility	
Work consistently with teacher through year	

of primary teacher-tutors. Among those who had some experience its frequency and nature were further indicators of the variations in expertise. Another was whether training had been undertaken in classroom observation techniques. A summary of information from the teacher-tutors (Table 5.9a–d) showed some of the variations.

The evidence provided by the new teachers and the teacher-tutors made it clear that the state of affairs with regard to the observation of teaching, and discussions about it, were mostly unsatisfactory. Most new entrants would have welcomed observation and discussion of both colleagues' teaching and their own. Few had the opportunity, for a range of reasons. Where observation of the new teachers' teaching did occur, it was sometimes for formal assessment purposes, and was thus conducted rather differently than it might otherwise have been. Sometimes observation was casual – other teachers 'came in and out'; adjacent rooms happened to be used; or someone glanced through the window occasionally. None of these arrangements could satisfactorily help the teachers to develop their teaching, or the observers develop their skills of observation and discussion. The following guidelines were developed to enable

Table 5.7 Classroom observation

(a) Observation of colleagues so far (November)	Number of teachers	
	Primary	Secondary
None	36	58
Once	5	–
More than once	2	22
No return	7	9

(b) Observation of new teachers so far (November)	Number of teachers	
	Primary	Secondary
None	33	44
Once	3	–
More than once	8	39
No return	6	6

Table 5.8 Teacher-tutors' opportunities to observe and discuss new teachers' teaching

(a) Opportunities to observe	Number of teacher-tutors	
	Primary	Secondary
None	15	2
Casual/occasional	14	21
Monthly	–	2
Weekly/regularly	3	8
When necessary	–	5

(b) Opportunities to discuss teaching	Number of teacher-tutors	
	Primary	Secondary
None	1	0
Casual exchanges	6	5
Occasional meeting		6
Half-termly meeting	1	0
Weekly/regular meeting in timetable time	4	16
Regular before/after school	23	19

Note: the figures include some who showed more than one type of opportunity.

Table 5.9 Teacher-tutors' experience and training in classroom observation

(a) Previous experience	Number of teacher-tutors	
	Primary	Secondary
None	13	3
Some	20	35

(b) Amount of previous experience	Number of teacher-tutors	
	Primary	Secondary
Regular	3	17
Occasional	15	16
	(2 no response)	(2 no response)

(c) Type of previous experience	Number of teacher-tutors	
	Primary	Secondary
Formal	3	9
Formal and informal	4	16
Informal	12	9
	(1 no response)	(1 no response)

(d) Training in observation	Number of teacher-tutors	
	Primary	Secondary
None	24	18
Some	9	20

dialogue with new entrants. It was obvious that in some schools such observation was undertaken by delegated personnel – especially heads of departments in secondary schools. Where that was the case it was agreed that the guidelines would need to be discussed with those colleagues by teacher-tutors.

Purpose The purpose of observation and discussion about teaching should be to enhance the professional development of the new teacher.

Procedure The procedure therefore should assume the nature of formative, sequenced events. These events should be based on prior agreement about what will be observed, what evidence will be sought, and how the observer can help the observed to clarify events and evaluate the teaching strategies.

Principles The observer should be a trusted colleague; credibility through regular contact and mutual discussion should be ensured, and observation should be negotiated and continuous. Sensitive listening and joint problem-solving should form the basis of professional learning.

Response Responses to evidence should first ensure explicit credit for good performance. Clear, manageable aims should be identified for problem areas, and appropriate courses of action decided after discussion of possible strategies.

The assumption about the place and value of the observation of teaching as part of professional learning was, within the project, closely linked to the aim to establish and support reflective practice as a main principle of induction. It was believed that the teachers themselves would often (though not always) be in the best position to judge their teaching, and in collaboration with colleagues to judge which aspects of it needed to be developed. That approach was seen as complementary to assessment procedures, and as potentially offering a good basis for longer-term professional development. Such an approach, coupled with the purposes and principles of observation by, of, or with colleagues set out above was seen as a way of guiding and supporting the 'strategic redefinition' of aspects of teaching.

However, before 'exposing' aspects of teaching which may need improving it was thought to be important that the new teachers should first identify the contributions which they made to the schools. Those contributions – the qualities and activities of the teachers – were a frequent topic of discussion and positive comment among teacher-tutors. Yet a feature of the new entrants' discussions was that they themselves consistently and predominantly talked of the 'problems' and 'difficulties' in their searches for 'improvement' in their teaching. Many seemed reticent about reporting solutions and successes. For example, the individual 'difficult' pupil often dominated discussions, disproportionately displacing report or comment about several hundred (in the case of secondary teachers) successes. In order to focus first on successes the teachers were asked to identify up to five aspects of teaching in which they had made or were making some significant contribution to the work of the school. Many said that they took all aspects of their work as 'normal', including aspects of skill, expertise, knowledge, personal qualities, or activities which they as individuals had brought to the school and which were likely to be appreciated by members of that school. We discussed how such contributions might be part of classroom teaching or stretch beyond it to other areas of school life. Some 127 teachers recorded identifiable contributions which were later collated within a number of categories. Those categories, which included a substantial number of responses, are listed in Table 5.10a.

Table 5.10 (a) Review of contributions made to the school/department by new teachers

	N	127 (%)
Specialist subject strength or specific knowledge within subject	90	74
Curriculum initiatives – subject matter, organization, visits, introducing new topics, preparing guidelines, etc.	78	61
Extra-curricula activities	61	48
New teaching methods	54	42
Leadership of colleagues in curriculum	51	40
Specific responsibilities – organization, management, resources, etc.	43	34
Resources – production, acquisition, organization	40	31
Pastoral tutoring/personal and social education	30	24
Introducing/using new technology for teaching	28	22
Children with special education needs	10	8
INSET participation/feedback to staff	9	7
Tracking national developments	4	3

Example

List up to five aspects of teaching in which you have made/are making special contributions to the work of your school. Show if these are known by colleagues.

1. Introduction of a weekly science club, open to all pupils. Provides opportunities to repeat experiments, try out new activities, watch videos, etc. Known about by most staff and pupils.
2. Introducing regular use of computer in science lessons. Pushing ahead with obtaining scientific software. Known about by head, science and computing staff.
3. Contributing to development of year group profiles; member of profile working party. Known about by deputy head and related staff.
4. Have set up string group, completely new (violins, viola, cello). Conduct, arrange music, fetch and carry music from county

Table 5.10 (b) Review of potential contributions to the school/department by new teachers

Area of potential contribution	N	92 (%)	127 (%)
Subject knowledge/qualification not used	76	83	60
Teaching method/organization of learning	40	43	31
Extra-curricula activity from special strength	28	30	22
New technology for teaching	19	21	15
Production, acquisition, organization of resources	11	12	9
Pastoral tutoring/personal and social education/careers	10	11	8
Use environment/arrange visits	9	10	7
Teaching special needs children	3	3	2
Multicultural education	1	1.1	0.8
INSET for colleagues	1	1.1	0.8
Fund-raising	1	1.1	0.8

hall. Known about by head, deputies, most staff and interested pupils.

5. Cultivating the display of pupils' work, together with relevant, up-to-date items of science news' in an attractive way. Known about by deputy head, head of science and most pupils.

It was also realized that some new teachers felt that they had skills and expertise which, for a range of reasons, were not being used in their schools. That problem was reflected in *The New Teacher in School* report (DES, 1988a). Within the project the extent of this problem was at first only an impression, derived from comment. It seemed important to determine how far potential contributions were lying dormant. Within the same notion of 'special contribution' – skill, knowledge, expertise, personal qualities or activities which individuals brought to the school – teachers were asked to identify up to five aspects of teaching in which they had contributions to make, but did not have the opportunity. Ninety-two teachers felt that they had unrealized potential of some kind. These 'talents' were later listed within categories which were almost identical to Table 5.10a and are given in Table 5.10b. An example of the responses following each table illustrates the kind of details provided by the teachers. It also shows that the perceived reasons for not being able to realize the full use of talents was recorded by the teachers. Those reasons, identified by 85 teachers, were also listed and formed a number of general and common categories of constraint (Table 5.10c).

Table 5.10 (c) Reasons for not making contributions

	N	85 (%)	127 (%)
Lack of time	38	45	30
Lack of resources, equipment, space	34	40	27
School structure/organization	29	34	23
Other staff expectations	28	33	22
Senior staff not supportive	27	32	21
Lack of confidence/status at this stage	13	15	10
Lack of competence to support an interest	12	14	9
Lack of interest/motivation among pupils	7	8	5.5
Parameters of curriculum guidelines	6	7	5
Parameters of job description	3	4	2
Legal constraint	2	2.5	1.5
Lack of children!	1	1.1	0.8

Example

List up to five aspects of teaching in which you have a special contribution to make, but do not have the opportunity. Show if you have tried to implement them or not. If possible give reasons why you have not been able to succeed.

1. Have a particular interest in, and reasonable knowledge of, astronomy. Would like to start club, visit observatories, etc. School has been given a large telescope which needs setting up. Not tried. Reasons: time does not allow at present.

2. Photography is available as a GCSE science module. Would like to do this, but insufficient materials and resources. Not tried. Reasons: no money (yet) for resources. Will be trying for it in future.

3. The aspect of pastoral care – counselling skills, etc. Tried. Am trying. Would like opportunities to attend courses, etc.

In seeking to make the induction year a basis for longer-term inservice professional development the idea of encouraging teachers to identify aspects of their teaching which needed developing, and supporting them in their development, was a key element. There was no reluctance to do so on their part. Indeed, the emphasis during discussions was on problematic issues which could be regarded as endemic in teaching, and which the teachers wanted to tackle. By the spring term they had been given a view of their progress from formal assessors. They had also had some time to 'sift out' from the initial plethora of teaching's immediate concerns some specific continuing ones. It was at that point in the initial and research project teachers' experiences that they were

Table 5.11   Aspects of teaching needing development

	N	127 (%)
Teaching methods in specific aspects of teaching or relating to specific course – e.g. reception class, A level, TVEI, pre-vocational	81	64
Providing for range of pupils' needs/levels of work	43	34
Knowledge of available resources	43	34
Pastoral care, tutor group, PSE, careers	10	8
New technology	35	27.5
Management of lessons – phasing, timing, resources, voice	32	25
Subject knowledge	28	22
Classroom organization – pupils, space, equipment, etc.	27	21
Discipline	23	18
Assessment, marking, record-keeping, report writing	23	18
Cross-curricular links	12	9
Planning curriculum and recording events	11	9
Display	7	5.5

often seen to be 'OK' by colleagues and when support effectively lapsed. In the extension project we aimed to maintain the impetus for learning in a supported environment, while shifting the opportunities and initiatives to the teachers. The aspiration was that such initiatives, taken up by the teachers themselves, would gain the support not only of teacher-tutors but of other colleagues in school or in other schools. We hoped that by this means the individual concerns of teachers would be addressed, rather than pursuing some illusory 'common issue' during support-programme meetings.

The teachers were asked to instigate a plan for a programme of self-development for the second half of the year and to identify up to five aspects of their teaching to which they would give priority for development. They were asked to give a brief description of the 'problem', to identify the type of support needed, and to indicate if the support was available (to the best of their knowledge). The range of aspects of teaching which were thus suggested, and the types of support perceived by the teachers as needed to help development in specific aspects are listed in Tables 5.11 and 5.12 respectively.

The tables were discussed with teacher-tutors, and the new teachers were

Table 5.12 Types of support identified as needed for developing aspects of practical teaching

	N	%
Advice from teacher-tutor/discussion with colleagues	54	42.5
Observation of colleague(s) teaching	46	36
Visits to other school(s) to observe/discuss teaching	42	33
INSET course	39	31
Material resources	37	29
Advice and information from advisers/specialists	29	23
Time for preparation	26	20
Experience, practice, reflection	6	5
Self-discipline	6	5
Team teaching	5	4
Liaison with other schools/transfer of pupils	5	4
Being observed by colleague(s)	4	3
Discuss with other new teachers	3	2.4
Safety training	2	1.6
Contact with other professionals attached to schools	1	0.78

asked to discuss their individual plans with the tutors, other colleagues or advisers, in order to refine and implement them. Implementation began in the latter part of the spring term and continued into the summer term. It was at that point that visits to other schools or use of time for observation within their own schools were supported by project funds to help to get the programme of self-development off the ground.

From the outset the project was conceived, and represented to all those who participated, as a development project. There was much to learn about the support needs of new teachers and of teacher-tutors, and of how best to provide for both. Some lessons had already been learned from the initial project, and some action had been taken to improve provision. In taking such action and to further the quality of support, it was intended that the work of the first year should be a collaborative venture, in which new teachers, teacher-tutors and project co-ordinators worked together to develop practice. The new teachers themselves contributed to the development, as well as receiving support, through information which gave a picture of their needs, their work, and their contributions to their own induction. Teacher-tutors contributed by defining a 'representative' view of their roles. It was a matter of faith on my part that the development of support for new teachers within their schools would result from the project. The activities did however provide a basis for future work, especially for schools which might at a later stage receive new teachers for the first time, or intermittently. My own actions were in co-ordinating the programme, and devising support and development activities which also contributed research, and collating the ideas and perspectives of new teachers and teacher-tutors which were fed back through the cycle of meetings. Through that collaboration it was possible to examine and begin to formulate both principles and practices, in ways which might 'ensure that induction is effectively arranged and delivered' (DES, 1988a).

I felt confident in claiming that most of the aims (see p. 162) were largely achieved. For example, a substantial picture of the basic needs of new entrants and teacher-tutors (aims 1 and 2) was gained. Co-ordination ensured that a teacher-tutor was available to support all new teachers (aim 3). The induction programme also provided information about the education service and national developments directly to the teachers (aim 4) and offered counselling support (aim 5). The framework for in-school support procedures and practices, agreed by a large number of teacher-tutors who can be seen as representative, was established (aim 6).

The achievement of aims 7, 8 and 9 depended largely on the work of the teacher-tutors in schools. Without question, effective induction depended first and foremost on the relationships and activities of the new teachers and their teacher-tutors (and other close colleagues). Of the nine aims of the project the biggest challenge was to articulate the vision of aims 7, 8 and 9 and to persuade all teacher-tutors and new entrants to adopt that vision. That challenge was based on the premiss that it was not sufficient to establish a scheme for teacher induction unless that scheme articulated clear principles for teacher professional development which were shared by participants. The particular principles were in turn based on a premiss that it would be possible to fulfil the potential professional development of new teachers by sustaining their learning through reflection, observation, discussion and collaborative enquiry. Once those principles could be widely established I hoped that the actions and conduct of the participants within the scheme might be consistent in quality across schools. Within the work of the project there was considerable evidence, some of which is included in this book, that these aims were not fully achieved.

In that work the teacher-tutors' previous experiences, current opportunities, visions, and competences were evidently very varied. Some had worked with new teachers consistently over many years, during which substantial detailed programmes of support had been devised and developed. They had time, as did the new teachers in their schools, to follow those programmes, including regular observation and discussion. They had visions of new entrants as contributors to school life who needed learning opportunities and support to sustain extended professional development. These were backed by tutoring qualities, acquired through experience and opportunities. Others had not had a new member of staff, let alone a new teacher, start in their school for many years. The teacher-tutor responsibilities had been allocated suddenly, and they needed to know what to do in circumstances where neither they nor the new teacher had non-teaching time. Those differences were matched by varying perspectives on how to work with new entrants. Yet within those differences the importance in principle of classroom observation, discussion and reflection upon practice was seen as central in the support and learning of the new teachers by all participants. There was consensus support for aims 7, 8 and 9 and project activities were characterized by debates about how to achieve them. Perhaps, as I will show later, the discussion should have been about precisely what the aims meant.

Activities were also characterized by expressions of considerable frustration by new teachers and tutors in trying to achieve those particular aims. That was because observation, discussion and reflection (however loosely defined their nature and purpose was), especially when developed concurrently with, and centrally to, building new relationships, were seen to require time which was often not available either to use or to develop the qualities and competences needed for those practices. Here the project involved the new teachers (and in some respects the teacher-tutors) in observation of, discussion about, and reflection on their own classroom practice. But in addition it asked both to observe, discuss and reflect upon their relationships, dialogue, and conduct of support programmes. It was a premiss of the work that participants should not simply use tutoring skills but should also be willing to investigate that use in order to improve the quality of support for new entrants, and to engage in open dialogue about the problematic nature of teaching.

A priority for that investigation might have been to seek clarification of the purposes, procedures and benefits of observation, discussion and reflection. These were often assumed, implicit, and unclear, despite the consensus about their importance among tutors. Of course, using and developing these activities also enabled tutors to question and investigate the premises and assumptions on which the aims were based. The focus of attention, however, was reflection on when and how tutor support of this kind was conducted, rather than why. This is illustrated in one recommendation from the project:

> [there is a need to provide] professional development for
> teacher-tutors in the qualities, skills, and techniques associated
> with tutoring — especially observation of and discussion about
> teaching ... matched by opportunities in which to develop
> those qualities and skills through practice.

The new teachers themselves did question the value and the conduct of observation. Table 5.12 clearly indicates that in the development of their teaching few listed being observed as a type of support needed. That is contrary to HMI's 1988 claims and to the views expressed earlier in the year by the project teachers themselves. The reasons for this low rating of observation were not investigated during the project. However, the indications did raise a challenge to the assumptions on which some crucial aspects of the project were based. The potential value of observation of teaching, to provide a 'shared agenda' or focus for discussion, had been central to the initial project. Recognition of the inadequacies in practice of classroom observation led to a proposal in the extension project that only one teacher-tutor should develop a close and sustained relationship, to replace the occasional visits of numerous 'tutors'. The question of the conduct of observation and discussion was a matter addressed by the tutors during the extension project in some detail, discussed above. Their value was merely assumed. Table 5.12 was devised from information gathered half-way through the year. The teachers had indicated that observation of their teaching, in their view, should be conducted early in the year to be of greatest benefit, by helping them identify initial 'problems'. At this later stage they were able to select substantial aspects of their teaching for development and to propose a range of means for pursuing their learning. The criteria and the quality of analysis on which such aspects of teaching were selected, and the appropriateness of means for learning, all remain problematic and deserve full investigation.

This project confirmed that, despite all aspirations to the contrary, it is likely that much of new teachers' practice and learning occurs, and will continue to occur, through private experience. That is the reality of the context of 'autonomous professional self-development'. Stenhouse (1975, p. 142) conceded that it would require a generation of work and changes in the teacher's professional self-image and conditions of work if the majority of teachers were to become teacher-researchers. His aspiration, like Lortie's, was for all teachers to become 'extended professionals' characterized by commitment to systematic questioning of one's own teaching as a basis for development; commitment and skills to study one's own teaching; and concern to question and to test theory in practice by the use of those skills. Within this 'capacity for autonomous professional self-development through systematic self-study', Stenhouse regarded readiness to be observed by others and to discuss one's teaching as 'highly desirable, though perhaps not essential' (Stenhouse, 1975, pp. 143–4). There was ambiguity in his position here:

> A teacher who wishes to take a research and development
> stance to his own teaching may profit at certain stages in the
> development of his research by the presence of an observer in
> his classroom.
> (Stenhouse, 1975, p. 155)

Cautiously treading the path of joint teacher research, open discussion and the establishment of 'unusual sensitivity and good personal relationships on both sides', Stenhouse also begged for the moon. He sought a 'general acceptance of the proposition that all teachers should be learners' and the creation of a 'public research methodology and accepted professional ethic' as a basis for observing the teaching of colleagues.

On professional self-image and conditions of work, teachers have not advanced in the generation which has since passed. Yet with regard to those commitments to professional self-development the evidence from this large group of new teachers is that professional self-development commitments exist and are acted upon. What was and is problematic is what is an appropriate research methodology for new teachers, given those commitments without conditions where observation by and relationships with tutors can become systematic and sustained? It was not a case of whether these teachers aspired to develop their teaching, but a question of how it might be developed. It was also clear from the teachers' responses (Table 5.12) that personal experience, practice and reflection were not seen as a valuable means of learning. Only 5 per cent included reflective practice among the types of support needed for developing their teaching. That represented a major challenge to the assumptions of aim 8 of the extension project: 'to establish and support reflective practice as a main principle of induction.' The identified need for time and material resources, unsurprisingly, featured as a high priority. Of the other types of support identified by 25 per cent or more of the teachers, all represented a recognition of more experienced colleagues as the source of learning. The colour of apprenticeship in its teaching-bastardized form – i.e. not with one master, but under or in search of many – appeared to be very bright. Yet I remained concerned that such an approach not only would not and could not enhance, but in some respects could serve to undermine, both aims 8 and 9: 'to make the induction year a basis for longer-term inservice professional development.' This presented an interesting conundrum alongside the initial and research project data which I needed to spend some time puzzling about. It was this puzzling that took the emerging constellations of concepts much further than after the initial project. This was especially so with regard to the question of reflective practice – both its conceptual adequacy as my central aim; and its place among the many players in the induction projects.

Chapter 6

Deliberations on Teacher Induction and Reflective Professional Practice

IMAGES OF TEACHER EDUCATION

It might have been expected that the review of research and analysis of policy on teacher induction would provide some guidance for the practical task with which I had been charged. As I have shown, what it revealed was several persistent issues. First, there are historical assumptions about the learner teacher as an apprentice to a master practitioner, which rest in tension with my own and others' aspirations for a different view of the long-term self-education of teachers. Secondly, economic and financial limits prevent either an apprenticeship scheme of induction, or provision for other longer-term education of teachers, leaving induction to be perceived as a test of competence, and learning in this period of professional development to chance. Thirdly, there is little conception in policy of what progress, development, or improvement in teaching quality is about. Fourthly, there is no single coherent academic/scholarly view of development in learning to teach. Combined, these left agreed principles and practice for induction unobtained (and possibly unobtainable). Since there is no consideration of the *education* of new teachers in recent reforms, that situation also appeared likely to continue. Practices have thus been left to chance, often amounting to whatever individual teachers can make of their circumstances. Not only did different concepts of teacher education seem to reside together uneasily, they were often tacitly held, in policy, in teacher education research, and among those responsible for induction. These formed another constellation of ideas which it seemed necessary to explore, and had a bearing on the nature of induction into teaching which was experienced by the projects' teachers. I believed, for example, that my own ideas about reflective practice and research-based teaching were clear. I soon came to question my views in the face of experience with the teachers, and also because attacks on teacher education from the political right intensified, as well as through reading a number of new publications on action research and reflective practice. It was important to elucidate the different 'images' or orientations to teacher education in order to appreciate more fully where my own ideas were located ideologically, as well as epistemologically, in the realms of teacher education. I detected several identifiably different sets of assumptions about teacher education.

The concept of *apprenticeship* in which the training of student teachers was carried out entirely by teachers in schools was a major feature of the nineteenth century. Its residual influence is manifest in the *practicum* aspect of more recent institution-based training. Under direct instruction or by example from the master, and with close monitoring of subsequent practice, the novice in this form of training is intended to learn to perform proven techniques of instruction. As a concept it has recently been brought to prominence again by some proposals to abolish institution-based teacher education in favour of a return to 'on the job' training (Hillgate, 1989; Lawlor, 1990). In practice, it seems that since the pupil-teacher and monitorial systems, only vestiges of apprenticeship have remained, and that these have been concerned with classroom technique alone, rather than with, say, the development of educational values.

That approach is reflected in the partial apprenticeship of institution and school-based programmes which proposed and operated systematized training in pre-specified teaching skills, with subsequent monitoring of observable performance against measurable objectives. This has been referred to as *competency-based* or *performance-based* teacher training. It has also been defined as *technical rationality* (Schon, 1971; Munro, 1989). Its foundation in behaviourism and rational planning or objectives-based curricula has been summarized by Munro (1989).

For the project teachers, a notable manifestation of these concepts was in the performance schedules used for the assessment of their teaching. Another was in their predominant concerns with the mastery of technique towards the 'capital T' mode of working, and the deproblematizing of practice. In terms of a mode of acquisition of competence, however, there was very little evidence of apprenticeship. The picture was one of self-reliant and largely solitary acquisition of technical competence, with occasional commentary and support but virtually no virtuoso performance from a master to be observed. Even 'sitting with Nellie' – the common image of observation in initial training – was rarely a part of their procedures for learning, though it remained an aspiration to utilize observation as a source of learning 'good practice'. Elliott (1991b) has called this the *social market* view of teacher education, one in which the outcomes of professional learning are seen as tangible, observable, and hence readily saleable, specific behavioural competences.

Both apprenticeship and performance-based approaches assume elements of skill development through practice, and improvement through experience in skill application. However, the formal structures of apprenticeship and monitoring by a master practitioner, and the pre-specification of programmes of purportedly identifiable and discrete skills, separate those modes from another notion of experiential teacher education. This rather more implicit or 'intuitive' view allows for the novice teacher to work alone in a classroom in the faith that he or she will act as a constructor of expertise based on that experience. It can thus be regarded as an *experiential/constructionist* image of learning teaching. Alongside apprenticeship for elementary school teachers, such unsupported experience was common for secondary teachers in the nineteenth century. It still pertains for some teachers in independent schools even now, and can be detected in some views of provision for new teachers. It is not always clear in some recent proposals of the radical right, which would abolish institution-based teacher education in favour of direct entry into teaching, whether they envisage systematic and sustained apprenticeship training, or experiential/constructionist learning. There are some who have suggested that no learning is necessary beyond the prior acquisition of subject knowledge.

Within the possible variants of the concept of experiential learning, it was this mode of acquisition of practical knowledge which predominated in these teachers' experience. It was also one which was presumed to be either inevitable, or adequate, or both, by the teachers and some support colleagues. However, it seems that whatever the intentions of providers of such experience, or inadequacies of provision which leave it as the *de-facto* mode of learning, it was from such circumstances that the extensive thoughtfulness of the teachers emerged. The question of what that reflection was about has already been addressed – a focus particularly on technical and clinical aspects of teaching, on practical problem-solving. Formulated crudely, the focus on what should be taught and how, rather than why features of education are as they are or ought to be different, characterizes the technical–rationality view of teacher education and its varied modes of skill acquisition. Perhaps because of the way in which that focus is conceived, and appears to predominate in widely held assumptions about teacher education, there have been perpetual debates in recent years about the relevance of theory to practice (Elliott, 1989, 1991a; Goodson, 1992).

Those arguments have been particularly noticeable since the increase in institution-based teacher education, both in terms of numbers of students and length of courses in the 1960s, and the shift toward all-graduate entry in the 1970s, which led to initial teacher training curricula adopting academic study in foundation disciplines of educational sociology, psychology, philosophy and history. This partial mantle of *theory-based teacher education* has been a butt of criticism ever since. Accounts of the growth and limitations (both in extent and conception) of theory-based teacher education were reviewed, summarized and discussed in Tickle (1987a). Its problems were perceived on the one hand by utilitarian-minded teachers as a lack of practical value in the theoretical perspectives, methodological concerns and substantive accounts of the disciplines. On the other hand, the New Right wanted what they called Marxist perspectives banned. Theory-based teacher education assumptions about rationality, based in questioning along the 'why?' axis of educational enquiry, seek to develop theoretical understanding of educational values and principles as a basis for good practice (Elliott, 1991b). I had not set out in the research to identify residual elements of learning from these kinds of theoretical perspectives. If there were such elements they were largely embedded in the teachers' aims and strategies rather than in overtly expressed beliefs. It seemed that alongside the focus on teaching technique and task-proficiency, more strategic considerations about how to realize aims in practice were based on pragmatic problem-solving, with some evidence of consciously explicated 'theory' (of the kind presented in initial training, and referred to explicitly as such) being applied and tested in classrooms.

From within the academic community a different kind of critique of the theory–practice relationship (Carr, 1987, 1988, 1989; Elliott, 1989, 1991a) emerged during the 1970s and 1980s. This led to what might be characterized as a *critical revisionist* view of teacher education. Proponents of this image would have teachers and teacher educators to be democratically active in the critique of institutional and social conditions in which schooling is located, as a means of advancing educational opportunity and achievement. A principal aspiration of this view is to make teachers more conscious of the structural limitations upon social progress toward 'true' democracy. The place of schooling as a state structure which limits the participation of individuals in processes of social change is a focus of attention; the idea that teachers may become agents of change is a focus of hope. Again, there was some suggestion that the initial and research project teachers adopted such perspectives, in so far as they might have been reflected in concerns that, for example, the achievement of maximum learning potential of every individual was being frustrated either by their own 'failings' or the circumstances in which they worked. These broadly expressed concerns seemed to pervade the views of the teachers. However, each seemed to see the possibilities of achieving such aims as residing mainly in their own efforts to devise 'the best' teaching strategies within their imagination, for the given circumstances in which they worked, or to make moderate adjustments to the facilities, for example, additional seating, multi-media resources, use of computers, and the supplementation of visual materials. While these were important priorities for change in the teachers' work, they rest within the range of technical means for achieving their aims, rather than changing the social context of schooling which a critical-revisionist approach would seek to promote.

In those circumstances it appeared that the route to 'the best' within the teachers' own capacities was to be the route of reflection as a means of self-criticism. Those modes of reflection represent, and I wish to claim illuminate, the *reflective/revisionist* image of teachers, teaching and teacher education. I have elaborated this view as *research-based teacher education* elsewhere (Tickle, 1987a). However, it now appears to be much more complex than I had assumed then, with nuances emphasized by different proponents, in greater and lesser clarity. Its general essence may be taken as incorporating and subsuming technical skills within professional practice which is based on effective judgement and action. In the development of skill, judgement and action, teachers are deemed to need to take comprehensive account of evidence in the situation, as well as the potential consequences of action. The mode of teacher education curriculum is to develop professional dispositions which constantly subject skill, judgement and action to scrutiny. This is the Stenhousian notion of professional development and the Schonian view adopted and reflected in numerous recent accounts of research and arguments for enhancing the education of teachers. It is an image elaborated by Elliott (1991b) as the *practical science* view of teacher education, which I want to explore in detail later on the basis of the data from the teachers presented so far.

The classification and labels which I have used are variants on other authors' analyses of teacher education (Munro, 1989; Zimpher and Howey, 1987). These images have different epistemological foundations and attract ideologically different disciples and proponents, as I have suggested already. They are often represented in the assumptions of policy or the aims, programmes and practices of teacher education curricula. Because the images only exist by virtue of the attachment of individuals to those differences and those individuals come together within institutions, it is likely that they will coexist as much as compete, and in some cases blend or form mergers. However, the different orientations have considerable implications for the educational experiences of teachers, since those different foundations and ideological attachments necessarily translate into particular policies, administrative arrangements, curriculum aims, programme content and pedagogical processes. Those implications apply to the induction and inservice education of teachers as much as they do to initial training. Initially I became conscious that aspects of these images were manifest among the participants in the development projects. Their elaboration might help to locate my aims for the projects and their underlying assumptions (the reflective/revisionist image) in relation to other approaches. What became especially clear to me through this analysis was that while the aims and my conduct of the project were located within the research-based image of teachers' learning which I personally held, this was not a clear and coherent image either in my own mind or in the literature. Nor was it necessarily understood, nor necessarily subscribed to, by the teachers themselves and others involved in their support and development. In particular I became quizzical about the relationship between technical competence in the skills of teaching and what had seemingly become a catchword for a mode of professional development: reflective practice. The relationship between the different orientations to teacher education, and the nature of each of them but especially of *reflection*, was considered partly under provocation from Zimpher and Howey's notions of competence.

COMPETENCES AND SOCIAL STRATEGIES

In the conduct and research of the initial project, the concepts of technical, clinical, personal and critical competences, explicated by Zimpher and Howey, were applied to the data, initially in detail in the case of Pauline. The use of that model of competences helped me to reveal aspects of the teachers' thinking and elements of practice which suggest that attention was grounded in the 'technical' and 'clinical' realms. 'Personal' competence, I argued, involved reflective testing of theory against evidence of classroom practice through being 'conscious of what I'm doing and why'. The application of personal competence in the form of increased confidence, and its development through a process of sensing success and feeling failure, seemed to lead to taking of initiatives, involving risk, and changes in teaching strategies which brought about further testing of technical and clinical competences. The interrelationship of these elements seemed intrinsic to the tasks of teaching, and to its improvement through clarification and understanding of actions and events.

It is these relationships which remain unclear in theoretical literature, as Zimpher and Howey point out. However, in the initial project (and also in the extension project) it appears that I was implicitly concerned with developing the technical and problem-solving reflectiveness of the teachers first and foremost. That, I can now see, may be why I was seduced by the ideas of Schon, reading them as I did as an elaboration of action research without attending to the complexities of the latter, or of Schon's ideas. But I was also implicitly concerned to effect systematic change in education in a more general sense, through the agency of critical practice by the teachers. That was the appeal of action research, and especially of the concept of strategic redefinition within the notion of social strategy explicated by Lacey.

The initial project teachers provided the opportunity to observe their practice in social and material contexts, making it possible to test out the concept of social strategies and to consider its importance in their professional development. On the basis of my work with all six new teachers, the concept of teaching competences was linked to the concept of social strategies, as I tried to make sense not only of what and how they learned, but also of their social interactions. The notions of strategic compliance, internalized adjustment, and strategic redefinition, as they had been developed and used by Zeichner and Tabachnick (1985), seemed appropriate for describing different responses of the teachers to their situations. One problem was that I was not simply concerned with describing those responses, but I had an implicit interest in fostering the capacity of teachers to redefine both their own work and their circumstances where appropriate. That interest was in the pursuit of aspects of my own educational aims, both for them as professionals and for the service of their pupils. Those aims are concerned with maximizing the educational advancement, and by inference the life chances of every individual in the economic and social structure. Such aims imply the necessary adoption of a critical perspective on the effects of teaching, of institutions, and of social structures, based on the premiss that such chances are denied to large sections of the population, and that schooling plays a part in that denial. It was in this respect that the concept of critical competence seemed to overlap in both its nature and its appeal with the social strategy of redefinition. However, I did not set out explicitly to pursue these interests, or to foster that strategy or type of competence. Those aims were submerged within the broad, and what I now regard as vague, aim of developing reflective practice. Although I had not previously voiced it, it is possible to make sense of my promotion of reflective practice only in terms of my own educational aims. Why else should I want to encourage reflective practice? In turn my interest in describing the work and learning of the teachers was to understand more fully where those aims were being realized, and where frustrated, in order to effect further action where that was deemed necessary.

However, implicit in Zeichner and Tabachnick's use of the concept of strategies is a notion of pre-formed and stable teachers' perspectives which were 'brought' to a school situation by new teachers. Data from the initial project teachers and analysis around the concept of competences suggested the need for a more dynamic extension of the idea of social strategies, to accommodate the intra- as well as inter-professional strategies of the teachers. So, for example, where technical and clinical competence were 'proven' (though not necessarily 'complete'), and evident to colleagues, these may have enabled the redefinition of the practices of colleagues. In Pauline's case the latter was achieved unwittingly very early in the year, as well as intentionally later.

On the other hand, where such competence was in doubt in the views of the teachers themselves, as in the cases of Diane and Richard, demands for compliance, and willingness to comply, in 'difficult' material and social settings, appeared to subvert and lose the potential of developing their practice, at the level of technical and clinical competences. In these instances there appeared to be a serious thwarting of initiative-taking, and of the possibilities of professional self-development. It is that element which seemed to be missing from the concept of social strategies, and which made the idea of compliance especially too simplistic. What it implies is teachers forgoing their predetermined perspectives in favour of practices in which they do not believe. Of course, that is a possibility in circumstances where very different power positions are held, as in Richard's case. But it is also possible that these new teachers were sufficiently attentive to a range of ideas and open to change, as in Lesley's case, for example, that neither compliance, internalized adjustment nor strategic redefinition satisfactorily conceptualize the dynamic of the interaction of ideas. That in turn signals an area of potential difficulty, for the teachers, and for induction generally. It is this. The conduct of teaching skills and application of clinical judgements represent the practical performance toward the realization of educational aims. Unless those competences are driven by well-formulated aims they would be educationally meaningless acts; mere technique, as used by Stenhouse, would mean the unthinking mimicry of craft labour, or the conduct of actions not based on educational principles. (I have in mind, say, keeping children busy for the sake of social order, or keeping children quiet for the sake of personal comfort.) But is it realistic, or reasonable, to assume that new teachers have well-formulated aims on which to base practice, or that even if they do, those aims should be treated as fixed?

While I came to ask that question, my interim analysis suggested that the teachers were mainly concerned with effecting action which was guided by often covert, sometimes overt, but established aims.

If my interim analysis of the data from the six teachers was correct, the relationship between technical, clinical and personal competences and their 'in-tandem' development would need to be considered within the notion of reflective practice toward further work in the extension project. So would the establishment of conditions which secured that development. It was for these reasons that in the extension project I attempted to take account of the individuality of teachers and teacher-tutors, and of the uniqueness of their circumstances, as a means of establishing structures within which those different realms of competence, and the possibility of redefining situations, could be addressed. Yet all of this left a persistent question still to be explored. I realized that my own conceptions of research-based teaching and of reflective practice were not clear. The nature of the project activities and the research of the teachers' experiences provoked a frequent challenge to address the conception of research which I had brought to 'research-based teaching'. For it seemed that personal competence, the development of aims and values, the redefinition of situations, and the critical appraisal of situations and ideas did not feature noticeably either in the conception of the project or the work and learning of the teachers. One question which arises is, was that an artefact of my own making? Or was I, like the teachers, more concerned with realizing aims than with clarifying and questioning them? Am I, as part of the profession, subject to the same limitations of imagination as I had begun to detect and implicitly to criticize among the teachers?

REFLECTIVE PRACTICE

The curiosity to explore what I increasingly regarded as vaguely held ideas (by me at least) – i.e. reflective practice and research-based teaching – was fuelled by my own experience of trying to research my actions and their effects. It was also affected by the dissection of images of teacher education, and the desire to explore the reflective-revisionist image further in its conceptual form. Perhaps more so, it was fuelled by the interpretive research of the new teachers' thinking and its relationship to practice, especially as this was revealed by the research group. That research, like my role in the induction projects, had been stimulated by an impression of Schon's concepts of reflection-in- and reflection-on-action. Consideration of orientations to educational research, elaboration of the conception of research-based teaching, and the development of what might be an appropriate view of teachers 'becoming effective researchers' seemed essential. The view I had gained of the teachers' reflectiveness did not square with conceptions of action research, at least as they were held residually in my mind. There were also paradoxes in the data from the teachers which suggested

that the development of technical and clinical competence led to deproblematization and lack of reflection about certain aspects of teaching. That
needed to be explored in relation to the theoretical concepts, in order to feed
back through my understanding into action in the projects, and in my teaching
more widely.

The apparent importance of reflection and its place in the redefinition of
individual teachers' professional practice was signified in the data from the
group of five especially, that is, Sue, Liz, Kathy, Debbie and Dave. This
revealed how professional judgements were made through modes of experimenting and attendant modes of reflection in relation to experience. There were also
manifest examples of this process observed among the initial project six.
Here, the concepts of reflection-in-action and reflection-on-action provided a
theme for the interpretation of data and a conceptual tool for showing how the
teachers examined their own practice. It was possible to elaborate the concepts by showing how reflection was invoked in different ways in making
judgements – through on-the-spot handling of information; mentally predicting events; immediately evaluating events; remembering critical incidents;
connecting evaluations to prior predictions; and so on. This elaboration of the
concept of reflection was seen in the context of the circumstances of learning
teaching largely in isolation. I developed a number of metaphors from the data
to illustrate that elaboration, especially those of being *en route* and *going
through it*. At this stage, being *en route* and *going through it* provided the
sources of data which the teachers needed to interpret in order to make sense
of experience. The metaphors of *playing it by ear* and *playing the hunch*,
through the performance of *mental gymnastics* in volatile and unpredictable
circumstances, were derived from the data to characterize the immediacy of
reflective practice, in a context of inaccessible and insecure data. Playing it by
ear and playing the hunch were modes of experimenting which incorporated
the various procedures of reflection described as mental gymnastics. The
metaphors of *minding, monitoring* and *mirroring* were derived from the data
to characterize the driving force behind the longer-term reflective process.
Minding, monitoring and mirroring were in a sense representative of the rules
of rigour in thinking about teaching and achieving 'effectiveness', as well as an
ethical dimension. My concern at this stage was with the challenge which this
data presented to my presuppositions about research-based teaching, and
especially to try to equate these reflective activities with the notion of research.

In terms of the notion of reflective practice the research group teachers'
accounts, like the work with the six initial project teachers, certainly provide
evidence of their thoughtfulness. Their deliberations on the detailed tasks of
teaching; particular incidents and actions; specific teaching strategies; longer-
term reviews of, and prospects for, schemes of work with students; their own
feelings at particular moments; and their image of themselves in relation to the
job of teaching, showed something of the range of phenomena which came in
for reflective attention. This was a busy reflective process. Of that, I think,

there can be no doubt. But it was not the focused, systematic enquiry assumed by 'models' of action research. Rather, it was a recognition of the pace of events of classroom life and the need to handle so much evidence at once, elicited by pragmatic methods. The unreliable nature of evidence also had to be handled. Its inaccessibility needed to be taken into account. These were problems of teaching being encountered extensively during the first year. Those problems applied to the self and the emotions as much as to practical teaching, for they were also about one's identity as a teacher, how one 'copes' emotionally with the tasks of teaching, and how one learns about that coping process.

In this informational anarchy there was, unsurprisingly I would suggest, a search for order. The attempts to deproblematize teaching, to 'know' that life could be secure in proven actions, seemed to be a major impetus underlying much of their reflective thinking. Given their view of teaching as a practical activity, learned from the experience of doing it, that search for security was mostly about minor (but myriad) administrative tasks, organizational arrangements, managerial proficiency, teaching techniques and pedagogical strategies. These realms of practice were largely what I had previously called the prerequisites of professional credibility (Tickle, 1987a), and what the teachers saw as the medals of 'capital T teaching'. So the question which arises is whether they were to fall in among the many teachers who are said to be

> locked into a view of themselves as technical experts, find nothing in the world of practice to occasion reflection. They have become too skilful at techniques of selective in-attention, junk categories, and situational control, techniques which they use to preserve the constancy of their knowledge-in-practice. For them, uncertainty is a threat: its admission is a sign of weakness. (Schon, 1983, p. 68)

In some respects there was evidence of the teachers locking themselves in to technical expertise, in the search for security and identity as 'expert'. Yet there were also continuous challenges to the barricades of inattention – 'surprising' evidence which drew them back from complacency; a decision to break out from routine and 'boring' teaching; the choice of new and risky strategies; and perpetual conditions of circumstances which affected the realization of their aims. In itself, the search to realize particular aims maintained a sense of puzzlement about those aims and the practices related to them. That is not to say that they were not clear or articulated. Diane's crisis was in part a result of confusion and mystification about educational aims. Others revealed aspects of their values and personal commitments either overtly in practices or implicitly in discussions about practices. For example, Lesley was overtly concerned with 'active' learning tailored to the needs of every individual, in ways which ensured maximum motivation, participation and achievement of each pupil. Anna was determined to ensure that standards of mathematical performance by each group were maximized. Mike's desire was to teach a particular, 'true'

CDT; Richard's concern was to effect a 'freer' primary practice; Kathy's intention was to maintain attention levels by 'reading' the responses of pupils and varying activities; Sue's was of devising activities to convey historical concepts; Dave's was of variations in explaining scientific concepts, to name a few more examples. Such examples however serve mainly to show that the articulation of values and beliefs was rare, let alone discussion about, and elaboration of, them. There was an identifiable 'level' of such discussion related to 'pedagogical knowledge' (Shulman, 1986a, 1986b), in the sense that these were 'ways of teaching' concerns, but not much evidence of reflection about aims.

Some interesting paradoxes are suggested by these data from the initial project teachers and the research group, which give cause to consider more closely the relationship between technical expertise and critical reflection (Stenhouse's 'mere technique' and 'reflexive' views of teaching; and Zimpher and Howey's technical and critical competences) and the nature of reflective practice and research-based teaching. In the aspirations of Stenhouse and Elliott which I had adopted in my earlier work, there were concerns not only for the long-term professional development of individual teachers, but also for institutional and social development to be brought about by teachers – a critical dimension. That dimension has been seen as a 'domain' of reflection, incorporating questions about 'which educational goals, activities and experiences contribute towards forms of life that can be characterised by equity, justice and concrete fulfillment for all students' (Tabachnick and Zeichner, 1991a, p. x). It is a view extended especially by Carr and Kemmis (1986), Van Manen (1977) and Zeichner and Tabachnick (1991). Theoretically the critical domain is said to sit alongside or subsume technical aspects of teaching and practical problem-solving, or else to come into play at certain times, or to interact with the other domains. It is this domain which constitutes the 'critical' in Zimpher and Howey's conception of competence.

Yet the teachers acknowledged that as they proceeded through the year they engaged in 'selective inattention' with respect to their own actions, even in the technical and clinical realms of competence, at least where circumstances were 'normal'. (Richard and Diane were significant exceptions.) How else could they have managed the pace of events and demands of the tasks before them? Being skilled implied being skilful at techniques of selective inattention, in the sense of coming to act quickly, intuitively, and without conscious thought, in the multitude of tasks to be done. In some tasks attention was regained when evidence emerged of a lack of skill or misjudgement, occasioning reflection on the actions they had taken, might have taken, or would in future take, and why. Shifts of this kind, between unconscious action and conscious reflection, were indicated throughout the discussions. On the other hand, there was still a good deal which remained problematic. So, while there was not (yet) a 'constancy of their knowledge in practice' *to* preserve, there was an apparent search *for* it, in the sense of wanting proven practical proficiency in classroom management and instruction.

In other respects, however, individuals from both groups engaged in 'uncertain' and risky practices, in the search for 'better' teaching strategies. In relation to these activities there was exploration of practice. The main constancy was of search for new or improved means of achieving aims, for sound judgements and skilful implementation of ideas. There were extensive reports of reflection in the events, and of the search for evidence of 'success' after the events. One paradox here is that an assessment that particular strategies 'worked' might lead to lack of reflection in future, and further deproblematization of teaching. There were indications that that was likely, at least in some of their work, as Debbie's notion of 'adjustments' to practice showed. If such teaching plans and strategies represented Schon's notion of experimenting, with the teachers attempting to make a hypothesis come true, then the activity of appreciation, action, reappreciation, further action, possibly amounted to the search for constancy and 'recipe knowledge'. 'Adjustments' amounted to fine tuning rather than to sustained reflection. Schon himself disparaged such knowledge.

Yet if these practitioners' experimenting is purposeful action aimed at achieving a desired state, the process of 'assessing' the experimentation was potentially the process of deproblematizing teaching. The 'selective management of complex information' allowed for such deproblematization. When information was unmanaged and uncontrollable, the constancy of unpredictability pertained. But even in those events there was a sense that the turbulence created was unwelcome. The search for the predictable was re-engaged. It is in this sense that the main paradox emerged. Can one doubt that these teachers were being reflective? I could not. Indeed, I believed that I had revealed substantial data on the substance and modes of their reflection as an illustration of Schon's reflective practice at a key stage of professional development. But perhaps what I was witnessing was an emergent non-reflective practice, as the teachers became embedded in capital T Teaching, judged by 'experience' of what 'worked'. If so, I wondered if Schon's notion of reflective practice is limited to the realm of technical and clinical proficiency, and unconcerned with the underlying personal values which drive social practices such as teaching, or with the critique of institutional and social contexts which might thwart educative experiences. Is his attention to practices which are relatively 'non-social' – design, engineering, architecture – misleading for professions which are essentially social in character?

Where such broad considerations did occur noticeably for some of the project teachers was in the face of difficulties. Richard came to reconsider his views in the face of his circumstances and pressure from teachers to be more 'traditional'. Anna responded to the challenge of low-achieving fifth form boys with extensive soul-searching, and sought examples of 'good practice' to model from. There seemed to be little opportunity for or interest in (except in Richard's case) discussing underlying aims. For others, reflection went some way beyond immediate practical problem-solving – Lesley liaised with a colleague and attended inservice meetings in search of discussion and others' perspectives. Pauline focused her attention on 'the challenge' of establishing evidence for why teaching techniques and strategies apparently succeeded (or did not). Sue and Debbie tested out new initiatives in a sense of exploration. Here, then, the attention of focus which occasioned reflection was very varied in detail, but where there was evidence of a sense of success in basic skills of teaching, or a search for more satisfying teaching, it occurred within the realm of pedagogical strategies and concerns to teach in the most 'effective' ways possible. It was within that broad aspiration that reflection on specific incidents, events and actions provided the tapestry of 'evidence' and 'experience' of practice deemed essential to judging that effectiveness and gaining a sense of success as a teacher. It was also in the realm of effecting teaching strategies that new ideas or innovations were tested by those who felt sufficiently confident in 'basic things'. It was in relation to these matters, of what reflection was about and whether it was sustained and sustainable, that clarification of my own aims and their theoretical base was needed.

REFLECTIVE PRACTICE AND TEACHER RESEARCH

The thrust of the work of Donald Schon (1971, 1983, 1987) has been influential at least to the extent that the rhetoric of 'reflective practice' has become widespread among teacher educators and some educational researchers. Zeichner and Tabachnick (1991) argue along with Calderhead (1989) that, at least within the North American continent and Britain, diverse views about teaching, schooling, and teacher education have been drawn together in a seamless way into a 'common rhetoric' of reflective practice which masks important differences. They suggest that the popularity of 'generic conceptions of reflection' is that they allow 'teacher educators of every ideological persuasion' to employ them. Zeichner and Tabachnick encourage the exposure of such persuasions in order to illuminate differences in 'motives and passions' held by teacher educators. Like Hayon (1990), they also attempt to identify the intended foci of reflection which can be detected, they assert, in the work of different proponents of reform in US teacher education. One branch of such reforms in Britain is action research to which I personally have subscribed. In that context I came to recognize that the term reflective practice is used sometimes in association with, or instead of, action research: 'Central to action research is the process of reflection ... Reflection is necessary because in our daily interactions each one of us is trapped in a web of ritualized responses and actions established through experience' (Somekh, 1990, p. 2). Somekh suggested that release from the trap will come 'through a systematic process of reflection on classroom action (often but not always involving problem identification, data collection, hypothesis generation and planning and implementation of action steps)' (Somekh, 1990, p. 2).

Hayon (1990) argued that despite the development of programmes of teacher education to encourage reflective teaching, the concept itself has remained vague and confusing. She advocated, and attempted to elaborate, 'the discovery of a language, or rather of languages of teacher reflection' (Hayon, 1990, p. 58). The result however does not move us far beyond the notion of thoughtful teachers with a mostly retrospective outlook on events.

Somekh, on the other hand, seems to associate reflection with the modes of action research which have become associated with 'models' (Kemmis *et al.*, 1982; Elliott, 1991a; Winter, 1989; Hopkins, 1985; McNiff, 1988) and with the essential elements of systematic rigorous enquiry through scientific procedures and techniques which derive largely from empiric/analytic and interpretive research. These are a long way from the experiences of the new teachers with whom I worked. So is the idea of them being already trapped in a web of ritualized responses and actions established through experience. That assumption pervades writings on action research, in which breaking out from ritualized practice into realms of problem-solving and innovation in their teaching is said to be the reason for research:

> A felt need, on the part of practitioners to initiate change, to
> innovate, is a necessary precondition of action research. It is
> the feeling that some aspect(s) of a practice need to be changed
> if its aims and values are to be more fully realized, which
> activates this form of inquiry and reflection.
> (Elliott, 1991a, p. 53)

What appears to have been manifest among these new teachers was certainly a felt need to achieve a mastery of practice. They were not yet in a position to initiate change or to innovate in their own work since it was not yet tried and tested. Their pre-condition for enquiry and extensive reflection *was* the trying and testing of practical strategies and immediate actions in response to events. The data from these teachers certainly show a sense of enquiry and reflective thought. In some cases, confirmed by a large number of teachers in the extension project, the concern to learn from such enquiry and to develop particular aspects of professional knowledge and practice was also evident. So was a widespread intention to introduce new practices – in a spirit of exploration – into their schools. It appeared that the potential for developing technical and clinical competence was considerable, and with them elements of personal competence too, in the way of increased confidence and sense of identity as a teacher.

Where the potential was being realized, it was not being developed through apprenticeship so much as partly through a form of osmosis as the teachers gleaned what was 'expected', as well as tested out in 'experience'. Where potential was still at the level of aspiration or intention, there, too, the hope was to learn either by experience or by 'models' of good practice from which practical propositions for teaching strategies could be gleaned.

So can their reflective practices be regarded as research? Certainly they don't follow the procedures of 'models' of action research, even less so controlled experiment. Their thinking is nearer to Schon's view of reflective practice in which research *is* an activity undertaken by practitioners. In the reflection-in-action mode, according to Schon, that research is conducted on the spot, triggered by practical problems and immediately linked to action. In the reflection-on-action mode it may be less immediate but none the less based in practice. Experiment and enquiry are conducted in each practice situation, which is said to be unique because of the instability and unpredictability of events. The pattern of appreciation of a situation, action, reappreciation of the newly created situation, and further action, eventually accumulating as an enriched repertoire of practical experience, is a key feature of Schon's view of research. The appreciation–action–reappreciation cycle becomes a feature of the construction of the theories and understandings of practitioners as a form of practical experimenting, he argues. Schon has defined different kinds of such experimentation in practice. These include 'exploratory experimenting', a kind of probing, playful, trial and error activity, which equates with 'playing it by ear'; 'move-testing experiment', in which action is taken with the intention of producing change, equating with 'playing the hunch'; and 'hypothesis testing' which involves discriminating between competing hypotheses and seeking confirmation or disconfirmation that they are correct, equating with 'monitoring' and 'mirroring'. He points out, and the new teachers demonstrated, that the practice context is different from the positivist research context in that the practitioner wants to understand the situation in order to change it. The intention of practitioners is to act in such a way as to make the hypotheses come true, by influencing and manipulating events. In this respect research-based practice does not and cannot provide an emulation of controlled experiment. Indeed, he argues, such experiments in practice necessarily violate the canons of positivistic research, residing more justifiably in the realms of 'artful inquiry' (Schon, 1983, p. 268).

Schon's reflective practice has been equated with action research (Elliott, 1991a, p. 50) in the form which uses the 'action-plan' model approach and a range of quantitative and/or qualitative research methods (pp. 69–89). But in the light of the evidence from these new teachers' thinking about their teaching, the equation would need some explication. If, for example, I had succeeded in encouraging the teachers to select, focus on and systematically (in the usual action research sense) study particular aspects of their work, what would happen to the myriad other 'problems' as they tried to realize their aims in practice? Might it be that many aspects of their teaching would indeed become subject to habituation and 'craft-culture' teaching techniques, consigned to the realm of technical competence without reflection, by virtue of the demands for attention to selected matters even sooner than they did? That would seem a real possibility. Yet Schon explicitly argues that his notion of reflective practice would potentially overcome the tendency toward 'selective inattention' and habituated practice. On the evidence from these teachers, for that to occur needs attention to multiple educational 'problems' to be maintained on a broad front. Even on a more narrow front, that of attending to a particular aspect of practice which needs to be changed in order to more fully realize its underlying aims and values, my considerations left me doubtful if or how such change might affect the construction of 'theories and understandings'. It was in that respect that my initial impressions of action research and of reflection seemed to correspond with aspects of the teachers' reflectiveness. But like that reflectiveness they seemed inadequately matched to my underlying aspirations for redefinition, critique, and the maintenance of a sense of the problematic in educational endeavours. It was here that I saw the significance of the dimension of depth in Schon's work, and in more detailed explications of action research. A 'depth' of attention, beyond questions of technique and classroom strategies which are subject to ritualization, would seem to be necessary in order to effect the development of theories and understandings.

Schon made his own appeal for 'depth' of reflection, and attention to matters other than techniques, though he is vague about what those matters might be:

> [T]he study of reflection in action is critically important. The dilemma of rigor or relevance may be dissolved if we can develop an epistemology of practice which places technical problem solving within a broader context of reflective enquiry, shows how reflection in action may be rigorous in its own right, and links the art of practice in uncertainty and uniqueness to the scientist's art of research. We may thereby increase the legitimacy of reflection in action and encourage its broader, deeper and more rigorous use.
> (Schon, 1983, p. 302)

My present attempt to elucidate how such enquiry was undertaken by new teachers illustrates the extent of the reflection involved in their learning, possibly confirming Schon's view of research-based practice as a distinctive activity:

> When the practitioner reflects in action in a case he perceives as unique, paying attention to phenomena and surfacing his intuitive understanding of them, his experimenting is at once exploratory, move-testing and hypothesis testing. The three functions are fulfilled by the very same actions. And from this fact follows the distinctive character of experimenting in practice.
> (Schon, 1983, p. 147)

Schon's critique of the rational/experimental model of research as inappropriate to application in social practice is supported by an elaboration of an alternative mode of knowing – existentialism. This equates with the basic phenomenological viewpoint of case study research discussed earlier: validity is found in the 'here and now', and theory drawn from experience cannot be literally applied to other situations (Schon, 1971, p. 231). The inherent uncertainty of experience from which knowledge of this kind derives, Schon argues, means that the generation and testing of knowledge in the here and now is essential. As a mode of research, case history and narrative, and the study of processes internal to a project, are important. And there are certain preconditions which are essential to the formation of existential knowledge: the maintenance of continuity over the learning process; recognition of the open-endedness of all situations; the subjecting of models derived from experience to testing, modification, explosion, or abandonment; a willingness of learners to make leaps in problem-solving; and an ability of learners to synthesize theory and formulate new models while in the situation (Schon, 1971, p. 235). The worlds of the new teachers, however, illustrate and exemplify, in my view, how such a mode of research-based practice existed in potential, but was also potentially displaced by the search for 'proven' practical strategies. The key conceptual question remained: what was the difference between the modes of reflection which the teachers displayed and which I had set out to encourage, and modes of research? What, in short, did Schon imply when he wrote of the 'broader, deeper and more rigorous use of reflection in action'? Elliott (1989) opened up a view on this question which takes me where the project teachers took me, though by a different route, into the realm of personal competence which incorporates understanding or at least articulation of the educational values on which practice depends:

> [T]he aim of action research is to generate *practical wisdom*
> defined as a holistic appreciation of a complex practical activity
> which enables a person to understand or articulate the
> problems s/he confronts in realizing the aims or values of the
> activity and to propose appropriate solutions ... conceived as
> an *educational theory* wisdom constitutes a complex structure
> of ideas which cannot be broken down into its constitutive
> elements – as propositions – without loss of meaning.
> (Elliott, 1989, p. 84)

This realm of personal competence is complex, more so than Elliott implies when he writes of problems confronted by a person in realizing the aims or values of an activity. For some teachers the complexity of theoretical understanding in itself provided what Pauline called 'the big question', and 'the challenge', i.e. to understand where and when, as well as how and why, some practices were succeeding in realizing her aims of motivating all pupils in foreign language learning as a means of enhancing language competences.

For others – exemplified by Diane's predicament – knowing what to do by way of practical activities for and teaching strategies with pupils was the problem. It was at this interface between practical action and understanding that the 'holistic appreciation' of teaching was not manifest. I am not suggesting that the teachers at this stage ought to have displayed 'practical wisdom' (as defined on page 216). Had I perceived action research in this way at the start of the initial project, perhaps I would have pursued this aim and sought to generate it more than I did. As it was, reflective practice was conceived by me, and reflective thinking pursued by the teachers, mainly within the 'constitutive element' of practical propositions. The elements of aims and values, of educational theory, were sufficiently addressed to qualify some of the thinking of the teachers as meeting the 'necessary pre-condition of action research', i.e. the realization that practice needed to be improved if its aims and values were to be more fully realized.

But there is a major challenge here which was not systematically pursued through my own actions in the projects, and which the 'necessary pre-condition' position held by Elliott did not address, but which his 'practical wisdom' position did. The importance of the 'personal' realm of competence, defined by Zimpher and Howey in terms of the clarification and development of values and of confidence, for the education of teachers and for the qualitative improvement of the education of pupils, is suggested by Salmon (1988). She points out that the teacher's personal constructs of understanding are crucial to the kind of education on offer to the pupils. The implication is that knowledge of self (Nias, 1989) as an element of professional knowledge needs to be more substantially part of the agenda of learning teaching. The relationship of self to theories of teaching would also follow in that agenda:

> Education, in this psychology, is the systematic interface
> between personal construct systems. This view of formal
> learning puts as much emphasis on teachers' personal meanings
> as on those of learners. Here a Kellyan approach stands apart
> from most educational psychology, which while generally
> focusing on distinctive ways in which individual pupils see
> things, tends to lump teachers together. The knowledge they
> represent, the meanings they offer are, it is implied, essentially
> standard. Underlying this definition of teachers, in terms of a
> standardised curriculum, are certain absolute assumptions
> about knowledge itself. If we believe that history, science or
> maths embody particular ultimate truths about the world, then
> we can see all teachers of these subjects as representing
> essentially the same sort of expertise. But we cannot take
> this view if knowledge is provisional. Learning, from this
> perspective, is not a matter of acquiring what Kelly dubs
> 'nuggets of truth', a treasure house of human certainties. In
> learning, we cannot ever achieve final answers; rather we find
> new questions, we discover other possibilities which we might

> try out. Knowledge is ultimately governed by constructive
> alternativism; everything can always be reconstructed.
> (Salmon, 1988, p. 22)

This is the 'constructionist, "worldmaking" view of the reality with which
the practitioner deals' (Schon, 1983, p. 35). That reality includes the self. An
illustration of the importance of this interface between technical and clinical
elements of competence, and personal elements, was displayed by the issue of
the emotions. The assumptions of much of the literature on learning teaching,
especially in the performance-based realm, is centred on teaching skills. The
literature on beginning teaching is often centred on acute feelings and subjec-
tivism. Can these world views be reconciled? The research group teachers
revealed the importance of the emotions as a specific element of personal competence, both in terms of their relationship to judgements, actions and events
and in terms of how the teachers learned to handle that relationship through
greater 'self-awareness'. From the data, as the research group teachers reflected
on it, they themselves identified how the professional self-development of that
aspect of personal competence had occurred. Some of the pilot project teachers
revealed, in different ways, the importance of the emotions and their relationship to personal confidence and classroom practice. But the 'things which
caused emotional disturbance in the first place', as Debbie had put it, *did*
include 'things' other than judgements and misjudgements within clinical
elements of practice. Richard's 'problems' were about being constrained in
implementing what he believed to be good educational practices. Mike had a
firm commitment to a set of ideas which he proposed to take to another school
if he could not implement them in his present location. Anna eventually did
just that. On the other hand, Anna had to formulate her ideas and aims for
the 'low achievers'; Mike had to rethink his ideas in the face of mixed-ability
grouping; and Richard questioned his beliefs as a result of comments from
colleagues and examples of their 'beliefs in action'. Diane had difficulty
formulating and articulating any aims for her reception class: a problem exacerbated by the breakdown in relationships. Lesley seemed to be constantly seeking practical strategies to help her realize her aims of equality of provision for
pupils within an activity-led, enquiry-orientated classroom.

The implications of these revelations for the development project brought
about the conception of a curriculum for supported self-education, which would
need to be developed to include a curriculum for the emotions (Tickle, 1991,
1992b). If the curriculum for the emotions which is needed is directly linked
to the agenda for the development of personal competences more broadly in
the sense of teachers' personal meanings, and to the enhancement of repertoires
of technical and clinical competences, then we might gain a sense of holistic
appreciation of the complex practical activities. As a part of a curriculum for
personal competence, as a means of enhancing technical and clinical competence, the place of the emotions in modes of experimenting and reflection can

be deemed to be central. It may be that the literature on beginning teachers is so replete with references to aversive trauma simply because this aspect of learning teaching has been overlooked in policy and provision. But if the links I have suggested above are unbreakable 'without loss of meaning', then individual teachers' personal constructs would also need to become part of curricula for professional development. This was the heart of the difficulty I had experienced with the concept of social strategy, what I saw as its inadequacy, and my attempt to link it to the concept of competences which I had found appealing.

In seeking to 'prove' the equation of Schon's reflective practice and his own action research, Elliott (1991a, p. 50) has argued that action research has been 'hijacked' and assimilated as a mode of positivist research. He has sought to substitute 'moral science' or 'practical philosophy' as a term more accurately representing the nature of reflective, educational practice as a 'more comprehensive' research paradigm. This is based on the notion that there are different kinds of practical reflection: that which is associated with realizing technical objectives in the curriculum, and which consists of technical reasoning about how to achieve pre-specified ends; and that which is associated with process values and consists of ethical and philosophical considerations in the judgements made in trying to realize values.

> The kind of reflection involved here is quite different to
> technical means–ends reasoning. It is both ethical and
> philosophical. Inasmuch as the reflection is about choosing a
> course of action in a particular set of circumstances, to realize
> one's values, it is ethical in character. But since ethical choice
> implies an interpretation of the values to be realized, reflection
> about means cannot be separated from reflection about ends.
> Ethical reflection has a philosophical dimension.
> (Elliott, 1991a, p. 51)

The location of this kind of reflection seems precisely equivalent to the realm of personal competence whose essence is about generating self-awareness and values clarification, which would provide a means of examining theoretical frameworks underlying teaching and thus open the way to researching 'practice'. The emphasis which these teachers provided offers some understanding of the relationship between technical competence (and even some aspects of clinical competence in so far as these include choices between different techniques for achieving objectives) and personal and critical competence. It now seems clear that what I set out to do emphasized the former, encouraging the focus on classroom practice and a search largely for technical improvement. The teachers on the other hand displayed the potential of, and need to operate according to, a more holistic view of teaching. A shifting emphasis between practical technique and practical philosophy was on occasion evident in some cases. But there also appeared to be differences between individual teachers in terms of the focus and kind of reflection.

It seems to me now that the development of personal competence, engaging teachers in reflection which 'itself modifies conceptions of ends in ways which change one's understanding of what constitutes good data about practice' (Elliot, 1991a, p. 51) is the key to intra-professional strategic redefinition. Perhaps it is this which constitutes the 'broader, deeper and more rigorous use' of reflective practice. Is it this which would distinguish 'reflexive' from 'reflective' practice? The distinction is an important part of the constellations of concepts.

The data from both the initial project and research groups certainly display reflective thinking on the part of the teachers. I believe I have shown how they engaged in a complex and extensive set of thought processes, which I equated with Schon's notions of reflection in and on practice. Yet there were only signals, indicators, in some cases in relation to specific problems, of the teachers examining their personal constructs. The actions and events which occasioned reflection were different from the underlying subjective conditions under which their actions were constituted by an 'I' as the object of reflection. They did not subject their driving aims and values to scrutiny to any noticeable extent. In this sense, so far as the data show, they engaged in *reflexivity*, which involves examining the 'I' which constructs actions as an object of conscious reflection, to the extent explored by Sue in the critical incident of the pupil who fell over. Others described this kind of reflexivity in relation to their emotional 'selves'. If Sue had pursued a reflexive approach to her actions in the critical incident, she might have examined why she had sent for the pupil at that particular time; why she was insistent on homework being produced on time; why the meeting took place before a class of pupils and standing in front of her desk; and so on. Each of these features displays implicit or explicit, conscious or unconscious, objects for reflexive scrutiny. Such scrutiny, in addition to Sue's reflections about what she did and said, would constitute broader, deeper and more rigorous reflection.

In a similar way the teachers' trial and error experimenting with teaching strategies could be seen, as Schon's reflective practice would have it, as the construction of practice by way of attempting to make a hypothesis come true. That could result in reading evidence to fit the case, given the inaccessibility of evidence and its unpredictability. At least it would tend towards demonstrating the 'truth' of 'what works for me' — which was described as a central criterion in judging the result of such experimenting:

> But an alternative account of the practitioners' experimenting
> [is that it is] not so much to make an hypothesis come true but
> to actualise an ideal. The hypothesis is not about what is the
> case (truth) but about how to realise values in action (or in
> other words how to define oneself in terms of one's own values).

And central here to hypothesis raising and testing is
reflexivity – the self folding back on itself to reconstruct itself
through action. Changing the self rather than actions is what
action-research is all about – or at least one form of action
research. The point about 'unstable' situations is that they
destabilize selves and require their continuous reconstruction.
Action is simply the material condition of this reconstructive
enterprise which is basically and fundamentally a reflexive and
not simply reflective one.
(Elliott, 1991, pers. comm.)

There is a further dimension to this matter. Sue could engage in this kind
of reflexivity privately and individually. Indeed she was tempted, even at the
level of reflection that she did engage in, to keep her thoughts to herself. The
implications of 'going public' were a matter of equal deliberation. Those considerations were replicated and reported many times by the teachers. This
creates another problem in terms of the status of their reflections. Such private
deliberations do not meet the criterion in action research, as it is often construed, of public enquiry. Schon's view of reflective practice carries no such
criterion. It does not anticipate that practitioners will necessarily engage in
collaborative discourse, which action research does. If the repertoire of
experience remains in the private domain, then it might not be subject to the
rigours of research: 'In justifying an interpretation of events, or of phenomena,
an action researcher must reflect about how s/he has subjectively constructed
it as a valid interpretation i.e. as one that others can be persuaded to accept'
(Elliott, 1991, pers comm.)

These dimensions of the process of learning teaching, of professional
development, are crucial to the way the project was, and might have been, conceived. They also help to explain what was going on in the manifestations of
thought and practice which I witnessed among the teachers. Was I witnessing
(and attempting to encourage) a process of self-construction of tried and tested
techniques and strategies for teaching? Or was I also witnessing and encouraging a reconstruction of the self, in terms of the values and personal qualities
of the teachers? If it was the former, then the processes of reflection and practice directed towards becoming 'capital T teachers' were about reflecting in
practice a self which was brought to the situation. Being *en route* had a fixed
destination in view, and the development of a repertoire of practice represented
strategies for reaching it. That view provides a distinctive interpretation to
the notion of 'what works for me' – a characteristic and powerful selection
mechanism when some of the teachers judged their actions and the advice and
ideas of others. For some, the 'me' was determined, and the task was to match
strategies to it. The strategies themselves thus became a by-product of the
values and aims of the self. Such a view would go a long way toward explaining
why these teachers' focus of attention was on the technical and clinical

221

competences of teaching. The important business was to see success in realizing aims, not to reconstruct those aims. There was also a different sense of aim playing a major part — the aim to be seen as and to feel proficient in the skills of teaching, those prerequisites to professional credibility which were part of the occupational culture which the teachers entered.

If on the other hand I was also witnessing (and encouraging) the reconstruction of the self in terms of personal values and qualities, then the reflexive process would have been directed toward maintaining instability and questioning aims, or enabling the teachers to develop their ideas within the destabilizing situations in which they worked. That process was also evident, in the cases of Richard and Diane particularly, but also with others to some extent. For them, and for others in respect to specific aims and values, the important business was to engage in soul-searching about their beliefs, and to try to define educational aims. But it also went much deeper in some cases: Sue's perpetual crisis about 'is this what life's come to?'; Dave's crisis of personal confidence in the face of colleagues who 'didn't understand' him; Anna's resignation, withdrawal of it, and eventual move to another post in a private school; and Debbie's emergent sense of isolation and self-doubt, were just some examples of the aspects of self which were deeper and more complex than aims, values, and teaching strategies.

These kinds of destabilization seemed to result in reflexiveness, but in instances of pain. Perhaps learning how to handle the emotions in relation to problem-solving strategies exemplifies the potential of reflexivity for handling these wider orientations of self as a teacher. Perhaps too, both in respect of teaching strategies and broader identities, the capacity to manage instability in a way which maintains the problematic nature of self, of education, and of teaching, is the key element for the maintenance of reflexivity. For it seems that in many respects the teachers also illustrate a tendency, or desire, to exit that mode of thinking in favour of termination of the learning process, closure of situations, firming up of models from experience, a desire to find trustworthy solutions, and a failure to address theory in favour of pragmatic responses to contexts. They aspired to some degree to enter what they denoted in various ways as the craft culture of 'capital T' teaching, seduced perhaps by a mirage of certainty in understanding 'what works' as a repertoire of technical and clinical competences.

That aspiration may have diverted them from the uncertainty involved in examining their own beliefs, personal philosophies and emotional selves which lay at the heart of their educational enterprise. In talking of becoming 'capital T' teachers the research group did seem to imply a possible escape from such reflexive practice as would be required by 'holistic appreciation'. The assessment of their teaching, based on a simple notion of technical and clinical skills, encouraged that endeavour to live by simple criteria of technical competence. So did their search for credibility. It may be that the holistic nature of teaching and the extent of 'problematics' was too great to handle at one time through rigorous research. The elusiveness of information or other forms of data was manifest; its accessibility exceptionally difficult. The means of interpreting data on the spot itself required deliberation and sophisticated judgement. Methods of recording it as evidence for later analysis or even recall was time-consuming and subject to technical difficulties. The development of understanding without opportunities to scrutinize ideas or to engage in discourse was limited (Richard in particular lamented this). Yet it is the development of these capacities which would constitute becoming effective researchers, and which would provide the basis for becoming effective teachers, if that is construed as an enhanced quality of educational encounters.

In their view there seemed to be a search for short cuts toward a repertoire of practical proficiency, a tendency to judge 'what works' without engaging too rigorously in research. If that is correct it seems to put the emotional curriculum potentially at centre stage. For the handling of insecurity in unique situations of instability and uncertainty could require particular kinds of emotional competence. To expect the teachers to have the ability to maintain control over the apparent anarchy of situations is a heavy demand to make. To expect them to engage in testing, exploding or abandoning models derived from experience when they are only in the process of constructing them seems like iconoclasm gone mad. Yet the development of these capacities as part of personal competence, as emancipatory in the sense of extending personal understanding, can be seen as essential to the education of new entrants to teaching.

When Elliott (1991a) writes of *educational* action research aimed at realizing educational values, the latter are linked with personal understandings of human nature and its powers and capacities for 'self-realization'. In this mode of research teachers engage in the resolution of practical problems, but also 'develop themselves in the sense of clarifying where their values lie and where their professional practice can be located in terms of them' (Elliott, 1991, pers. comm.).

This focus on means and ends simultaneously would have engaged the teachers, much more fully than was evident, in reflection on the problems of the personal dimension of competences as much as on the problems of the technical. It is in that sense that Elliott argues that when teachers engage in action research they are essentially becoming practical philosophers of education and not simply empirical researchers. This is also Stenhouse's (1975) notion of a unified educational practice. In terms of the constellations of concepts this 'holistic' view appears as a support structure for several dimensions: the weld point between Zimpher and Howey's technical/clinical and personal competences; the extension point from Lacey's social strategies into my concern with intra-professional development; the link (or cut-off point) between different conceptions of teacher education and training; and a point of extensic beyond the conception of reflective practice offered by Schon and into a more thorough consideration of its basis and that of action research.

EXTENDING THE CONSTELLATIONS OF CONCEPTS

The ideas of Habermas provided an opportunity for the extension of my own understanding in that respect. I sought to link notions of competence which I had adopted in the projects, and my quest to understand action research as a more complete view of reflective practice, with Habermas's notions of knowledge and human interests. The concurrency of ideas was seductive. Habermas (1968) was concerned in part with the relationship between theory and practice, which he discussed in the context of a critique of positivist science and also of Husserl's phenomenology. That concern, and his own interest in developing an emancipatory view of knowledge, was summed up in the statement: 'The conception of theory as a process of cultivation of the person has become apocryphal' (Habermas, 1968, p. 304).

By relating how, from its Greek origins, a traditional view of theory had penetrated scientific thought in a way which either presumed or aspired to value freedom, Habermas sought to return to what he regarded as a more authentic relationship between knowledge and human interests. He argued that the psychological commitment of the sciences (including the social sciences) to theory in a 'pure' form, and the epistemological severance of knowledge from interest, did not correspond to the classical meaning of theory. That did not dissociate abstract laws from a sense of being, but was, rather, orientated toward the concept of being. Positivism, on the other hand, represented in logic by the distinction between descriptive and prescriptive statements, filtered out emotive from cognitive contents of knowledge (Habermas, 1968, p. 303). It was thus that he asserted that theory was once supposed to comprise practical efficacy, but that it had 'fallen prey to methodological prohibitions' (Habermas, 1968, p. 304). From the perspective of a rehabilitation of such practical efficacy Habermas postulated three categories of possible knowledge (1968, p. 313), which appear to correspond to the dimensions of competence which I had addressed in the data from the teachers. The first concerns 'information that expands our power of technical control'. This technical interest is invoked in an attempt to describe our relationship to nature, and to control our circumstances through understanding the world we inhabit. The second is a practical interest, associated with problem-solving through intersubjectivity and communication. It is concerned with 'interpretations that make possible the orientation of action within common traditions'. This is the historical-hermeneutic aspect of life in which the practical interest is encountered in reaching communal understandings and an understanding of self in the conduct of our daily lives. Thirdly, Habermas posits an emancipatory interest, which is concerned with analyses that free consciousness and enable our ability to reflect critically on our circumstances and our own presuppositions. He relates these directly to an interest structure of the human species which is rooted in different means of social organization: work, language, and power. Habermas drew on Popper's three-world theory, in arguing that persons 'exist simultaneously in (1) an external world of states of affairs and objects; (2) an internal world of ideas, thoughts, emotions; and (3) a normative world of inter-subjectively determined norms and values' (Holub, 1991, p. 13). The implications of this for the idea that teachers should become effective researchers lie in the proposition that when we engage in the investigation of 'society' (or, in the teachers' case, of events or phenomena) the research process and presuppositions of the researcher must also be subject to self-reflection. If we operate only in the realm of technical interest, focused on the external, through empirical/analytical procedures, then the work would have limited validity in Habermas's terms. A more 'comprehensive' approach would include the discussion of propositions through argumentation. Such argumentation involves different but interconnected types of statement which would bring together the descriptive (in order to describe states of affairs), the postulatory or prescriptive (in order to establish rules of procedure), and the critical and self-reflective, through which to justify ideas, decisions, and actions.

Is it possible to equate the teachers' search for closure and the security of what works in practice with the technical interest of Habermas? The focus of the teachers' attention appeared to be in large measure on the external world of states of affairs, as they wrestled for control and stability and sought to manipulate situations. That was not the only focus of attention but it was a predominant one. There were signs of the potential for intersubjectivity and for critical reflection which often went unrealized – Debbie's personal challenge was the most fully articulated; Liz's quest to be given the chance to ask herself the right question was presented, but curtailed; the lack of opportunity for Richard to discuss philosophy was a source of frustration for him. These were just a few examples. Such discussion would be a prerequisite to intra-professional strategic redefinition through the development of critical competence. However, such critical competence would perhaps need to be achieved first within the internal world of ideas, thoughts and emotions, to the point of clarification and understanding, though with a willingness to maintain the dynamic of change. If that level of emancipatory interest had been achieved and supported within each school community, then there might have been the possibility of the teachers participating in argumentation, and thus in strategic redefinition in the inter-professional sense. In the light of the clarification of values and reflexiveness about them and the means of realizing them in practice, the teachers could have examined the context in which that realization was to be tested to better effect. As it was, realization depended on the acquisition or application of appropriate political competences in the inter-professional realm. That seemed to depend on feeling at ease with the uncertainties of questioning and modifying one's personal understandings and practice. Only then, perhaps, would it be possible to engage ingenuously in dialogue and the development of communal practical knowledge. This offers an opening into a shared professional culture of openness, critique and collaboration at the individual and inter-professional level within schools. That would both depend upon and raise the potential of reflexiveness in the public domain, thus incorporating features of rigour.

It was that which was so noticeably curtailed, with so many opportunities lost. The complete lack of dialogue between Lesley and her headteacher (as teacher-tutor) was replicated in almost all cases. Mike's teacher-tutor's view that there were no problems (an acknowledgement of Mike's classroom competence) ignored the very deep issues about multi-media teaching and resources which concerned Mike himself. Mike would not raise the issues with senior personnel. Sue was unable to discuss her feeling of isolation among colleagues for fear of giving the wrong impression of herself (even though privately it was a critique of the interpersonal relations among staff which she engaged in — there seemed no chance of raising that publicly). Again, these are but a few examples which illustrate the problem of the personal competences — from the handling of emotions, social confidence, sense of status, and even geographical relocation, to the explication and elaboration of educational aims and values as a key aspect of the teachers' professional development which was not consciously attended to in the practice of the projects.

Let me recall Schon's view that essential pre-conditions to the formation of existential knowledge include the maintenance of continuity over learning processes; recognition of the open-endedness of all situations; the subjecting of models derived from experience to testing, modification, explosion or abandonment; a willingness of learners to make leaps in problem-solving; and the ability to synthesize theory and formulate new models while in the situation. These entail predispositions toward the study of personal beliefs in situations of uncertainty and instability. But they also entail applying the emancipatory interest to the external world of states of affairs and to the normative world of intersubjectively determined norms and values. However, it seems from the evidence of these teachers that while their worlds invoked conditions of instability they may be regarded as temporary, to be 'suffered' by new entrants (Nias, 1987, p. 179). The search for 'capital T' teaching could well bypass the opening into shared professional dialogue and argumentation in favour of an assumed, or narrow, craft knowledge which deflects evidence and deforms the capacity for rigorous reflection across these worlds.

A move toward a different professional culture would need to embrace the ontological aspects of experience, as well as the epistemological, beginning with the immediate, complex instability of feelings, of teaching experiences, and of teaching contexts. The disposition to manage and even exploit instability and opportunity by risking the unconventional, maintaining a desire to be surprised, and achieving a 'sense of comfort in the ambiguous' (Webb, 1985), would be important characteristics of such a movement. This would recognize the fact that teaching is problematic, and would keep it so, without making it aversively traumatic for individuals. It would potentially maintain the power of experiences like Pauline's, and displace the power of experiences like Diane's. In order to go beyond personal experience and have some impact on institutions and teaching in general, these personal competences would need to become a central feature of the new teachers' curriculum.

However teachers' learning and practice occurs within the social, intellectual and cultural limitations of existing forms of practice (Wolff, 1981). This is not therefore simply a matter of the professional development of individuals, as I had originally tended to emphasize in the design of the initial project. The implication of what I am now arguing, from a more invigorated perception of the problem, is that the aspiration of developing reflective practitioners through a focus on personal competences could provide the opportunity for developing the profession as a social force. This was explicit in the more 'collective' aims of the projects which prompted action to change school circumstances and induction policy through the work of teacher-tutors. Yet it is a relationship which might easily be lost sight of, as has happened, I believe, in Schon's work. His initial concerns (Schon, 1971) were with 'ways of knowing in public'; with modes of social enquiry which might enable communities to become better at learning from social endeavours manifest in policy and programmes for change. His interim work (Schon, 1983) then focused on how professionals reflect as individual practitioners. More recently (Schon, 1987), he has focused on how students of the professions can be educated in and through such modes of thinking as individuals, at the 'level' of technical problem-solving.

This shift from social to individual learning may be understandable in western cultures which emphasize individualism. But it is in my view unfortunate, because it implies that learning is an individual enterprise. Schon's early work stressed how poor social groups are at learning from experience and how they fail to engage the pre-conditions for the development of existential knowledge. Given that, it might be considered unjust to expect individuals in isolation to hold the dispositions deemed essential for such learning, which would imply requiring them to engage permanently in attempts to subvert existing forms of their own practice. It was clear that while the teachers were encouraged to maintain and enhance reflective dispositions toward their work, that was undertaken mostly as private introspection. The development of teaching, it seems, requires that it might be enhanced both individually and collectively in a professional climate of more confidence, openness and dialogue about professional problems within schools and more widely in the community. That might provide both individual and social restructuring of education through the growth of a community of reflective practitioners.

Bibliography

Alexander, R. J., Craft, M. and Lynch, J. (eds) (1984) *Change in Teacher Education: Context and Provision Since Robbins*. London: Holt, Rinehart & Winston.

Altrichter, H. and Posch, P. (1989) Does the 'grounded theory' approach offer a guiding paradigm for teacher research? *Cambridge Journal of Education* 19 (1), 21–32.

Andrews, I. (1979) Induction programmes: staff development opportunities for beginning and experienced teachers. In Wideen, M. F. and Andrews, I. (eds), *Staff Development for School Improvement*. Lewes: Falmer Press.

Applegate, J. H. (1989) Readiness for teaching. In Holly, M. L. and McLoughlin, C. S. (eds), *Perspectives on Teacher Professional Development*. Lewes: Falmer Press.

Ashcroft, K. and Griffiths, M. (1987) The 3 faces of school experience: teaching teaching skills in an enquiry-based initial teacher education course. Paper presented to the annual conference of the British Educational Research Association, University of East Anglia, September.

Auld, R. (1979) *Report of the Public Enquiry into the Organisation and Management of the William Tyndale Junior and Infants School*. London: Inner London Education Authority.

Ball, S. (1981) *Beachside Comprehensive*. Cambridge: Cambridge University Press.

Bennett, N. (1976) *Teaching Styles and Pupil Progress*. London: Open Books.

Bennett, N. and Desforges, C. (1984) Ensuring practical outcomes from educational research. In Shipman, M. (ed.), *Contemporary Analyses in Education: Educational Research, Principles, Policy and Practice*. Lewes: Falmer Press.

Berger, P. L. and Luckmann, T. (1967) *The Social Construction of Reality*. London: Allen Lane.

Berliner, D. C. (1987) Ways of thinking about students and classrooms by more and less experienced teachers. In Calderhead, J. (ed.), *Exploring Teachers' Thinking*. London: Cassell.

Berliner, D. C. and Tikunoff, W. J. (1976) The California beginning teacher evaluation study: overview of the ethnographic study. *Journal of Teacher Education* 27 (1), 24–30.

Beynon, J. (1987) Ms Floral mends her ways. In Tickle, L. (ed.), *The Arts in Education*. London: Croom Helm.

Blumer, H. (1962) Society as symbolic interactionism. In Rose, A. M. (ed.), *Human Behaviour and Social Processes: An Interactionist Perspective*. London: Routledge & Kegan Paul.

Blumer, H. (1969) The methodological position of symbolic interactionism. In Hammersley, M. and Woods, P. (eds) (1976), *The Process of Schooling*. Milton Keynes, Open University Press.

Bolam, R. (1973) *Induction Programmes for Probationary Teachers: A Report of an*

Action Research Project Funded by the DES and Carried out at Bristol University 1968-72. Bristol: University School of Education.

Bolam, R., Baker, K. and McMahon, A. (1975) *The Teacher Induction Pilot Schemes (TIPS) Project: a National Evaluation Report*. Bristol: University School of Education.

Bond, D., Keogh, R. and Walker, D. (1985) *Reflection: Turning Experience into Learning*. London: Kogan Page.

Booth, M. B., Furlong, J. Hargreaves, D. H., Reiss, M. J. and Ruthven, K. (1989) *Teacher Supply and Teacher Quality: Solving the Coming Crisis*. Cambridge: University of Cambridge Department of Education.

Brown, M. H. and Willems, A. L. (undated) Lifeboat ethics and the first year teacher. ERIC database unpublished manuscript.

Brown, S. and McIntyre, D. (1986) The qualities of teachers: building on professional craft knowledge. Mimeo, Scottish Council for Research in Education/University of Oxford.

Brown, S., McAlphine, A., McIntyre, D. and Hagger, H. (1988) Gaining access to experienced teachers' professional craft knowledge. Paper presented to the annual conference of the British Educational Research Association, University of East Anglia, September.

Bruner, J. (1977) *The Process of Education*. Cambridge, Mass: Harvard University Press.

Bullough, R. V. (1989) *First Year Teacher: A Case Study*. New York: Teachers' College Press.

Bullough, R. V., Knowles, J. G. and Crow, N. (1991) *Emerging as a Teacher*, London: Routledge.

Busher, H., Clark, S. and Taggart, L. (1988) Beginning teachers' learning. In Calderhead, J. (ed.), *Teachers' Professional Learning*. Lewes: Falmer Press.

Calderhead, J. (ed.) (1987) *Exploring Teachers' Thinking*. London: Cassell.

Calderhead, J. (ed.) (1988) *Teachers' Professional Learning*. Lewes: Falmer Press.

Calderhead, J. (1989) Reflective teaching and teacher education. *Teaching and Teacher Education* 5 (1), 43-51.

Calderhead, J. (1992) Induction: a research perspective on the professional growth of the newly qualified teacher. In General Teaching Council, *The Induction of Newly Appointed Teachers*. London: General Teaching Council Initiative for England and Wales.

Callaghan, J. (1976) Speech made at Ruskin College, Oxford, 18 October. Printed in full under the title Towards a national debate. *Education*, 22 October.

Cameron-Jones, M. and O'Hara, P. (1990) Getting the measure of new teachers in Scotland: does the system work? *Scottish Educational Review* 22 (1), 38-44.

Carr, W. (1987) What is an educational practice? *Journal of Philosophy of Education* 21 (2), 163-75.

Carr, W. (1988) The idea of an educational science. Paper presented at a plenary session of the International Congress of the Philosophy of Education, Madrid 23-26 November.

Carr, W. (1989) *Quality in Teaching: Arguments for a Reflective Profession*. Lewes: Falmer Press.

Carr, W. (undated) Theories of theory and practice. Mimeo, School of Education, University College of North Wales.

Carr, W. and Kemmis, S. (1986) *Becoming Critical: Knowing Through Action Research*, Lewes: Falmer Press.

Chilver, Lord (1988) *Report of the Interim Advisory Committee on School Teachers' Pay and Conditions*. London: HMSO.

Chisholme, L. (1990) Action research: some methodological and political considerations. *British Educational Research Journal* 16 (3), 249–57.

Clandinin, D. J. (1986) *Classroom Practice: Teacher Images in Action*. Lewes: Falmer Press.

Clark, C. M. and Yinger, R. J. (1987) Teacher planning. In Calderhead, J. (ed.) *Exploring Teachers' Thinking*. London: Cassell.

Clark, K. (1992) Speech to the North of England education conference. Southport, 4 January.

Clark, R. P. and Nisbett, J. D. (1963) *The First Two Years of Teaching*. University of Aberdeen, Department of Education.

Collins, M. (1969) *Students into Teachers*. London: Routledge & Kegan Paul.

Copeland, D. W., Birmingham, C., de la Cruz, E. and Recht, B. (1991) The reflective practitioner in teaching: towards a research agenda. Symposium presented to the annual meeting of the American Educational Research Association, Chicago, April.

Corcoran, E. (1981) Transition shock: the beginning teacher's paradox. *Journal of Teacher Education* 32 (3), 19–23.

Cormon, L. (1970) Hangman or victim? In Ryan, K. (ed.), *Don't Smile Until Christmas*. Chicago: University of Chicago Press.

Cornwell, J. (1965) *The Probationary Year*. Birmingham University, Institute of Education.

Cox, C. B. and Dyson, A. E. (eds) (1969) *Fight For Education: A Black Paper*. London: The Critical Quarterly Society.

Cox, C. B. and Dyson, A. E. (eds) (1970) *Black Paper Two*. London: The Critical Quarterly Society.

Davis, D. J. (1979) *The Liverpool Induction Pilot Scheme: Summative Report*. School of Education, University of Liverpool.

Day, C., Pope, M. and Denicolo, P. (eds) (1990) *Insights Into Teachers' Thinking and Practice*. Lewes: Falmer Press.

Dent, H. C. (1977) *The Training of Teachers in England and Wales 1800–1975*. London: Hodder & Stoughton.

Department of Education and Science (DES) (1968) *Probation of Qualified Teachers: Administrative Memorandum 10/68*. London: DES.

DES (1972) *Education: A Framework for Expansion*. London: HMSO.

DES (1976) *Helping New Teachers: The Induction Year*. London: DES.

DES (1977a) *Education in Schools: A Consultative Document*. London: DES.

DES (1977b) *Teacher Induction: Pilot Schemes Progress*. London: DES.

DES (1982a) *The New Teacher in School*. London: HMSO.

DES (1982b) *Education (Teachers) Regulations 1982*. London: DES.

DES (1983a) *The Treatment and Assessment of Probationary Teachers: Administrative Memorandum 1/83*. London: DES.

DES (1983b) *Teaching Quality*. London: HMSO.

DES (1983c) *Teaching in Schools: The Content of Initial Training*. London: HMSO.

DES (1984) *Initial Teacher Training: Approval of Courses: Circular 3/84*. London: DES.

DES (1985a) *Quality in Schools: Evaluation and Appraisal*. London: HMSO.

DES (1985b) *Better Schools*. London: HMSO.

DES (1987) *Quality in Schools: the Initial Training of Teachers: An HMI Survey*. London: HMSO.

DES (1988a) *The New Teacher in School*. London: HMSO.

DES (1988b) *Qualified Teacher Status: Consultation Document*. London: DES.

DES (1989a) *The Education (Teachers) Regulations 1989*. London: DES.

DES (1989b) *Initial Teacher Training: Approval of Courses: Circular 24/89*. London: DES.

DES (1990) *The Treatment and Assessment of Probationary Teachers Administrative Memorandum 1/90*. London: DES.

DES (1991a) *School Teacher Appraisal: Circular 12/91*. London: DES.

DES (1991b) *School Teacher Probation: Circular Letter*. London: DES, September.

DES (1992a) *Reform of Initial Teacher Training: A Consultation Document*. London: DES, 28 January.

DES (1992b) *School Teacher Probation: Circular Letter*. London: DES, 4 March.

DES (1992c) *The Induction and Probation of New Teachers 1988-1991*. London: DES.

Doyle, W. (1985) Learning to teach: an emerging direction in research on preservice teacher education. *Journal of Teacher Education* 36 (1), 31-2.

Draper, J., Fraser, H., Smith, D. and Taylor, W. (1991) The induction of probationer teachers: implications of an industrial model. *Scottish Educational Review* 23 (1), 23-31.

Draper, J., Fraser, H., Smith, D. and Taylor, W. (1992) *A Study of Probationers*. Edinburgh: Scottish Office Education Department.

Earley, P. (1992) *Beyond Initial Teacher Training: Induction and the Role of the LEA*. Slough: National Foundation for Educational Research.

Elba_, F. (1983) *Teacher Thinking: A Study of Practical Knowledge*. London: Croom Helm.

Elliott, J. (1978) How do teachers learn? In Porter, J. (ed.), *The Contribution of Adult Learning Theories to the In-service Education and Training of Teachers*. Paris: OECD.

Elliott, J. (1980) Implications of Classroom Research for Professional Development. In Hoyle, E. and Megarry, J. (eds), *Professional Development of Teachers, World Year Book of Education*. New York: Kogan Page.

Elliott, J. (1985) Educational action research. In Nisbet, J. (ed.), *Research, Policy and Practice, World Year Book of Education*. New York: Kogan Page.

Elliott, J. (1988) Educational research and outsider–insider relations. *Qualitative Studies in Education* 1 (2), 155-66.

Elliott, J. (1989) Educational theory and the professional learning of teachers: an overview. *Cambridge Journal of Education* 19 (1), 81-101.

Elliott, J. (1991a) *Action Research for Educational Change*. Milton Keynes: Open University Press.

Elliott, J. (1991b) Three perspectives on coherence and continuity in teacher education. Mimeo, School of Education, University of East Anglia.

Elliott, J. (1992a) A model of professionalism and its implications for teacher education. *British Educational Research Journal* 17 (4), 309-18.

Elliott, J. (ed.) (1992b) *Reconstructing Teacher Education*. Basingstoke: Falmer Press.

Elliott, J. and Adelman, C. (1976) *Innovation at the Classroom Level: A Case Study of the Ford Teaching Project, Unit 28 Open University Course E203: Curriculum Design and Development*. Milton Keynes: Open University Press.

Elliott, J. and Adelman, C. (eds) (undated) *Ways of Doing Research in Your Own Classroom*. Ford Teaching Project. Cambridge: Cambridge Institute of Education.

Elliott, J. and Ebbutt, D. (1985) *Facilitating Educational Action Research in School*. York: Longman.

England, H. (1986) *Social Work as Art*. London: Allen & Unwin.

Evans, N. (1978) *Beginning Teaching in Professional Partnership*. London: Hodder & Stoughton.

Feiman-Nemser, S. and Buchmann, M. (1985) *The First Year of Teacher Preparation: Transition to Pedagogical Thinking*. Michigan State University, The Institute for Research on Teaching, Research Series No. 156.

Flude, M. and Hammer, M. (eds) (1990) *The Education Reform Act 1988*. Basingstoke: Falmer Press.

Gadamer, H. G. (1975) *Truth and Method*. London: Sheed & Ward.

Gadamer, H. G. (1976) *Philosophical Hermeneutics*. London: University of California Press.

Gaede, O. G. (1978) Reality shock: a problem among first year teachers. ERIC database, unpublished manuscript.

General Teaching Council (1992) *The Induction of Newly Appointed Teachers*. London: General Teaching Council Initiative for England and Wales.

General Teaching Council for Scotland (1990a) *Assessment of Probationary Teachers: Guidance for Headteachers*. Edinburgh: GTC for Scotland.

General Teaching Council for Scotland (1990b) *The Management of Probation*. Edinburgh: GTC for Scotland.

General Teaching Council for Scotland (1991) *What About Probation?* Edinburgh: GTC for Scotland.

Gilroy, P. (1989) Professional knowledge and the beginning teacher. In Carr, W. (ed.), *Quality in Teaching: Arguments for a Reflective Profession*. Lewes: Falmer Press.

Gittins Report (1976) *Primary Education in Wales, Report of the Central Advisory Council for Education (Wales)*. London: HMSO.

Golby, M. (1989) Teachers and their research. In Carr, W. (ed.), *Quality in Teaching: Arguments for a Reflective Profession*. Lewes: Falmer Press.

Goodson, I. (1992) The devil's bargain: educational research and the teacher. Mimeo, Faculty of Education, University of Western Ontario, Canada.

Grant, C. and Zeichner, K. (1981) Inservice support for first year teachers: the state of the scenes. *Journal of Research and Development in Education* 14 (2), 99–111.

Griffin, G. A. (1985) Teacher induction: research issues. *Journal of Teacher Education* 36 (1), 42–6.

Guardian (1989a) Doing it is not enough. London: *Guardian*, 7 February.

Guardian (1989b) Baker beams on a back to front reform. London: *Guardian*, 14 February.

Habermas, J. (1968) *Knowledge and Human Interests* (English translation 1971). Boston: Beacon Press.

Hall, G. E. (ed.) (1982) Induction: the missing link. *Journal of Teacher Education* 33 (3), 53–5.

Hammersley, M. (1977) 'Teacher Perspectives', Units 9 and 10, Schooling and Society, Course E202, Educational Studies. Milton Keynes: Open University.

Hammersley, M. and Hargreaves, A. (eds) (1983) *Curriculum Practice: Some Sociological Case Studies*. Lewes: Falmer Press.

Hannam, C., Smyth, P. and Stephenson, N. (1976) *The First Year of Teaching*. Harmondsworth: Penguin.

Hannam, C., Smyth, P. and Stephenson, N. (1988) The whole experience: Diane Elliot's first year. In Dale, R., Ferguson, R. and Robinson, A. (eds), *Framework For Teaching*. London: Hodder & Stoughton.

Hanson, D. and Herrington, M. (1976) *From College to Classroom: The Probationary Year*. London: Routledge & Kegan Paul.

Hargreaves, A. (1978) The significance of classroom coping strategies. Paper presented at the Westhill Conference, Westhill College, Birmingham, January.

Hargreaves, A. (1986) *Two Cultures of Schooling: The Case of Middle Schools*. Lewes: Falmer Press.

Hargreaves, A. (1988) Teaching quality: a sociological analysis. *Journal of Curriculum Studies* 20 (2), 211–31.

Hargreaves, A. and Fullan, M. G. (eds) (1992) *Understanding Teacher Development.* London: Cassell.

Hargreaves, D. H. (1967) *Social Relations in a Secondary School.* London: Routledge & Kegan Paul.

Hargreaves, D. H. (1989) Merit and market. *Times Educational Supplement.* 7 April, p. A15.

Harrison, G. N. and Sacks, S. R. (1984) Student to teacher: novel strategies for achieving the transition. *Journal of Education For Teaching* 10 (2), 154–63.

Hayon, L. K. (1990) Reflection and professional knowledge. In Day, C. *et al.* (eds), *Insights Into Teachers' Thinking and Practice.* Lewes: Falmer Press.

Henry, M. A. (1988) Multiple support: a successful model for inducting first-year teachers. *Teacher Educator* 24 (2), 7–12.

Hermanowicz, H. J. (1966) The pluralist world of beginning teachers. In *The Real World of the Beginning Teacher*, National Commission on Teacher Education and Professional Standards, The National Education Association.

Hillgate Group (1989) *Learning to Teach.* London: The Claridge Press.

Holly, M. L. and McLoughlin, C. S. (eds) (1989) *Perspectives on Teacher Professional Development.* Lewes: Falmer Press.

Holub, R. (1991) *Jurgen Habermas.* London: Routledge.

Hopkins, D. (1985) *A Teachers' Guide to Classroom Research.* Milton Keynes: Open University Press.

Howey, K. (1983) *The Education of Teachers: A Look Ahead.* New York: Longman.

Hoyle, E. (1969) *The Role of The Teacher.* London, Routledge & Kegan Paul.

Huling-Austin, L. (1990) Teacher induction programmes and internships. In Houston, W. R. (ed.) *Handbook of Research on Teacher Education.* New York: Macmillan.

Hunt, D. W. (1968) Teacher induction: an opportunity and a responsibility. In *The National Association of Secondary School Principals Bulletin*, Reston, Virginia, October, p. 13.

Hustler, D., Cassidy, R. and Cuff, T. (eds) (1986) *Action Research in Classrooms and Schools.* London: Allen & Unwin.

Independent (1989) Schools should 'be allowed to train teachers'. London: *Independent*, 13 March.

ILEA (Inner London Education Authority) (1980) *The ILEA Induction Scheme: A Survey of Probationers' Experiences and View of The First Year of the Scheme.* London: Research and Statistics Division, ILEA.

ILEA (1984) *Improving Secondary Schools: Report of the Committee on the Curriculum and Organisation of Secondary Schools.* London: ILEA.

ILEA (1985) *ILEA Induction Scheme: Five Years On.* London: Research and Statistics Division, ILEA.

Jackson, P. (1968) *Life in Classrooms.* Eastbourne: Holt, Rinehart & Winston.

James Report (1972) *Teacher Education and Training.* London: HMSO.

Johnston, J. E. and Ryan, K. (1983) Research on the beginning teacher: implications for teacher education. In Howey, K., *The Education of Teachers: A Look Ahead.* New York: Longman.

Kemmis, S. and McTaggart, R. (eds) (1982) *The Action Research Planner.* Victoria: Deakin University Press.

Kerry, T. (1982) *The New Teacher.* London: Macmillan.

Kinchloe, J. L. (1990) *Teachers As Researchers: Qualitative Inquiry as a Path to Empowerment.* Basingstoke: Falmer Press.

Kroath, F. (1989) How do teachers change their practical theories? *Cambridge Journal of Education* 19 (1), 59–70.

Lacey, C. (1970) *Hightown Grammar: The School as a Social System*. Manchester: Manchester University Press.

Lacey, C. (1977) *The Socialization of Teachers*. London: Methuen.

Lamber, J. (1992) Induction of newly trained and appointed teachers. In General Teaching Council, *The Induction of Newly Appointed Teachers*. London: General Teaching Council Initiative for England and Wales.

Lawlor, S. (1990) *Teachers Mistaught*. London: Claridge Press.

Lomax, D. E. (ed.) (1973) *The Education of Teachers in Britain*. London: John Wiley.

Lortie, D. (1975) *Schoolteacher*. Chicago: University of Chicago Press.

Lowyck, J. and Clark, C. M. (1989) *Teacher Thinking and Professional Action*. Leuven: Leuven University Press.

McCabe, C. (1978) *Induction in Northumberland: An Evaluation*. School of Education, University of Newcastle upon Tyne.

MacDonald, B., Argent, M. J., Elliott, J. E. and May, N. H. (1986) *The Final Report of the Stage 2 Review of Police Probationer Training*. Norwich: Centre for Applied Research in Education, University of East Anglia.

Macintyre, A. (1990) *Three Rival Versions of Moral Enquiry*. London: Duckworth.

McIntyre, D. (1980) The contribution of research to quality in teacher education. In Hoyle, E. and Megarry, J. (eds), *Professional Development of Teachers, World Year Book of Education*. New York: Kogan Page.

McIntyre, D. (1988) Designing a teacher education curriculum from research and theory on teacher knowledge. In Calderhead, J. (ed.), *Teachers' Professional Learning*. Lewes: Falmer Press.

McKernan, J. (1988) The countenance of curriculum action research: traditional, collaborative, and emancipatory-critical conceptions. *Journal of Curriculum and Supervision* 3 (3), 173-200.

McKernan, J. (1991) *Curriculum Action Research*. London: Kogan Page.

McNair Report (1944) *Teachers and Youth Leaders*. London: HMSO.

McNiff, F. (1988) *Action Research: Principles and Practice*. London: Macmillan.

Morton, B. (1988) Ceremony of innocence. Unpublished MPhil thesis. Norwich: School of Education, University of East Anglia.

Munro, R. G. (1989) A case study of school-based innovation in secondary teacher training. Unpublished PhD Thesis, University of Auckland, New Zealand.

National Union of Teachers (NUT) (1969) *The Future of Teacher Education*. London: NUT.

NUT (1971) *The Reform of Teacher Education; A Policy Statement*. London: NUT.

Nelson, B. L. (1989) *Mentor Teachers' Thinking About Teaching and Mentoring*. Winnipeg: University of Manitoba.

Newsam, P. (1989) Bucking the market. *Times Educational Supplement*, 24 March.

Nias, J. (1987) Teaching and the self. *Cambridge Journal of Education* 15 (1), 17-24.

Nias, J. (1989) *Primary Teachers Talking*. London: Routledge.

Nixon, J. (1981) *A Teacher's Guide to Action Research: Evaluation, Enquiry and Development in the Classroom*. London: Grant McIntyre.

Oberg, A. and Blades, C. (1988) The sound of silence: reflections of a teacher. Paper presented to the fourth International Study Association on Teacher Thinking conference, Nottingham, September.

O'Hear, A. (1988) *Who Teaches the Teachers?* London: Social Affairs Unit.

Open University (1981) *Course E323 Management and The School, Block 6: The Management of Staff, Part 4: Staff Development, Section 2: The Induction of Probationary Teachers*. Milton Keynes: Open University.

O'Rourke, B. (1983) Lion tamers and baby sitters. *English Education* 15 (1), 17-24.

Patrick, H., Bernbaum, G., and Reid, K. (1984) The PGCE and the probationary year. *British Journal of Inservice Education* 10 (3), 47–54.

Phillips, D. C. (1987) *Philosophy, Science, and Social Enquiry*. London: Pergamon.

Phillips, D. C. (1988) On teachers' knowledge: a skeptical dialogue. *Educational Theory* 38 (4), 457–66.

Plowden Report (1967) *Children and Their Primary Schools* (2 vols) *Report of the Central Advisory Council for Education in England*. London: HMSO.

Pollard, A. (1985) *The Social World of The Primary School*. London: Holt, Rinehart & Winston.

Pollard, A. and Tann, S. (1987) *Reflective Teaching in the Primary School*. London: Cassell.

Rich, R. W. (1933) *The Training of Teachers in England and Wales During The Nineteenth Century*. Cambridge: Cambridge University Press.

Richardson, G. (1970) X is for the unknown. In Ryan, K. (ed.), *Don't Smile Until Christmas*. Chicago: University of Chicago Press.

Rudduck, J. (1985) The improvement of the art of teaching through research. *Cambridge Journal of Education* 15 (3), 123–6.

Rudduck, J. (1988) The ownership of change as a basis for teachers' professional learning. In Calderhead, J. (ed.), *Teachers' Professional Learning*. Lewes: Falmer Press.

Rudduck, J. (1991) *Innovation and Change*. Milton Keynes: Open University Press.

Rudduck, J. and Hopkins, D. (1985) *Research as a Basis for Teaching*. London: Heinemann.

Russell, T. L. (1987a) Research, practical knowledge, and the conduct of teacher education. *Educational Theory* 37 (4), 369–75.

Russell, T. L. (1987b) Learning the professional knowledge of teaching: views of the relationship between 'theory' and 'practice'. Paper presented at the annual meeting of the American Educational Research Association, Washington, DC, April.

Russell, T. L. (1987c) Reframing the theory–practice relationship in inservice teacher education. In Newton, L. J., Fullan, M. and McDonald, J. W. (eds), *Re-Thinking Teacher Education: Exploring The Link Between Research, Practice and Policy*. Joint Council on Education, Faculty of Education, University of Toronto/The Ontario Institute for Studies in Education.

Russell, T. L. (1988) From pre-service teacher education to first year of teaching: a study of theory and practice. In Calderhead, J. (ed.), *Teachers' Professional Learning*. Lewes: Falmer Press.

Ryan, K. (ed.) (1970) *Don't Smile Until Christmas*. Chicago: University of Chicago Press.

Ryan, K., Newman, K. K., Mager, G., Applegate, J. H., Lasley, T., Flora, U. R. and Johnston, J. (1980) *Biting the Apple: Accounts of First Year Teachers*. New York: Longman.

Salmon, P. (1988) *Psychology for Teachers: An Alternative Approach*. London: Hutchinson.

Salter, B. and Tapper, T. (1981) *Education, Politics and the State*. London: Grant McIntyre.

Sanger, J. (1986) Naturalistic enquiry on trial: an exploration of the issues in the practice of naturalistic enquiry in educational settings. Unpublished PhD thesis. Norwich: Centre for Applied Research in Education, University of East Anglia.

Schlechty, P. C. (1990) *Reform in Teacher Education: A Sociological View*. Washington: American Association of Colleges for Teacher Education.

Schon, D. (1971) *Beyond the Stable State*. San Francisco: Jossey Bass.

Schon, D. (1983) *The Reflective Practitioner*. New York: Basic Books.

Schon, D. (1987) *Educating the Reflective Practitioner*. London: Jossey Bass.

Schon, D. (1991) *The Reflective Turn: Case Studies in and on Educational Practice*. New York: Teachers College Press.

Schrag, F. (1989) On teacher knowledge – expanding the dialogue. *Educational Theory* 39 (3), 269–72.

Schwalenberg, R. J. (1965) *Teacher Orientation Practices in Oregon Secondary Schools*. Oregon: University of Oregon Press.

Sharp R. and Green, A. (1975) *Education and Social Control*. London: Routledge & Kegan Paul.

Shulman, L. S. (1986a) Those who understand: knowledge growth in teaching. *Educational Researcher* 15 (4), 4–14.

Shulman, L. S. (1986b) Knowledge and teaching: foundations of the new reform. Mimeo, Stanford University.

Sikes, P. (1987) A kind of oasis: art rooms and art teachers in secondary schools. In Tickle, L. (ed.), *The Arts in Education*. London: Croom Helm.

Simons, H. (1987) *Getting to Know Schools in Democracy: The Politics and Process of Evaluation*. Lewes: Falmer Press.

Smith, D. C. (ed.) (1983) *Essential Knowledge for Beginning Educators*. Washington, DC: American Association of Colleges for Teacher Education.

Sockett, H. (1986) Teacher professionalism and curriculum research. Mimeo, University of East Anglia School of Education.

Sockett, J. (1987) Has Shulman got the strategy right? Knowledge and teaching: foundations of the new reform: a critique. Mimeo, University of East Anglia School of Education.

Somekh, B. (1990) Some thoughts on action research. Mimeo, University of East Anglia School of Education.

Stenhouse, L. (1975) *An Introduction to Curriculum Research and Development*. London: Heinemann.

Stenhouse, L. (1979) Research as a Basis for Teaching. Inaugural Lecture, University of East Anglia, February.

Stenhouse, L. (1984) Artistry and teaching: the teacher as focus of research and development. In Hopkins, D. and Wideen, M. (eds), *Alternative Perspectives on School Improvement*. Lewes: Falmer Press.

Tabachnick, B. R. and Zeichner, K. M. (eds) *Issues and Practices in Inquiry-Oriented Teacher Education*. Basingstoke: Falmer Press.

Tabachnick, B. R. and Zeichner, K. M. (1991b) The reflective practitioner in teaching and teacher education: a social reconstructionist perspective. Paper presented to the annual conference of the American Educational Research Association, Chicago, April.

Taylor, W. (1969) *Society and the Education of Teachers*. London: Faber.

Taylor, W. (1978) *Research and Reform in Teacher Education*. Slough: Council of Europe, European Trend Reports on Educational Research, NFER.

Taylor, W. (1984) The national context 1972–82. In Alexander, R. J. *et al.* (eds), *Change in Teacher Education: Context and Provision Since Robbins*. London: Holt, Rinehart & Winston.

Taylor, J. K. and Dale, I. R. (1971) *A Survey of Teachers in Their First Year of Service*. Bristol: University of Bristol School of Education Research Unit.

Taylor, J. K. and Dale, I. R. (1973) The first year of teaching. In Lomax, D. E. (ed.), *The Education of Teachers in Britain*. London: John Wiley.

Tickle, L. (1979) A sociological analysis and case study of the organisation and evaluation of art design subjects, for third and fourth year pupils in a 9–13 middle school. Unpublished MA (Ed) Thesis, University of Keele.

Tickle, L. (1983) One spell of ten minutes or five spells of two . . .? Teacher–pupil encounters in art and design education. In Hammersley, M. and Hargreaves, A. (eds), *Curriculum Practice: Some Sociological Case Studies*. Lewes: Falmer Press.

Tickle, L. (1987a) *Learning Teaching, Teaching Teaching: A Study of Partnership in Teacher Education*. Lewes: Falmer Press.

Tickle, L. (ed.) (1987b) *The Arts in Education*. London: Croom Helm.

Tickle, L. (1987c) Constructing teaching knowledge: out of training and towards the education of new teachers. Paper presented to the Annual Meeting of the British Educational Research Association, Manchester, England, September.

Tickle, L. (1988) Professional skills assessment in classroom teaching. Paper presented to the Annual Conference of the British Educational Research Association, University of East Anglia, September.

Tickle, L. (1989a) New teachers and the development of professionalism. In Holly, M. L. and McLoughlin, C. S. (eds), *Perspectives on Teacher Professional Development*. Lewes: Falmer Press.

Tickle, L. (1989b) On probation: preparation for professionalism. *Cambridge Journal of Education* 19 (3), 277–85.

Tickle, L. (1990) The reflective practitioner in the first year of teaching. Paper presented to the Annual Conference of the British Educational Research Association, London, August.

Tickle, L. (1991) New teachers and the emotions of learning teaching. *Cambridge Journal of Education* 21 (3), 319–29.

Tickle, L. (1992a) The assessment of professional skills in teaching. *Cambridge Journal of Education* 22 (1), 91–103.

Tickle, L. (1992b) Capital T teaching. In Elliott, J. (ed.), *Reconstructing Teacher Education*. Basingstoke: Falmer Press.

Tickle, L. (1992c) The first year of teaching as a learning experience. In Bridges, D. and Kerry, T. (eds) *Developing Teachers Professionally*. London: Routledge.

Tickle, L. (1993) The wish of Odysseus: new teachers' receptiveness to mentoring. In Wilkins, M. (ed.), *Issues in Mentoring*. London: Kogan Page.

Times Educational Supplement (1988) On-the-job training the best solution. London, *TES*, 16 December.

Tisher, R. P. (1982) Teacher induction: an international perspective on research and programs. Paper presented to the annual conference of the American Educational Research Association.

Tom, A. (1985) Inquiry into inquiry-oriented teacher education. *Journal of Teacher Education* 36 (5), 35–44.

UCET (1988) *Working Party Report on the Desirability and Feasibility of a Two-year PGCE Course*. London: Universities Council for the Education and Training of Teachers.

Van Manen, M. (1977) Linking ways of knowing with ways of being practical. *Curriculum Inquiry* 6 (3), 205–28.

Veenman, S. (1984) Perceived problems of beginning teachers. *Review of Educational Research* 54, 143–78.

Vulliamy, G. and Webb, R. (1991) Teacher research and educational change: an empirical study. *British Educational Research Journal* 17 (3), 219–36.

Walker, R. (1985) *Doing Research: A Handbook for Teachers*. London: Methuen.

Waller, W. (1932) *The Sociology of Teaching*. New York: Russell & Russell.

Webb, N. (1985) Borderline creativity. *Interchange* 16 (1), 94–102.

Webb, R. (1990a) The origins and aspirations of practitioner research. In Webb, R. (ed.), *Practitioner Research in the Primary School*. Basingstoke: Falmer Press.

Webb, R. (ed.) (1990b) *Practitioner Research in the Primary School*. Basingstoke: Falmer Press.

Western Australia Education Department (1977) *The Induction of Primary School Teachers: A Report*. Perth: Research Branch, WAED.

Whitehead, J. (1989) Creating a living educational theory from questions of the kind, 'How do I improve my Practice?' *Cambridge Journal of Education* 19 (1), 41–52.

Wilson, S. M., Shulman, L. S. and Richert, A. E. (1987) 150 different ways of knowing: representations of knowledge in teaching. In Calderhead, J. (ed.), *Exploring Teachers' Thinking*. London: Cassell.

Winter, R. (1987) *Action Research and the Nature of Social Enquiry*. Aldershot: Gower Publishing.

Winter, R. (1989) *Learning From Experience: Principles and Practice in Action Research*. Lewes: Falmer Press.

Wolff, J. (1975) *Hermeneutic Philosophy and the Sociology of Art*. London: Routledge and Kegan Paul.

Wolff, J. (1981) *The Social Production of Art*. London: Macmillan.

Zeichner, K. (1981) Reflective teaching and field-based experience in pre-service teacher education. *Interchange* 12, 1–22.

Zeichner, K. M. and Tabachnick, B. R. (1985) The development of teacher perspectives: social strategies and institutional control in the socialization of beginning teachers. *Journal of Education for Teaching* 11 (1), 1–25.

Zeichner, K. M. and Tabachnick, B. R. (1991) Reflections on reflective teaching. In Tabachnick, B. R. and Zeichner, K. M. (eds), *Issues and Practices in Inquiry-Oriented Teacher Education*. Basingstoke: Falmer Press.

Zeichner, K. M., Tabachnick, B. R. and Densmore, K. (1987) Individual, institutional and cultural influences on the development of teachers' craft knowledge. In Calderhead, J. (ed.), *Exploring Teachers' Thinking*. London: Cassell.

Zimpher, N. L. and Howey, K. (1987) Adapting supervisory practices to different orientations of teaching competence. *Journal of Curriculum and Supervision* 2 (2), 101–27.

Zimpher, N. L. and Howey, K. R. (1990) Scholarly inquiry into teacher education in the United States. In Tisher, R. P. and Wideen, M. F. (eds), *Research in Teacher Education: International Perspectives*. Basingstoke: Falmer Press.

Name Index

Subject Index